# THE ROAD TO
# OHIO STATE

# THE ROAD TO
# OHIO STATE

Incredible Twists and Improbable Turns
Along the Buckeyes Recruiting Trail

**Doug Lesmerises**

TRIUMPH
B O O K S

Library of Congress Cataloging-in-Publication Data available upon request

This book is available in quantity at special discounts for your group or organization. For further information, contact:

**Triumph Books LLC**
814 North Franklin Street
Chicago, Illinois 60610
(312) 337-0747
www.triumphbooks.com

Printed in U.S.A.
ISBN: 978-1-62937-926-5
Design by Nord Compo

Jim Otis photo in Chapter 17 is courtesy of Getty Images. All other photos are courtesy of AP Images.

*For my mom, Kay, who always thought I should write a book, and my late dad, Leo, who always took me to every game.*

# Contents

# Foreword

Recruiting is like any other business. It's relationship based. So when you're on the road recruiting, it's about relationships and how you treat people. You have to figure out who you trust and who you believe in and you're constantly gathering information. I think great recruiters gather information, and then they're able to process the situation and identify people. You want to find people who would fit your culture and ultimately help your team. But asking the right questions is important. You also have to be willing to listen.

But you don't always get the whole story when you ask a coach a question. It's based on how many years you've known him or her and their trust in you, and that determines how much information you're truly going to get about each kid. Then you have to try to process and find out how much more you have to dig because most high school coaches are going to give you a little bit of the party line. They're going to advocate for their kids and tell you that they deserve a scholarship to Ohio State. And that's for a lot of reasons.

One is because the parents at the high school are pushing to get their kids scholarships and sometimes think that high school coaches can give kids scholarships. But I think a good recruiter can figure out those situations. It's like anything. When you walk in a room, can you figure out the dynamics of a room? Can you figure out the dynamics of a team? Can you figure out if this kid is going to help your team? The more questions you ask and the more information you get, it helps you to be more accurate about the people you'll ultimately bring into your program.

As you go through recruiting, you can usually tell the way people are talking about somebody. Maybe one person—if he or she really likes somebody—will give a good recommendation. And then you go to somebody else, and they say the same thing. By the time you get to the third or fourth person, if they're talking really highly about somebody, you need to pay attention.

That's what happened with Chris Olave in the Class of 2018. As Ohio State's offensive coordinator and quarterback coach, I was recruiting a quarterback named Jack Tuttle at Mission Hills High School in the San Diego area. Jack and his Mission Hills coach, Chris Hauser, were saying they had this great receiver coming in and I said, "Do you have his film?" They informed me there wasn't any film because he transferred in. But while I was out there, I was able to see him do some things on the field that day—not a whole lot—but he was able to catch the ball a little bit. He didn't look very big to me, kind of an undersized guy. But then I saw some of his track times. And then I saw his film as he started to get into those first couple games of his senior year. And we could just see somebody who had an unbelievable ability to track the ball, great ball skills, great spatial awareness, and obviously top end speed. So we jumped on him right away.

I think a lot of guys felt like why are you going all the way to California to get a kid who's 6'0", probably 168 pounds at that time? But we knew Chris was worth it. We went out and saw him practice. He had missed his junior year, and we felt like if he had played his junior year, he'd have everybody in the country after him. We were able to get in on that one pretty early on. And again, recruiting is about relationships, and when you can start building relationships early on, especially when you identify players before others do, it really helps in the end.

When I was an assistant at Boston College, I recruited a safety from Florida named Justin Simmons. I went to one of his spring games and nobody was really recruiting him. Gary Blackney, the former coach at Bowling Green, was coaching him in high school and really felt like he could play almost anywhere. Since he was a former college coach, I really listened to him. So Justin came to Boston College with very few offers and he had a great career and now he's in the NFL. It was just us and a couple small schools, and the biggest concern was that he wasn't being recruited by anybody. But you've got to trust the film and trust the people in the area who believe in the kid, and that one worked out.

There are great stories like that, and then there are the ones that you miss on. But when you err on the side of the high school coaches, the people in the area, and what they have to say, you're going to end up with great kids and great people. That matters. Because at Ohio State, we shouldn't have to compromise. We should not only get great players, but also great people, great students, and great leaders. That is one of the most exciting parts about being part of Ohio State. Then, using the expertise about quarterback play that I feel like I was able to acquire coaching in the NFL, I take a lot of pride in being able to recruit some of the best quarterbacks in the country and make that room one of the best.

In the recruiting process, families and recruits want to know that you're going to be able to really make them better because you have an expertise at what you do. Then it's building a culture where the parents can send their son here and feel good that you're going to take great care of them and maximize them in all areas of their life. That's really what it comes down to: how do we maximize young men? There's already great talent, but how do we take that talent and turn it into skill and discipline?

That is the exciting part of being back in college at Ohio State. In the recruiting process, we can handpick who we bring into the program and then watch them grow as players and as people. That process—and all of its twists and turns—is depicted in *The Road to Ohio State*. Whether it's a current guy like Olave or a great Buckeye from the Woody Hayes days, you'll learn how and why your favorite players joined our great program.

*—Ryan Day*
*Ohio State head coach*

# Editor's Note

The Road to Ohio State *is part of a series of books created by Tom VanHaaren.*

## CHAPTER 1

# Joey Bosa, Class of 2013, and Nick Bosa, Class of 2016

Joey Bosa's road to Ohio State began with something Mark Pantoni had done hundreds of times before. He scouted a great high school football player in the state of Florida, liked the film, and took it to the University of Florida coaches.

But for the first time in the fall of 2011, the head coach that Pantoni worked with wasn't Urban Meyer. Pantoni, who started as an intern in the Gators football office after earning his undergraduate degree in 2004 and master's in 2006 from Florida, had taken on an elevated role in the Florida football recruiting operation under Meyer in 2007. By 2008 Pantoni was running the recruiting for the Gators, and as Florida signed top 10 classes in 2008 and 2009 and the No. 1 class in the country in 2010, Pantoni absorbed more from Meyer, and Meyer relied more on Pantoni.

But Meyer stepped down as Florida's coach in December 2010, which meant when Pantoni took the early junior season film of a defensive end from Fort Lauderdale, Florida, to the Gators coaches during the 2011 football season, it wasn't Meyer evaluating Bosa. It was first-year coach Will Muschamp and his staff. "I really liked him and thought he was obviously physically advanced, and he was a really good player," Pantoni said. "So I took two game cut-ups to Muschamp and some other coaches, and I was like, you guys have got to watch this guy. This kid's a really good player. And I think at the time he may have had Florida State and Alabama, but those were the two only really big offers. And they liked him, but they didn't want to offer him because they thought he was too stiff. I completely disagreed. So I'm like, I'm not gonna take no on this guy."

Pantoni texted Bosa and his father, John, and invited them to visit Florida. Pantoni told them how much he liked what he saw on film. "The dad you could kind of tell was like, well, are you guys gonna offer if we visit? And I tried to play it up: they just want to see Joe in person. And so they came up for the first game, and obviously I was building a really good relationship with them," Pantoni said. "But they came up, and Will still wouldn't offer him. So in a good way, that was about the end of it for Florida…So they left there not very happy. And three months later, I moved to Ohio State."

The Gators did offer later in the fall but to no avail.

Less than five years later, Pantoni sat with the Bosa family in Chicago at the 2016 NFL Draft as Joey was taken with the No. 3 pick by the San Diego Chargers, the kickoff to a record-setting draft that saw the Buckeyes set a new mark with 10 players picked in the first three rounds.

Between that first film and that first-round selection, Pantoni helped Meyer reshape the face of Big Ten recruiting; Joey Bosa helped the Buckeyes win their first national championship in more than a decade during the 2014 season; Nick Bosa followed his older brother to Columbus and later into the top three of the NFL draft to create arguably the greatest defensive end pipeline in college football history; and the Bosas' mother, Cheryl, was in the midst of what she called the best six years of her life with one of her sons playing for her Buckeyes from 2013 to 2018.

But by the time Pantoni had taken the Joey Bosa film to the Gators, Alabama coach Nick Saban had already entertained a 15-year-old Bosa in his office and offered him a scholarship.

George Smith, his legendary high school football coach at St. Thomas Aquinas, one of the top high school football programs in the country, said the ease of the recruitments of the Bosas was matched by only one other player he coached. "Of all our great players," Smith said, "probably those two guys and Michael Irvin were the easiest."

Bosa and Bosa were that obvious as Buckeyes in the recruiting Classes of 2013 and 2016, and future Hall of Famer Irvin was that obvious for the Miami Hurricanes in the Class of 1985.

It could have been even simpler for Joey Bosa if he'd said yes to that initial Alabama offer. He wanted that to happen, and it would take something seismic to shake him off that first impression from Saban, who had won his first national championship at Alabama in 2009 and now was telling a teenager the Tide wanted him to help chase more titles. After that offer in July 2011 at the first team camp he ever attended, Bosa and his father were in a sandwich shop in Tuscaloosa, Alabama, going over what had just happened: from Bosa taking outside linebacker snaps for the first time to Saban opening and shutting his office door with the click of a button, leaving Joey feeling like he was in a movie. "How could it get any better than this?" Bosa asked his father. "I probably should just commit right now."

The Alabama affection was real. To change it would take something like a two-time national championship coach at Florida accepting the job at Ohio State, which happened to be his mother's alma mater. It would take something like his father telling an eager son enamored with Saban that the recruiting process would be long, and this was just the start. All that happened, and for Joey Bosa, it brought together his family connections and his championship aspirations, which was maybe the only combination that could have beaten Saban at the peak of his powers.

Meyer was wondering if he'd be able to rekindle his recruiting powers after taking the Ohio State job in November 2011, less than a year after stepping away at Florida. His final recruiting class at Florida in 2010 had included five five-stars among 28 players, including the top-ranked players in the states of California, New York, Pennsylvania, Colorado, and Maryland, according to 247Sports.com.

In accepting the Ohio State job, Meyer was coming home to the state where he'd been raised on Buckeyes football. But he was also leaving the blue skies and abundant talent in Florida. "The player at the end of the day—and the family at the end of the day—has got to select Ohio State," Meyer said. "And so there's got to be a reason why. At Florida a lot of times, it's the sunshine, the stadium, The Swamp. You have such a plethora of incredible athletes in a 300-mile to 500-mile radius. Ohio's completely different. With the population shift, there's great players, but there's not a ton of them anymore. There was a time in Northeast Ohio and Western [Pennsylvania], you'd have 25 Ohio State- or Notre Dame-level athletes. The reality is there's five now, and you can't build your team from just those areas. The

[Midwest] footprint is so important, but if the goal—and ours was—to beat Alabama, you're gonna have to go do this. So I would just lie awake and say, 'How can we get this kid?' Is it a phone call? Is it writing a letter? Obviously not. Ohio State never really had a national presence. They did good, but it wasn't what it became."

Meyer went to work implementing a plan he believed would increase the appeal of the Buckeyes to players around the country. But first they had to get out offers. Days after Meyer hired Pantoni and his other key employees from his Florida tenure, one of his first offers was to Bosa. "I told Urban right away," Pantoni said, "'There's this kid at St. Thomas, and he's gonna be a freak.' And then you found out Cheryl went to Ohio State, and there's a lot of ties. But Cheryl had always said Joey would be the tough one because he was kind of a homebody. She said Nick would always be the easy one because he just loved Ohio State."

Cheryl Bosa further expounded upon the difference in her sons' affinities. "Nick has always been a Buckeye," she said. "Nick was a Buckeye from the time he could walk and talk. He was always my buddy, sitting and watching games with me on Saturday. Joey, on the other hand, was the anti-Buckeye. He would cheer for whoever Ohio State was playing, just to give me and Nick a hard time. So when the recruiting process started, we're talking early, like Joey's freshman year. Joey would say to me all the time, 'You know, I'm not visiting Ohio State, Mom.' And I kept a poker face the whole time because I wanted my kids to make their own choices and be happy with their choices and I was never going to push them in a direction where they could be like, 'Well, you made me go here.'

"So he used to tell me, 'I'm not going there, I'm not going there,' but I knew deep down in my heart, if he ever visited there, it would be a done deal because I know how fantastic it is. I knew that it was just a matter of him making a choice to take a trip there. But early in high school, Joey was 100 percent going to Alabama. It used to just kill me. I'd be sitting in the stands, and he'd make a good play, and he'd be like, 'Roll Tide,' on the field. I'd be sitting with my friend, and I'd be like, oh my God, he just did Roll Tide. I'm gonna die. And then, thank God on Earth, all of a sudden, the news came out that Urban Meyer got the job. And I'll never forget Joey coming home and saying to me, 'Urban Meyer got the job at Ohio State.' And I'm like, *Really?* Poker face, poker face. And he's like, I might want to go visit there. I had to go in the other room and do a dance."

There was a Buckeyes presence in the Bosa home. But as Joey Bosa acquiesced about the idea of Ohio State, it had to be about more than the bloodline. John and Cheryl are amicably divorced and they were both involved in all aspects of their sons' lives and college decisions. "They weren't fans of my alma mater either at Boston College," John said. "Joey really was kind of interested in Florida schools and he wasn't a huge college football fan growing up."

The bloodline for playing defensive end, however, ran deep and strong. After John Bosa played defensive end at Boston College, the Miami Dolphins selected him as their first-round draft choice (pick No. 16 overall) in 1987. In 1988 the Dolphins picked at No. 16 in the first round again and selected another defensive end—Ohio State's Eric Kumerow, the younger brother of Cheryl Kumerow.

The Kumerows were from the Chicago suburbs, and Cheryl, a year older than Eric, attended the University of Illinois her freshman year. Their older brother, Craig, played football at Indiana, and after going to watch Craig play a road game at Ohio State, Cheryl was sold. Eric was viewed as the best player in Illinois in the Class of

1983, and the Illini wanted him as a quarterback. But at 6'6" and 215 pounds, he also potentially projected as a tight end, linebacker, or defensive end in college. Wherever he played, he could name his school. "I sat in that stadium, and my jaw hit the ground," Cheryl said of that initial visit to Ohio Stadium. "We were a football family, but if you've been in The Shoe, you know there's nothing in the world like it. I was like, holy cow, this is the coolest! And Eric at the time was being recruited everywhere."

His inclination was to stick close to home. He had a strong relationship with his sister, so going to the same college she attended also had an appeal. Kumerow sat at the top of the recruiting board for the Illini and head coach Mike White. "He was going to Illinois. That was done," Cheryl said. "[With] me being at Illinois, Mike White used to call me 50 times a day. The football office was constantly asking if there was anything they could do for me."

Illinois assistant Rick George spoke to the *Quad-City Times* in December 1982. "We've made it clear Kumerow is the only quarterback we're recruiting," he said. Kumerow narrowed his choices to Illinois, Penn State, Michigan, and Ohio State.

When he picked the Buckeyes in February of 1983, George told United Press International that the Illini coaches were "shocked" by the decision. "Ohio State is a nice school and all that," George said. "But Illinois athletes should go to school in Illinois."

Cheryl had won the recruiting battle for the Buckeyes. In the fall of 1983, Eric and Cheryl Kumerow both enrolled at Ohio State. "I had told him, 'If you want to go to Ohio State, I'll transfer,'" Cheryl said. "And that was it. He went to Ohio State, and I transferred."

The Kumerows loved Columbus, and Eric did make the move to pass rusher. When he arrived in the NFL, he introduced his sister to his new teammate, John Bosa. Those two first-round defensive ends playing in South Florida led to two more first-round defensive ends growing up in South Florida. John Bosa said he didn't want his sons to start football too early, so they were basketball and baseball players first. But they asked to play football, and John remembers the day he dropped them off at football practice. Joey was around the sixth grade, and Nick was maybe in third, and as they walked opposite ways to their teams, he knew this was the start of something.

They chose St. Thomas Aquinas in Fort Lauderdale for high school, which through 2020 had sent nearly 40 alumni on to the NFL. John Bosa said the program was more like a junior college than a high school when it came to the football instruction and structure. As the head football coach, Smith went 361–66, including six state titles and two national titles, over 34 years. He continued on as athletic director before retiring in 2021. He knew talent when he saw it and he saw that the Bosas were bound for the NFL. "They had a weight room ethic they probably got from John," Smith said. "Here these guys are killing people in high school, and yet they're our hardest workers."

What the Bosas learned about Smith's program, Meyer had known for years. One of Smith's players in the early '80s was the son of the Miami Dolphins' director of pro personnel. That son didn't last long at St. Thomas Aquinas because that father, Bill Davis Sr., was soon hired to be the Cleveland Browns' vice president of player personnel in 1981. Davis acquired players such as Bernie Kosar, Earnest Byner, and Frank Minnifield as the Browns were built into an AFC power in the mid-1980s. His son, Billy Davis, graduated from Berea High School outside Cleveland and went on to play college football at Cincinnati, where his roommate and soon-to-be best friend was Meyer. Long before Meyer hired Davis as Ohio State's linebackers coach in 2017, Davis and Meyer went to spring break in Florida, where one day Smith stumbled upon a group of players using the St. Thomas weight room. He knew they weren't in high school because they were too big. "I said, 'Get the hell out of here,'" Smith said, "and one of them was Urban."

Davis went on to coach in the NFL for decades, and Meyer went on to build a relationship with Smith while recruiting for Notre Dame, Bowling Green, Utah, and Florida. When the Gators played Oklahoma in the BCS National Championship Game on January 8, 2009, Florida did its walkthrough the day before at Aquinas. Tim Tebow jokingly almost pulled Smith into the post-practice ice tubs. "We became extremely close even before Florida," Meyer said of Smith. "But when I got to Florida, that kind of became my place. Every year I'd go hang out with them. The one thing about recruiting, it's labor intensive. It's all about time, it's all about invest-ment—and not just in the person you're recruiting but in the schools, in the influencers. First of all, I love George Smith, but I also realized he was the No. 1 influencer at one of the top one or two schools in America, at a place where I needed to become invested. We could not lose people at St. Thomas. So every year everybody knew to clear my schedule when I went to St. Thomas because when I go there I'm not going to bump in and leave. I'm going to be there for a while and get to know him and get a personal relationship with him."

In the five recruiting classes from 2006 to 2010, St. Thomas Aquinas had 11 players ranked among the top 50 players in the state by 247Sports.com. Florida State, Georgia, Auburn, North Carolina, Notre Dame, and Ohio State each landed one of them. (The Buckeye was Duron Carter, the son of OSU legend Cris Carter who helped coach at St. Thomas Aquinas.) Miami got two players. And the Gators got three: Marcus Gilbert, Major Wright, and Cody Riggs. "So when I got hired at Ohio State," Meyer said, "George was one of the guys I was very close with. And I know about Joey Bosa right away."

So Meyer knew Bosa's high school coach, and Smith vouched for Meyer with the Bosas. But that wouldn't have been enough. Pantoni, who also grew close with Smith, made an early connection with the Bosa family, but that wouldn't have been enough. Cheryl Bosa loved her alma mater. But that wouldn't have been enough. There were multiple strings in Bosa's life pulling him toward Columbus. But Ohio State still had to prove it was worthy of the interest of a pass rusher and quarterback wrecker made for the modern game. "There's a challenge that a lot of players and a lot of parents have in getting their sons visibility," John Bosa said. "We had none of those challenges. There would be 15 college scouts standing on the sidelines at St. Thomas. A lot of parents have to take their kids to different camps, but I knew from the minute we stepped on St. Thomas' campus that would never be a question for us."

So the Alabama trip the summer after Joey's sophomore season was a test, a toe in the recruiting waters. John Bosa saw a Tide staffer filming his son a lot during the camp. "There was one guy with a camera the whole camp watching Joe's every move," John Bosa said, "so I knew something was up."

After the camp, Bosa found himself sweaty, shirtless, and shivering in Saban's office. Saban asked for a towel for Bosa to put across his shoulders. "He pushes this button that automatically closes his door," Bosa said. "I heard about the door. He just clicked it, and it shut. I was pretty scared. It was a super nice door."

After the door shut, Saban opened another one by extending the offer. Once John Bosa made it clear a commitment wasn't happening right away, father and son flew home, and soon the mail started flooding the St. Thomas football office from every program in the country. Well, most every program. "This is how dysfunctional Boston College was," John Bosa said of his alma mater. "They never offered him."

Actually, they offered during Joey's senior year when John was at an alumni event. While pulled into a football office, John said he told his old school what he thought of them missing the boat on his son by two years. By then, the Bosas had mapped out their plan.

John told his sons that he would never be their coach or their agent. Instead he would always try to surround them with the best. But John did tell Joey he'd help whittle down the options. "The realistic options didn't include Texas, Oklahoma, or USC, schools like that. That really just wasn't it," John Bosa said.

He thought those schools knew their own territories well, but when it came to South Florida, they were tossing out offers without much investment behind them. "What I wanted to look at was what are the schools that really fit you and that you fit? Realistically, what's a school that you could go and thrive?" John said. "So obviously, Alabama was one. Ohio State was another. Michigan was in there. We looked at Wisconsin, Florida State, Florida, schools that kind of made sense for a South Florida kid with his skillset. It was really schools that do recruit Florida boys. So the Big Ten was obviously a natural fit for him and then Florida schools."

Beyond the schools, John was very interested in the people. He pushes back against anyone in recruiting who says a player should commit to the school and not the coach. Bosa believed the people were the deciding factor, so he dug hard into the schools, trying to figure out which coaches might be looking to leave for the NFL or another job. "Once I got it down to a workable list, I said, 'You cannot make a mistake.' I said, 'Listen Joey, the final decision is you. I will be happy and support wherever you want to go,'" John said. "'But you're just going to have to feel it in your heart. You're gonna wake up one morning and you're gonna know.' And that's exactly what happened."

That first OSU visit came in April 2012 during his junior year, when the Bosas made a Midwest swing that hit Wisconsin, Ohio State, and Michigan. They flew up from Florida, then roadtripped from Madison to Columbus to Ann Arbor with both parents and both sons. "We looked like the Griswolds," said Cheryl, imagining the recruiting trip as a version of *National Lampoon's Vacation*. "We rented a minivan, and I laugh thinking about it because the tires on this van were completely bald. Every time we turned a corner, it screeched. We had Nick with us, too. So it was me and John, and then these two giant mammals in the back of the minivan."

When the Bosas arrived in Columbus, Cheryl observed in her son what John said they had been looking for—that moment when you just know. "I saw it in his face," Cheryl said. "I saw it in his face."

With defensive line coach Mike Vrabel, linebackers coach Luke Fickell, secondary coach Kerry Coombs, strength coach Mickey Marotti, Meyer, and Pantoni, the Buckeyes believed they had the kind of people in the program who would make Bosa feel at home. "There's all of a sudden this really good vibe going on," John said. "There was just something about that group."

It was so good that Joey didn't want to make the Michigan trip that was planned to end the Midwest tour. "We're driving to

Michigan, and Joey's going, 'I wanna go home, I don't wanna go to Michigan,'" Cheryl said. "But we had to go to Michigan. And it was a good visit."

But it wasn't Columbus. "I learned this over the years: that the best recruiters are the ones that listen," Meyer said, "to find out what's important to that person. The worst recruiters I've been around are the ones that are scared of empty space in conversations. They talk through empty space and they're usually terrible recruiters, and I've had a few of those. I'd say, 'Listen, will you shut up and just let this kid or this family talk so we can find out what's important to them?' Selling is not always about talking. Before you talk you've got to listen and find out what's important. And so Joey and that whole family was rather clear right from the get-go that this is a father who was a first-round draft pick, this is a mother whose brother was a first-round draft pick, and I knew Eric Kumerow from my days at Ohio State, and they had dreams for this player, and this player had dreams, and those were to be the best in America. So I had to really make sure we had the best coaching, the best training, and our focus was right on because we listened to what this kid was. And I think that's important: that the worst recruiters are scared. I'd lecture my staff, 'The worst recruiters are scared of the empty space in a conversation. The best recruiters embrace that because that's when you get to find out what's important.'"

That trip made one thing clear. "All of a sudden, it's a two-horse race," John said. "It's Ohio State–Alabama."

That horse in Ohio was ready to ride. "The relationship Joey and I had was becoming very strong," Pantoni said. "He was a different kid, kind of like he is now, and somehow I just connected with him in some weird way. So after the visit, Joey and I were texting all day

Monday morning, and John calls me on Tuesday and says, 'Mark, you need to calm down. I don't know what you and Joey are talking about, but he wants to commit, and he needs to take his time with this.' And I was like, John, we'll do whatever you ask."

Cheryl laughs about what it was like to be recruited by Pantoni. "When Pantoni started recruiting the boys, he looked like he was younger than them," she said. "But he's easy. He's so easy. You can rib him, but he's always there for you. And then he's smart. And he's just a great dude. And we just connected with him immediately. Everybody does."

What Joey wanted to do at that point was come back the next weekend for the Ohio State spring football game on Saturday, April 21, 2012. When Joey asked Cheryl if they could go back to Columbus that quickly, her mind began to race. "I'm thinking to myself, *I went to Ohio State. I know what that means.* We're talking about 80,000 people in the stands. We're talking about trying to get a flight, trying to get a hotel room," Cheryl said. "Anywhere else it's like: big deal, it's the spring game. Columbus, you know it's crazy. But in my head, I'm going, *I will spend any amount of money on a hotel room to get him to the spring game.*"

They got there. And Joey made a decision. When Joey and Cheryl went back to the Woody Hayes Athletic Center after the game, he said he wanted to commit to Ohio State. The only problem was that John, who was so involved in every aspect of the process, wasn't on the trip. "He kind of felt bad I wasn't there," John said. "And I said, 'This was a process, and if you feel it in your heart, this is your deal. If you want to commit, then do it.'"

They all decided a FaceTime call would do the trick. So Joey and Cheryl went into Meyer's office, and with John watching over video,

Joey committed to the Buckeyes. "Urban went absolutely bonkers," Cheryl said. "Everyone's freaking out, and it was a blast, an absolute blast."

As they celebrated, everyone, who saw the recruitment through their own personal point of view, was correct. John saw the conclusion of a thorough, comprehensive process. Meyer saw the outcome of listening to a family and providing the best. Pantoni saw the value of a special, innate connection with a player he'd seen something in from the start. And Cheryl saw her son embrace her alma mater the same way she'd done decades earlier. All were true.

Once the first Bosa committed, Pantoni was ready. "I joked with Joey, 'The only reason we took you is to get Nick.'"

As a freshman in 2013, Joey Bosa accrued 7.5 sacks and was named a freshman All-American. He helped the Buckeyes through an undefeated regular season before an upset loss in the Big Ten Championship Game kept them out of the national title game and sent them instead to South Florida to play Clemson in the Orange Bowl. That made it easy for 16-year-old Nick Bosa, who had made first-team All-State as a sophomore at St. Thomas—where he had broken the school sack mark with 14.5—to come by and watch his brother practice. Carter, the Hall of Fame NFL receiver who played for the Buckeyes from 1984 to 1986, was at OSU practice that day as well. With his status as a respected Buckeye and St. Thomas Aquinas assistant coach, Carter had rare insight into the Bosas. "I can't say it because Joey will get mad," Carter said that day. "But the little brother might be better than Joey."

Nick at the time had several offers, including one from Ohio State that had arrived on October 23, when Meyer had called him on his 16th birthday and offered. The Buckeyes were clearly in the lead. The relationship between the brothers was so tight that attending the same school was only a plus. Nick said they did everything together. "It would definitely be cool to keep the legacy going," Nick said then.

Something else was happening that would ensure that the Buckeyes would add another Bosa. The Buckeyes loved Vrabel during recruiting, but after the 2013 season, he left to become an assistant coach with the Houston Texans. After four seasons there, he'd be named the head coach of the Tennessee Titans. His replacement was longtime Penn State defensive line coach Larry Johnson, and it didn't take long for "Coach J" to become almost a member of the Bosa family. "With Joey we didn't know that Coach J was going to be coming there, and oh my God, that's like the best thing that ever happened," Cheryl said. "Vrabel was great, too, but Coach J— look what he's done."

What he's done is develop NFL defensive ends with the detail of a technician and the wisdom of a grandfather. He did it for 18 years at Penn State with players like Tamba Hali and Courtney Brown and he continued it at Ohio State with the Bosas, Chase Young, Tyquan Lewis, Sam Hubbard, and Jalyn Holmes. "I trusted that Urban would get the best of the best as assistant coaches," John said. "I didn't know that my sons would end up loving Larry Johnson more than any coach they ever had. To this day, I just love that guy and what he's done for my sons and I just love him as a person, a mentor, and as a teacher."

That connection grew quickly with Joey in his sophomore season, but it also grew with Nick while he was a junior and senior at St. Thomas. By the time he committed to Ohio State in July 2015 before his senior football season, he practically was a Buckeye. "There was an underlying thought by a lot of the schools that, *Hey, we're gonna offer him, but he's probably gonna follow his brother,"* John said. "So schools were still offering, but their expectations were kind of limited. And I'll be brutally honest: at this point Nick had already sat in on numerous film studies with Coach Johnson, he had already been taught a bunch of techniques at the high school level by Joey and by Coach Johnson. So I say this—and Nick knows it now—but there was no way in hell that Nick was going anywhere but with Larry Johnson. That was done in my mind."

Nick made official visits to Florida State and Florida, but the Bosas didn't want to string any schools along. Nick had always been the Ohio State fan, and now his brother's experience made him want to be a Buckeye even more. "They're so close. Joey being there would only influence him to go there," Cheryl said. "And if it wasn't a good choice, Joey would sit down with him and say, 'I think there's better options.' They're together all the time. They train together. They're always together."

"If you think about it, it would be very natural for a younger son to not want to go to the same school," John said. "Your brother is a Big Ten Defensive Player of the Year, he won a national championship, he's a consensus All-American. Do you really want to follow that? So a lot of guys would want to take a different path. Obviously, that didn't scare Nick."

Not at all. He committed to Ohio State in the summer of 2015 before his senior year of high school. He was named the Big Ten Defensive Lineman of the Year as a sophomore in 2017 before a core muscle injury in 2018 ended his junior season after three games. He was still selected in the 2019 NFL Draft by the San Francisco 49ers at No. 2—one spot higher than his brother three years earlier. He helped lead San Francisco to Super Bowl LIV in his rookie year. "It would be a mistake to say they're not competitive with each other," John said, "but it's a healthy competition."

When Nick, a five-star player and a top 10 overall recruit in the Class of 2016, arrived in Columbus, he was ranked slightly higher than Joey had been. According to the 247Sports.com team rankings, the Buckeyes had the No. 4 class that year—about par for the Meyer era.

Meyer had wondered early on how he could recruit like he had done at Florida. One of the solutions was a program implemented in 2013 called "Real Life Wednesdays" that brought in leaders from the real world to talk to the football team and provide advice about getting jobs and growing as leaders. That became the thing that Meyer believed separated Ohio State from other schools, that allowed them to compete with better weather and larger local recruiting bases to still gather one of the two or three best classes in the nation. "No one had Real Life Wednesdays," Meyer said. "That was so powerful. Still is. I would say 99 percent of the big-time players that signed, that was reason either one or two why they came to Ohio State."

Now the head football coach of the Jacksonville Jaguars, Meyer pulled together six full recruiting classes at Ohio State from 2013 to 2018 that in the 247Sports rankings were No. 2, No. 3, No. 7, No. 4, No. 2, and No. 2. He'll likely never recruit again after spending 30 years doing it as an assistant and head coach. When he arrived in 2012, Meyer's belief that committed players should be recruited right up until Signing Day and until their commitment was official ruffled feathers in the Big Ten. Talk of a previous "gentleman's agreement" between conference coaches to leave committed players alone took up an entire an offseason. Michigan State coach Mark Dantonio and Wisconsin coach Bret Bielema expressed dissatisfaction with

Meyer's tactics after Ohio State flipped players away from the Spartans and Badgers in the Class of 2012. Meyer responded by telling a group of Ohio school coaches at a clinic that he expected his nine assistants to do it again. Soon, the Big Ten entered a new era of recruiting that was more aggressive and more national. The strategy employed by Meyer was copied and became commonplace. Big Ten recruiting never looked back.

When Meyer retired from Ohio State after the 2018 season, he'd sometimes wake in the morning missing the everyday fight of recruiting. He always cared about recruiting rankings, always loved that it was evaluation friendly, always craved the competition that recruiting provided out of season. "But it's never been harder," Meyer said, "because recruiting is about relationships."

When the signing period for football players moved from February to December for the Class of 2018, Meyer thought coaches and schools lost time to get to know players because the entire recruiting calendar moved up as a result. "I loved recruiting a player that we got to know for a couple years because we'd never lose him," Meyer said. "In my mind we would never lose a player if we got to spend time. It's the quick ones, where you get one shot at them and they're committing their sophomore year—those are hard."

With the Bosas it wasn't quick. It was a process. It seemed easy and it seemed right because so many strings pulled together. After Joey Bosa committed, he told Meyer the same story he'd told his family all along: that he had never planned to be or wanted to be a Buckeye. He always wanted to find his own school, the right place for him, one with the right people. It turned out…that was Ohio State.

CHAPTER 2

# Donte Whitner, Class of 2003

Donte Whitner's focus was in place from the start—maybe because he wasn't at Ohio State only for himself. He was there with his own NFL objective but also with an opportunity to create a path for players from his community to follow. By the time he left Columbus as the No. 8 overall pick in the 2006 NFL Draft, the safety from Glenville High School in Cleveland had fundamentally changed how Ohio State football operated in two long-lasting ways. To achieve that required dedication from Day One. "I'm not sure I ever saw him smile in the three years he was with us. I don't think he ever had a day of fun," Jim Tressel said of the five-star player he recruited as part of his second full class at Ohio State and then coached for three seasons. "He was just on a mission and he had it all planned out. He knew what he had to do and he was going to learn the game."

When Whitner arrived at Ohio State in January of 2003, he was 17 years old and enrolling early at a program playing for a national championship. Whitner's stay in Columbus began at The Blackwell Inn on Ohio State's campus as he prepared to become the second high school senior to ever enroll early at Ohio State. He started school in January in order to take part in spring football practice. Only running back Maurice Clarett had done it the year before.

Then Whitner watched Clarett help lead the Buckeyes to a victory against the Miami Hurricanes in the National Championship Game in the Fiesta Bowl on Friday night, January 3, 2003. By Monday morning Whitner was out of The Blackwell and into his dorm, starting classes for the winter session at Ohio State. "I skipped senior basketball, senior track, everything because I was on this fast pace to go to Ohio State and be a first-round pick," Whitner said. "At this point I'm in a new environment, coming from a primarily African American environment. So now I'm integrating by myself virtually to Ohio State, and it's a culture shock for me. So I'm dealing with a culture shock, I'm dealing with this big campus, I'm dealing with the curriculum, which I felt like I hadn't been prepared for. I have to figure out classes and I have to teach myself the nuances of the college game."

He was joining a team flying high off the program's first national championship in three decades and a team that wasn't accustomed to freshmen joining the team so soon. Whitner existed in this new realm alone, a kid trying to add to a program that had just proven it had everything it needed to win it all. "I'm competing against guys who are three, four years ahead of me and hearing this top high school guy is coming in early to take your job," Whitner said. "So now I'm not only dealing with competition on the field. I'm dealing with guys who don't even want to show me where my class is, who don't even want to show me what building I'm supposed to be in, who don't want to give me a ride when they know I'm gonna be late. So all these things I have to figure out at 17 years old."

He did figure it out, and now incoming OSU freshmen leaving high school early and enrolling in the winter is so normal that it's almost expected. That's recruiting in this era. The best players often get to college as fast as they can. In Ohio State's Class of 2021, 15 of the 21 players enrolled in January and took part in spring practice. The success of players like Whitner 18 years earlier helped create that new normal.

That was one change Whitner helped usher in. And there's the Glenville pipeline and the new normal that Whitner, Tressel, Troy Smith, Ted Ginn Sr., and Ted Ginn Jr. created for a Cleveland high school and an Ohio State football program that became linked by talent, commitment, and a shared view of the world. That connection started between Ted Ginn Sr., the coach and patriarch of the Glenville football program, and Tressel, a Northeast Ohio native who vowed to get the best players from the Cleveland area to Columbus.

What Tressel and Ginn formed led to a Glenville High School football player being part of Ohio State's recruiting class for 13 straight years from 2002 to 2014. Over that time 22 Tarblooders signed with the Buckeyes. The last group in 2014 included future NFL first-round draft pick and 2017 NFL Defensive Rookie of the Year Marshon Lattimore. The Glenville pipeline for the Buckeyes started with three players who proved beyond a doubt that Ohio State's faith in them was justified. The first was Smith in the Class of 2002, who took over as the starting quarterback for the Buckeyes in 2004, won the Heisman Trophy in 2006, and was selected in the fifth round of the 2007 NFL Draft by the Baltimore Ravens.

Next was Class of 2003's Whitner, who became a two-year starter at safety and made first-team All-Big Ten in 2005. He was drafted by the Buffalo Bills in the first round in 2006 and went on to an 11-year NFL career as a starting safety that included two Pro Bowl selections. Then came Ginn Jr. in the Class of 2004, the receiver and return man with blazing speed who scored 27 touchdowns in his three-year OSU career, was drafted at pick No. 9 by the Miami Dolphins in the 2007 NFL Draft, and went on to a 14-year NFL career. "When you have three hit like that," Tressel said, "then the younger kids in the school see that."

Whitner is proud of that Glenville legacy. "That means everything to me, I know that it means everything to Ted Ginn Jr., and I know that it means everything to Troy Smith because at that point we didn't have anybody to look at and say, 'Hey, I can do that,'" Whitner said. "So we had to go strictly on belief from Coach Ginn."

Glenville players had their role models and they saw they were wearing scarlet and gray. The connection for Tressel and Ginn Sr., though, went beyond football. Tressel remembered meeting Ginn at a Fellowship of Christian Athletes camp in Erie, Pennsylvania, in the 1990s. Tressel was there as the Youngstown State head coach, a position he held from 1986 to 2000. "I'd gotten to know Ted and I just admired so much what he was trying to do for those players," Tressel said. "At Youngstown State maybe we got one kid over the course of time, but we just didn't quite have the star power that could attract some of those kids. But I periodically noticed that a couple really good players had gone to Michigan."

Tressel, in particular, noted defensive end Pierre Woods, one of the top 50 players in the country in the Class of 2001, who picked the Wolverines and signed with Michigan weeks after Tressel was hired to replace John Cooper. Tressel was introduced as Ohio State's head coach on January 18, just 20 days before Signing Day in 2001. That would be the first and last time the Buckeyes signed a class on Tressel's watch that didn't include a Glenville player. "Tress," Ginn Sr. said in 2014 as the Glenville-OSU run was ending, "that's my friend."

Always an advocate for his players, Ginn Sr. wondered why more colleges didn't actively recruit players from inner-city Cleveland. So to spread the word on their talent, he organized summer tours where Ginn drove a van of Glenville players and others from Cleveland to camps at colleges around the Midwest. "In those early days, there was a little bit of nervousness because we didn't know until we actually got to the camps that we would match up against anybody else in the country," Whitner said. "So there was a little bit of nervousness, a lot of talking from Coach Ginn on demeanor and how to act in front of certain people and how to handle certain situations and how to always compete and go through the whistle. So he would constantly beat that in our heads over and over. And once we got to our first couple camps, we started to have success, and the scholarship offers started to flow."

Ginn wanted those offers from everywhere. He wanted his players to get to college and get an education. That was the first priority. If Ohio State was interested, all the better.

To encourage that interest from Ohio high schools, Tressel had hired 29-year-old defensive backs coach Mel Tucker, a Cleveland native, to recruit Northeast Ohio. Tucker held maybe the most important recruiting job on the new staff. "There was an issue there with Michigan poaching players out of Northeast Ohio," Tucker said. "So that was my charge: to not let anyone out of Northeast Ohio that we wanted."

Tressel had grown up in Berea on the West Side of Cleveland, and Tucker had grown up in Cleveland Heights on the East Side. Between the two of them, they figured they had Cleveland covered. "I can honestly say in my four years at Ohio State: no one ever got out of there that we wanted," said Tucker, who left Ohio State for the Cleveland Browns after the 2004 season, the first of several more steps in a coaching career that would eventually lead him to become the head coach at Michigan State in 2020. "Between Coach Tressel and myself, we were able to partner up and get it done. And we felt we just had to get it done in Northeast Ohio. At that time, that needed that to be a foothold for Ohio State."

It became very clear in the early 2000s that recruiting the best football talent in Cleveland required recruiting Glenville. "Mel was a Cleveland guy, and I was a Cleveland guy, and we said, 'Obviously, we have to develop a relationship with Coach Ginn,' and again, I just admired the guy," Tressel said. "What he did for kids was unheard of."

"I think that he understood that there was something missing from our neighborhood," Whitner said of Ginn. "You might be the best athlete, but if you don't have the grades and you don't have the parental background, then you don't have that guidance to be able to make it. So he's that father figure. So he understood that there's a need in the community."

That first summer after Tressel was hired, the Ginn Bus Tour stopped in Columbus. Outside the Woody Hayes Athletic Center, the first Glenville-Ohio State connections were made. "We were out behind the Woody on what used to be the old field hockey field," Tressel said. "It was like concrete. And the kids were out there, and I was talking to Ted and I said, 'Man, that guy can throw it.'"

Tressel was getting his first glimpse at his future Heisman winner. "Troy was being recruited but not crazy high," Tressel said. "West Virginia, I think, was where he was leaning a little bit."

Ohio State was already on to Justin Zwick as its quarterback for the Class of 2002. "I wanted to be honest with Troy that Justin was highly ranked on our board," Tressel said. "But if he'd like to come and compete, it probably wouldn't be that first fall because there are only so many reps to go around. So come in and do some other things. We're going to sign you as an athlete. So Troy felt like we were up front with him and he was enjoying his experience, and that got us kicked off. And Coach Ginn appreciated that we were working with him just as we said we would and he was confident we were going to give him a chance to be a quarterback when the time was right. So that really began."

Two years behind Smith, Ginn's son looked like a sure thing for the Buckeyes. "Recruiting young Ted was a no-brainer," Tressel said.

In-between was Whitner, who had emerged as one of the top defensive backs in the country after lighting up those summer camps between his junior and senior year. He narrowed his choices down to Ohio State, Michigan, Notre Dame, Miami, and USC. The Hurricanes and Trojans offered better weather, and Notre Dame had that Golden Dome tradition and an Ohio quarterback in its 2003 class in Brady Quinn who was eager to have Whitner join him. "He'd call me every day like, 'Come on, man, you've got to go to Notre Dame with me,'" Whitner said. "They had a lot of talent, which is why I put them on my list. But I didn't go there because you couldn't have girls in your dorm room. That's why I chose not to go there. That was my reason."

That left Ohio State and Michigan, and the Wolverines' history of success and recruiting in Ohio and at Glenville mattered to Whitner.

"They were a hard-nosed, tough football team and they were really welcoming to us when we went to all the Michigan camps," Whitner said. "So we had really tight relationships with all the Michigan coaches from Lloyd Carr all the way down to the strength staff. We had a bond."

Although Smith was the first Glenville player to choose Ohio State, Whitner was the first where it was really a battle. Smith would become a Buckeyes legend, but he was an under-the-radar recruit. Whitner—a cerebral, serious, physical, fast safety who could hit—was wanted by everyone. "I chose Ohio State because it was the hometown team," Whitner said. "Coach Tressel, Mel Tucker, I knew they would always have my back, and going to Ohio State, they always had my back. Mel Tucker, he really taught me the nuances of: okay, you have the talent, but now let's use your mind. So he's the first person who got me looking at keys and certain things on the football field to make me one step faster to make those plays. He was especially hard on me and making sure I was always communicating... So I would say it started with Mel Tucker, and then it trickled down, and then Coach Tress was a big part as well. But you have boots on the ground and a guy who's as trusted and knowledgeable and who is as respected as Mel Tucker, and then he works harder than anybody. And you can trust him. He built that trust with Coach Ginn, let him know that he would take care of his kids. And that's what really did it: Mel Tucker building a relationship with Coach Ginn and building that trust, and that's why a lot of guys ended up at Ohio State."

That trust between Glenville and Ohio State continued after Tucker was gone. It led to players such as offensive lineman Bryant Browning, safety Jermale Hines, offensive lineman Marcus Hall, safety Christian Bryant, quarterback Cardale Jones, linebacker Chris

Worley, and Lattimore, among others, playing for Glenville first and Ohio State next. Tressel said his recruiting philosophy at Ohio State included providing opportunities to players from Ohio. He found a school with a coach looking to give his players just that kind of chance. "I've had a ton of kids come here, and they've given them hope, been an example for my kids, and treated them really well," Ginn Sr. said after accepting an "Ohio's Finest" award from Ohio State at a coaching clinic in 2019. "More importantly, I know what it means and I teach kids what it means to be an Ohio State person."

Whitner helped make it happen. "Donte was totally different than Troy and Teddy," Tressel said, "but just a special, special player and special kid. Totally motivated."

Whitner said when he called Carr at Michigan to tell the Wolverines coach that he had picked Ohio State, Carr hung up the phone. "Never talked to him or heard from him again to this day," Whitner said. "You don't forget that."

Neither Glenville nor Ohio State will forget what Whitner did. After 157 NFL games—152 of them starts—with the Bills, San Francisco 49ers, Cleveland Browns, and Washington Redskins, Whitner retired after the 2016 season and is now involved in sports broadcasting as an analyst. He's also been working on a documentary about Coach Ginn and all the NFL players he helped produce. With Smith's Heisman Trophy and the NFL success of Whitner and Ginn Jr., the Glenville story has been told in many ways and by many people. But few can tell it like Whitner. And the story can't be told in full without Ohio State. "Think about it. Think about the community that they took a chance on," Whitner said. "They took a chance on inner-city kids from an impoverished community out of Cleveland, Ohio. So they came into our school where nobody else believed, came to our games, came and sat on our couches when nobody else was coming. And they came there and they said, 'Hey, you guys have talent. We believe in you. If we follow this plan, everybody's gonna be successful.'"

CHAPTER 3

# Ryan Shazier,
# Class of 2011

Wednesday, December 8, 2010, started like any other day in South Florida for Plantation High School senior Ryan Shazier, one of the fastest, nimblest, fiercest linebacker recruits in the country and a loyal Florida Gators commit for the last half year. By the end of the day, his future head coach had resigned, assistants from two other college football programs were camped out at his high school, and the meticulous recruiting process of the Shazier family had been blown up just one month before Shazier planned to start college as an early enrollee in January. Over the next year, Shazier would lose his head coach three times, only to wind up back where he started.

Safety Jeremy Cash, Shazier's friend and teammate, committed to Ohio State eight months earlier. The Buckeyes had also been after Shazier, but he'd pledged to Urban Meyer and the Gators in June. Then rumors circulated during the school day that Meyer, who had briefly resigned as Florida's coach for a day in 2009, was again going to step away. "Cash was like, 'Hey Ryan, you know

Coach Meyer's resigning,' and he was laughing at me," Shazier said, "I was like, 'You're lying.' And then I Googled it.'"

Early afternoon reports were out that Meyer was stepping down. By 2:00 PM Florida made it official. Meyer held a news conference that evening to announce his resignation. As word started to leak, assistant coaches from Ohio State and LSU were at Plantation High ready to speak to Shazier, and those schools knew they were back in the game for a top 150 national recruit.

Shazier and his parents, Vernon and Shawn, had undertaken every step of the recruiting process together. They evaluated together and decided together, but in this moment, Ryan was taking matters into his own hands. He met with OSU assistant Paul Haynes and LSU assistant Billy Gonzales and made his intentions clear. "I didn't even tell my dad," Shazier said. "I was like, 'I just want to let y'all know that my recruitment is open. We can talk. I'm all ears. I will listen to whatever you've got to say now.'"

Shazier had always listened to his dad. A pastor, leadership speaker, and chaplain for the Miami Dolphins, Vernon Shazier also coached his son early in his football career, and there was a way of playing the game that he wanted to instill in Ryan, something Vernon saw firsthand from Dolphins All-Pro defensive end Jason Taylor. "I call it dog training," Vernon Shazier said.

In junior high and high school, Ryan would get into a pass rush stance, sprint 20 yards, take a 30-second break, and do it again over and over, simulating the burst and recovery of a football game. The goal was explosion and pursuit and then reloading and then exploding and pursuing again. "In the NFL and college, players take off plays," Vernon said. "You want to be a dog? You don't take off plays. You tell that tackle before the game starts, 'You better not take off a play because I'm not taking one off. You take a play off, you're gonna lose your quarterback.' Ryan was trained to be a monster. I trained him to be a monster."

He, though, was a skinny monster. "He had a problem maintaining weight," Vernon said. "We did everything we could to maintain Ryan at 180 pounds in high school."

Vernon Shazier always saw his son as a linebacker—a 6'2" safety body with a linebacker physicality and attitude. But during his junior season for the good of the team, Ryan played defensive end for Plantation. In a 12-game season, he missed two games because of injury and still had 19.5 sacks. "He just destroyed Broward County," Vernon said of one of the most talent-rich pockets of high school football in the country.

"I was just so fast," Ryan said. "And the linemen in high school just aren't technique-sound. They just blocked everybody the same, so they really weren't prepared for my speed coming off the edge. They tried to block me as if they were blocking a regular D end, so I was able to just run around them and cut off one side of the field because I got off the ball so much faster than these guys they were normally going against."

Blazing fast 180-pound defensive ends can tear up high school football opponents, but they don't translate to the next level. Both Ryan and Vernon knew he'd play linebacker in college, and Ryan worked out in linebacker groups during summer camps and he did his father's linebacker drills on his own. But some schools had a hard time seeing past the lack of in-game proof to make a linebacker evaluation. With that possibility in the backs of their minds, the Shaziers made the 40-minute drive from their home in Pompano Beach to the University of Miami during the summer between Ryan's junior and senior season. Vernon, a huge fan of the Hurricanes, hoped for the best. "He was going to go to Miami," Vernon said, "just because I loved Miami."

"Growing up, I was never a Miami fan. I didn't want to go there," Ryan said. "But I wanted their interest because I was like, hey, I would seriously consider this school because my father loved this school, and my family was close. But they were like, 'Hey Ryan, you never played linebacker in high school, so how do we know you're going to be good at linebacker in college?'"

That's not the kind of question you want to ask a rare athlete playing out of position only to help his high school team. Shazier, who had at least 30 offers already in hand, did everything he could to get the Miami offer he wanted in his heart, the one he thought he earned with his talent. "Miami said, 'Well, we haven't seen him play linebacker. We want to see him play some linebacker his senior year,'" Vernon said. "So we leave Miami. He's pissed off they don't offer him. I've got a big Miami magnet on my front door at the house. To this day, I don't know where it's at. Ryan smashed it down. I don't know what he did with it."

"Yeah, I was like, 'I'm not going to Miami,'" Ryan said, "'So let's just take that off.'"

Not everyone had questions about Shazier at linebacker. Since taking over as Ohio State's linebackers coach in 2004, Luke Fickell had coached standouts such as A.J. Hawk, Bobby Carpenter, James Laurinaitis, Marcus Freeman, Ross Homan, and Brian Rolle. But Fickell, who attended each one of Shazier's spring practices at the end of his junior year, saw that Shazier was different. At one of the practices, he stood next to a Miami assistant. "I literally said to him, 'This kid right here is my favorite kid anywhere in the country I've seen all year,'" Fickell said. "He said to me, 'Yeah, we've got a bunch of guys like that who just run really fast.' And I'm like, 'Yeah, well I don't think we do.'"

It wasn't just out-of-state schools willing to take Shazier without linebacker experience. There was another school in Florida that didn't have a make-or-break issue with Shazier's position. "He had come to a camp and run something like a 4.4, a 4.3, something really crazy," said Mark Pantoni, who was running Meyer's recruiting operation at Florida at that point before later following Meyer to Ohio State and reshaping the Buckeyes' recruiting office. "But you always wondered because he was this 185-pound kid playing defensive end in high school and just this raw athlete. You saw the flashes on film with how explosive he was, but you never really knew could this guy play linebacker because there was no film of it. But for us at Florida, he was an in-state kid, he came from a great family, so he was a no-brainer for us."

The idea for the Gators was to take the great athlete and then figure out the details. That's what the Shaziers were doing on the other side—figuring out the details. Vernon set up a recruiting control center in their home with flip charts for each contending school hanging from the walls. Florida State had been the first offer, followed by Oklahoma, Alabama, and Florida, and soon after, Ohio State. The issue was narrowing down options, so Ryan centered on a top five that his father researched in every way: Florida, LSU, Ohio State, North Carolina, and UCLA. Program history, coaches' backgrounds, linebacker depth chart, academics—the data was all there. Florida State, for instance, the school Ryan had liked growing up, was hurt by having too many young linebackers that might block his path to the field. Armed with that info, the Shaziers drove to Gainesville, 300 miles away, for an unofficial visit in June 2010.

Shazier was lured by Meyer's success, winning national titles in 2006 and 2008. Everything else about the successful home state school, which is the No. 1 option for most players in most recruiting situations, just fit. "My mom loved the school, how close it was," Ryan said. "They're a top five school right now. They have one of the best coaches of all time. I have a legit shot of winning a championship. And I'm right here at home. So my family fell in love with it."

The decision even made sense to Ohio State coach Jim Tressel, who knew his linebackers coach was enamored with Shazier. "I remember how much Luke liked him all along," Tressel said, "just the kind of person he was. When you're going into another state that's got great programs, you're going to have to have a little bit of luck. The natural thing—I always felt for kids—was to play at the greatest place they could where their parents could be a part of it. And so I never questioned a kid not wanting to venture further if that were the case. But in his case, it was Luke's stick-to-itiveness. I think Luke liked being around the kid and I don't think we thought we were gonna get him."

With those feelings about a big-time school an easy drive away and with the charts giving the Shaziers the comfort that this decision was both heart and head, Ryan called Meyer on the drive home from the unofficial visit and committed to the Gators with the start of his senior high school football season more than two months away. "It was super exciting," Shazier said. "The whole offseason during camps or seven-on-seven camps, I'm one of the guys who's super supporting the Gators. While we're doing the camp, I'm having a Gator hat on and I'll wear Gator gloves when I catch a pick. Everyone knew: Ryan Shazier is going to the Gators."

That fall Shazier would regularly drive to Florida home games on unofficial visits. The family grew accustomed to the trip. Shazier had committed to Florida after an unofficial visit and he never took any official visits, the trips when schools can pay for a recruit and then put their best foot forward. In the name of having that official visit experience, even though he was locked in on his choice, Shazier said he asked Florida if he could make an official to Ohio State on November 27, 2010, for the Michigan game. A recruit can make five official visits to five different schools, and Shazier wanted to use this trip to Columbus to watch the No. 8 Buckeyes basically for fun.

It didn't happen, though the stories differ as to why. Shazier still remembers it was the game when the Buckeyes' alternate uniforms were scarlet jerseys and scarlet helmets with gray pants. But he remembers it from what he saw on TV. Shazier said he asked Florida, and the Gators asked him not to go. "They were just like, 'Hey, Ryan, you're committed to us, we're committed to you, we don't really have any other linebackers committed right now, we supported your commitment,' so I was like, 'Cool, I'm a man of my word. I'm not gonna visit anywhere else,'" Shazier said.

Fickell recalled the discussion he had with Shazier a bit differently. "We were still recruiting him a little bit, still talking to him and trying to bring him up," Fickell said. "He wanted to come up to go to the Michigan game. So he was going to do an official visit to the Michigan game, and I called him the week before and I was like, 'Is your dad gonna come?' And he was like, 'No, my dad's a pastor for the Dolphins, and they have a game, so he can't come.' And I was like, 'If he can't come, I'm not bringing you.' If your dad has never been here, you're gonna go home after this weekend and say, 'Dad, I really like it. I want to go there.' And there's no way he's going to say okay. So if you can't bring your dad, then we're not doing it."

Dan Herron ran for 175 yards, and Terrelle Pryor threw two touchdown passes as the Buckeyes beat Michigan for the seventh straight time, winning 37–7. It was, unsurprisingly, the last rivalry game for Michigan coach Rich Rodriguez, who would be fired in January. As Tressel moved to 9–1 against the Wolverines, there were no indications yet that this would also be his final game in the rivalry. By not taking the visit, Shazier maintained an official visit option to Ohio State if he would ever need it for some reason. "That was the best thing that ever happened," Fickell said, "because then we could do an official visit after everything went down."

Ten days later, Shazier realized he would need it. Under Tressel the Buckeyes were not in the habit of spending a lot of time recruiting players who were verbally committed to another school. But two things were at play with Shazier. One was how much Fickell liked him. The other was that Cash was an Ohio State commitment, which gave Haynes and Fickell reasons to stop by Plantation High School and perhaps keep the Buckeyes in the back of Shazier's mind.

"We didn't normally do a whole bunch if they'd committed elsewhere," Tressel said. "But when you're back in the area recruiting other kids and you're fond of a kid, Luke would stop by and that type of thing."

Once the recruiting door opened again, the Buckeyes were running through it. "The day Urban resigned—Bam!—it was a beeline to the school and to the house," Fickell said.

The Buckeyes were in SEC country, back taking on the SEC. Ohio State had lost to Florida and Meyer in the 2006 national title game and then lost the first recruiting round to the Gators for Shazier. The Buckeyes lost the 2007 national title game to LSU and coach Les Miles and then faced the Tigers again in this renewed battle for Shazier. Ohio State would go all out. "Both of them went at him like a tiger that hadn't eaten in six months," Vernon Shazier said.

Beyond the renewed vigor from LSU and Ohio State, Florida tried to keep Shazier after hiring Texas defensive coordinator Will Muschamp as its new coach three days after Meyer's resignation. That included Muschamp visiting the Shazier home. "I remember trying like heck when Urban left to keep him in the fold," Pantoni said. "I know Will loved Ryan and his family, and they tried to hold on as much as they could."

But the ground had shifted. Miami had hesitated, Florida had changed. Now it looked like it was time for Shazier to take a hard look beyond the borders of his home state. The family went back to the flip charts. It seemed like a two-school race with LSU and Ohio State, so they started planning trips. Knowing he wanted to enroll at his new college in less than a month, Ryan told the schools he needed to visit immediately. Meyer resigned Wednesday, and Shazier was in Baton Rouge, Louisiana, starting an official visit on Friday. "I had a great trip," Shazier said. "I told everybody, 'I'm going to LSU. I love LSU.'"

He was back from LSU on Sunday and scheduled to fly with his father to Ohio State on Wednesday and he wasn't sure why they were bothering. "I was like, 'Dad, I'm gonna be honest. I don't know why we're going to Ohio State,'" Shazier said.

Vernon told his son to remain open-minded and to stick by the plan and his promise to visit Columbus. Even in his momentary certainty about LSU, Ryan had always considered Ohio State an interesting outlier. "If I ever went up north, Ohio State would be the only school I would go up north to," he said.

Upon touching down in Columbus, Shazier got a real feel for the north. "It was like 10 degrees or -4. It was crazy cold," Ryan said. "When I had left home, it was 80 degrees."

"I guess Vernon had never really been north," Fickell said. "And it was the coldest week of the year. The two-and-a-half days Ryan was here with his dad, it was zero or below. And his dad, before they got on the plane, took something that supposedly raises your body temperature. He sweated the entire time. But it was zero degrees, and I was like, we'll never get this guy."

It was cold, there weren't many people on campus, and he wasn't able to spend much time with the team, which was preparing to play Arkansas in the Sugar Bowl. "I'll be honest. My visit at Ohio State wasn't a super great visit," Shazier said.

But he liked the few players he did meet. "It feels like me. These guys feel like me. I feel comfortable around these people," Shazier said.

"It was a midnight hour thing because he was going to school in January, but I know the connectivity he had with our kids was important," Tressel said. "But, gosh, he looked to me like he was 180 pounds, and I kept thinking, *Luke, are you sure this guy is all that you say he is?* And Luke said, 'I promise you he's all that I say he is.'"

Particularly with an academic calendar that had more LSU students on campus when Shazier was there, Baton Rouge and Columbus in December were very different places. But Shazier tried to move his decision beyond a winter's first glance. "If I was going strictly off a good time and this is the most fun place, I probably would have gone to LSU," Shazier said. "Ohio State is a fine place. But my two visits: one had all the students there, and it was warm, and it had a bunch of parties, while the other one was like nobody there, and it's freezing cold…I had to weave through what's fun to what is actually important."

Ohio State made an impression in that way. Whenever they visited a school, Vernon Shazier said he would ask everyone he met a simple question: "What makes your program special?"

"At every school I got a variety of answers," Vernon said. "On the Ohio State visit, every single person I asked that question said, 'Jim Tressel.' I'm a leadership coach, and that said a lot to me. Every single person said 'Jim Tressel.'"

The Shaziers got on the plane home on Friday with a choice to make. Ryan wanted to finish high school early so he could start college in January and take part in spring football. He was making his final announcement at a graduation party that night. "My visit to LSU was definitely better," he said. "But when me and my dad were talking, I felt like for my life it would be better if I came to Ohio State."

Then came the party. Since Ryan had committed in June, and the plan to graduate early had been known for months, the party colors had previously been established—orange and blue for Florida. Once his mother had heard the report from the LSU visit before Ryan and Vernon had taken off for Columbus, the new lean had been relayed. So there was some expectation that Ryan was now returning from Columbus for a Florida-themed party where he would announce he was attending LSU. "Everybody was waiting," Vernon said.

Instead Shazier chose the Buckeyes. It was just 10 days since Meyer stepped down, and the Shaziers had done everything to shuffle their lives and prepare Ryan for the next step. And then life was shaken again.

Five days after Shazier picked the Buckeyes, the fact that several Ohio State players had received extra benefits in the form of tattoos and money in exchange for memorabilia came to light. Less than six months later on Memorial Day 2011, Tressel was forced to resign from Ohio State as a result. Shazier had gone from committing to Meyer to committing to Tressel—only to see both head coaches resign. "I seriously thought about transferring," Shazier said. "When Coach Tressel resigned and all those sanctions went down, I was like I don't want to go into a school with a bunch of sanctions."

Ohio State self-imposed two years of probation and a small reduction of scholarships in July, but the NCAA didn't hand down a one-year bowl ban, which the Buckeyes took in 2012, until late December. In May, Shazier figured—probably correctly—that since he hadn't yet played for the Buckeyes, he could transfer and apply for a waiver that would allow him to play immediately at a new school. But Shazier didn't want to uproot his life. And after losing two head coaches for whom he planned to play, Shazier would now be coached by Fickell. The longtime linebackers coach was tapped to lead the Buckeyes for the 2011 season. They had maintained a relationship even while Shazier was committed to Florida.

That relationship would help keep Shazier in Columbus during a freshman season where he proved he wasn't like any other Ohio State linebacker. Playing behind senior Andrew Sweat (a fact that the Shazier family flip charts had anticipated), Shazier was blowing up thanks to big plays on special teams. That drove a conversation all season about why he wasn't playing more. After Sweat was injured, Shazier started the last three games against Penn State,

Michigan, and in the Gator Bowl against...Florida. In his only fully healthy start of the season against the Nittany Lions, Shazier made 15 tackles—more than any Buckeye had made in a game in two years—and he was named the Big Ten's Freshman of the Week. Battling a knee injury, he made eight tackles against Michigan and 10 against the Gators.

And he changed head coaches again. After a season under Fickell, the coach who believed in him as a recruit, Shazier was back to... Meyer. After a year away from the game, Meyer was hired by Ohio State on November 28, 2011—12 days shy of a year from his resignation at Florida. College football head coach No. 4 for Shazier was the same as college football head coach No. 1. There, however, was one issue. "This isn't any knock to Coach Meyer or anything, but when Coach Fickell got demoted or whatever, I really loved Coach Fickell during the whole recruiting process, and he was the main reason I went to Ohio State because he's a great linebackers coach, and I really support him," Shaizer said. "He's a great coach. I love him a lot, and when he got demoted, I was like, that sucks. I was excited to play for Coach Meyer when he came in, but I was just having questions about what the future looked like at Ohio State."

In 18 months of making college decisions, Shazier went from commitment, to coach resignation, to decommitment, to commitment, to coach resignation, to not starting, to starting, to coaching change, to bowl ban. Now he once again was thinking about a transfer. But Meyer kept Fickell on staff in his previous role as co-defensive coordinator, and Shazier decided to stick with the decision he had made in the first place—to play for Meyer. "Me and Coach Meyer had some talks, and we just talked about everything that was leading me to going to Florida," Shazier said. "I just remembered how great of a coach he was and how excited I was going to be to play for him at Florida. And I was like, why would I not be excited to play for him at Ohio State?"

Meyer had a built a connection, going back to Shazier's original pledge to Florida. "I got so close with his mom and dad," Meyer said. "Obviously, his father was a team pastor. So I knew his faith was so important. Faith was obviously important to me, too. So that was big. So to get to coach him at Ohio State, I love that family."

Shazier also realized he had found a home as part of the Ohio State defense. "We've got a lot of great talent here and talking to myself, I was like, *I would be a dummy to transfer from a school where I'm starting.* I was a guaranteed lock," Shazier said. "Nobody was going to take my spot away."

No one did. And for the next two seasons, Shazier played linebacker for the Buckeyes like few ever have. That dog training had created a linebacker with a rare mix of intelligence, instinct, speed, and strength. Shazier led the Buckeyes in tackles in 2012 with 115 and was named first-team All-Big Ten. Banned from the postseason, the Buckeyes went 12–0 with Shazier as arguably their best player.

In 2013 Shazier led the Buckeyes with 143 tackles, the most by an Ohio State player since Chris Spielman 26 years earlier. Shazier was named first-team All-Big Ten and first-team All-American, and the Buckeyes started 12–0 and were on track for a BCS National Championship matchup with Florida State before they were upset by Michigan State in the Big Ten Championship Game. Shazier was arguably their best player again. "We were the better team. We just had a terrible game," Shazier said. "So we probably could have had a national championship."

Shazier wouldn't win a title at Ohio State. He turned pro after three seasons in Columbus, and the Buckeyes won it all the next season in 2014. But after the twisting way he made it to Columbus and the complicated reality of his freshman season, Shazier as a sophomore and junior gave the Buckeyes exactly what Fickell said during recruiting—a player unlike any other they had. Once Shazier decided to go north, it unfolded the way his father expected. "You can find some Ryan Shaziers in the SEC," Vernon said. "It's going to be very hard to find them in the Big Ten. In the Big Ten, it's going to look like you're playing with high school kids. Your speed is going to be that fast. It's like a father chasing his child."

The dominance led to the next obvious outcome—the NFL. Shazier was chosen by the Pittsburgh Steelers with the No. 15 pick in the 2014 NFL Draft. Over four seasons in Pittsburgh he played in 46 games and was named to the Pro Bowl twice. On December 4, 2017 on *Monday Night Football*, Shazier made a tackle against the Cincinnati Bengals that ended his football career.

A severe spinal injury required surgery and initiated fears that Shazier may be paralyzed. A couple of months later, he regained movement in his legs. Seventeen months later on May 3, 2019, he danced with his bride, Michelle, on their wedding day.

In September 2020, Shazier officially announced his retirement from the NFL at age 28. A husband, a father of two, a son, a star, a Steeler, and a Buckeye, he would move to the next stage of his life, which included ventures in the media world. Over the last decade, the game he loved had taken him down paths beyond his control. Wherever he landed, even if not by his choice, Ryan Shazier made that place better. "I wouldn't do anything different," Shazier said. "If I knew Coach Meyer was going to Ohio State, I probably would have committed to Ohio State a lot earlier and stopped all the drama. But if I had to look at it all over again, I don't think I would have changed anything."

The final Ohio State outcome of his son's journey provided Vernon Shazier with one of his favorite jokes. When it all shook out, he liked to say with a smile that Meyer in the end followed Ryan to Ohio State. "Urban," Vernon said, "knew he was a champion."

## CHAPTER 4

# Cornelius Green,
# Class of 1972

In the fall of 1969, a young Black high school quarterback named Cornelius Green and a young Black college football assistant coach named Rudy Hubbard made changes that set them on a path toward each other and toward Ohio State history. One changed high schools, one knew he had to change recruiting areas, and the result three years later would break barriers in Columbus and set the Buckeyes on the last great run of the Woody Hayes era. What one of them didn't know until more than 50 years later was how close the two of them were to not making that final connection, as another college assistant was ready to block that path. But back then Green was just concerned with getting the snap.

Growing up in Washington, D.C., Green, who initially spelled his name Greene before changing it later in life, played tackle football for the first time in eighth grade in 1967. A wisp of an athlete at quarterback, brushing 100 pounds and learning the game, he was accustomed to a shotgun snap from his touch football days at a local rec center. Touch football was the game he stuck to while he felt he wasn't ready for tackle football. But then he'd decided to try out, and it came time for him to walk up and receive a snap directly under center. "I didn't want my hands on the guy's behind," Green said. "The first two plays, I had my hands close to his behind, but I didn't have them right on his behind, so I fumbled the first two snaps, and the ball just went everywhere. By the time I realized what was happening, the coach had popped me upside my helmet. It was a good pop, too. Back then you could put your hands on kids. I immediately was embarrassed and feeling tearful, but I went up and put my hands on his behind and caught all the rest of the snaps." At the end of practice, Green said the coach apologized and asked him not to quit.

That same fall an Ohio State running back was finishing what he considered a disappointing college football career. Hubbard grew up in Hubbard, Ohio, on the northwest side of Youngstown in the northwest corner of Ohio, just a few miles from the Pennsylvania border. A star in football, basketball, and track, Hubbard was omitted from the Steel Valley All-Star team in a vote of area coaches following his senior season, and that snub drew the curiosity of *The News-Reporter*, the local newspaper. "By-Passed in All-SVC Voting, Rudy Sought By 19 Colleges," read the headline over a story from reporter Tony Angelo on December 19, 1963.

Hubbard was listed at 6'0" and 185 pounds, and his father, George, was a township constable focused on his son receiving a strong college education. Among the schools listed as interested in Hubbard were Ohio State, Purdue, Michigan State, Wake Forest, Ohio, and Miami (Ohio). "As of this writing, Rudy is leaning toward Purdue, but Ohio State is sending an assistant coach this week to talk again with the Eagle halfback," Angelo wrote. "Ruby Hubbard, who must be considered among the top Eagle athletes in the last

20 years, although he missed the All-Steel Valley selections, will be heard from again."

Of that, there was little doubt. Hubbard just had to decide where he would make some noise. "Purdue came in on me first," Hubbard said. "I always liked Ohio State and the guy I really liked was Paul Warfield. But it was either going to be Purdue, Ohio State, or the University of Michigan."

Hubbard took a trip to Purdue, which included a Ray Charles concert, but there were some crossed wires stemming from Hubbard's high school coach. What probably should have been a good trip wound up feeling like a weird trip because Hubbard's coach and the Purdue coach weren't on the same page, and Hubbard felt caught in the middle. One of Hubbard's high school teammates accompanied him, and Purdue wasn't sure why he was there.

Next was Ohio State, which had produced Warfield, a star halfback from Warren, Ohio, which was 20 miles from Hubbard's hometown. Warfield was about to be picked by the Cleveland Browns in the first round of the 1964 NFL Draft and would embark on a career as a receiver that would lead him to the Pro Football Hall of Fame. Hubbard thought he could be next. "Paul Warfield was greased lightning fast," Hubbard said.

Around that time Hubbard said he was introduced to Dr. Joe Logan, a local wealthy Black doctor and loyal Ohio State fan who helped the Buckeyes recruit. Knowing Hubbard was a Browns fan, Hubbard said the doctor invited him to a Browns game. Hubbard said the doctor picked him up in a Corvette, drove him to a local airport, got into a private plane, and then flew them to Cleveland. Dr. Logan was also a pilot. "That did it for me," Hubbard said, laughing at the memory. "At that point, I was sold."

Logan had helped Ohio State land Warfield as well during a time when boosters were allowed by NCAA rules to be involved in recruiting. "Dr. Logan, who graduated from Ohio State University, is now an OSU recruiter and can take credit for obtaining the services of Paul Warfield," wrote the *Mansfield News Journal* in 1968.

Hubbard later visited Michigan, but Ohio State, entering its 14th season under Woody Hayes, was the choice. Hubbard enrolled as a freshman in the Class of 1964, when freshmen weren't eligible to play varsity. He had knee surgery in May 1965, which limited him to two games and one carry as a sophomore. In 1966 he played more than any halfback but carried the ball just 18 times, while used mostly as a blocker. As a senior in 1967, he played more than any member of the backfield, but the Buckeyes slogged through a 6–3 season, averaging just more than 16 points per game. In the first eight games, Hubbard carried 30 times for 116 yards and scored once. In the final game against Michigan, he carried 15 times for 103 yards and scored two touchdowns in the first 11 minutes. Ohio State won 24–14 in Ann Arbor. Hayes told *The Columbus Dispatch* afterward that Hubbard had "a heck of a day. The kids gave Rudy the game football."

"This was my last game, and we were supposed to lose by two touchdowns," Hubbard said. "It was almost anticipated that they were going to fire Coach Hayes. It was my best game. And we came back [to Columbus], and I was through with him. I was really pissed off, to be honest with you."

Hubbard felt his talent had been wasted at halfback. "We ran a T-formation, and the fullback was the focus of the offense," Hubbard said. "If we ran right, I was the blocker. If we ran to the left, I was the blocker. I was stronger than the rest of the running backs, except the fullback. But the other guys were not going to block. So I wasn't really that happy. I had a mediocre career when I thought I was gonna have a great one."

After the season Hubbard High School held a football banquet and presented Hubbard with a plaque to commemorate his Ohio State career. Hayes was invited as the guest speaker. When Hubbard accepted his award, he looked at his coach and let him know how he felt about the last four years. "I unloaded," Hubbard said. "I'm telling him if I had it to do over, I don't know if I would go to Ohio State. But I'm thinking I'm not gonna have to see him again."

Hayes' response? Two weeks later while Hubbard was on campus finishing classes, Hayes asked Hubbard to come by his office. Hubbard thought his coach was going to get him back. Instead, Hayes offered him a job as the first Black assistant football coach in Ohio State history. "I never knew if it had anything to do with the Michigan game," Hubbard said. "I never asked him that."

What Hayes may have appreciated was a player who wasn't afraid to speak his mind and stand up to his coach. There was the banquet, and Hubbard also described one early practice altercation as a player when Hubbard made clear to Hayes there were some things he would not tolerate. They never had an issue again. But if Hubbard had helped save Hayes' job, maybe it was only right to reward Hubbard with a job of his own. In his first coaching season in 1968, the Buckeyes won the national title. Hubbard stayed for six seasons as an OSU assistant before leaving after the 1973 season to take the head coaching job at Florida A&M. His 12-year run with the Rattlers produced a record of 83–48–3 and included the 1978 Division I-AA national title, when FAMU beat Massachusetts in the championship game. That success led to Hubbard's induction into the 2021 College Football Hall of Fame class.

If Hubbard was going to work for Hayes, he was going to have to recruit. Hubbard said he was first assigned to southern Ohio, an area from which the Buckeyes had not been drawing many players. On an initial trip there, Hubbard had trouble getting a hotel and was finally told to get a room on the Black side of town. "When I went back to Columbus, I was steaming," Hubbard said. "Woody said, 'To hell with them, we won't recruit there.'"

Hubbard knew he needed to work recruiting areas where he'd be free to scout talent, develop relationships, and do his job. Hayes assigned him two new territories. One was Columbus itself. The other was the Maryland; Virginia; Washington, D.C., area. Hubbard would soon be recruiting a young running back from Columbus and a young quarterback from Washington for the Class of 1972. The running back was Archie Griffin. The quarterback was Cornelius Green.

Green was raised by his biological father's sister and her husband, calling his aunt and uncle "Mom and Dad." They were 40 years older than Green and had eighth-grade educations. The father he knew, William Floyd, lost his eyesight to diabetes when Green was in eighth grade and never saw his son play football, though he'd hear him. During his Ohio State days, his parents would watch the games on TV together. "My mom would be his eyes," Green said.

His mother, Jinnie Green Floyd, worked as a hotel maid. When Green burst onto the scene as a sophomore at Ohio State, the hotel manager promoted her and paid for her to fly to a game in Columbus. By then, they'd felt the pride of their son racing through the Washington high school athletic scene, taking the city by storm.

That happened because of one change, when Green took in the lay of the land at high school football practice before his sophomore season and saw nothing but roadblocks. Green estimated he was the sixth-string quarterback in practice at McKinley Tech, working with players who barely knew the game. "I was with running backs who didn't know what they were doing, so we looked like the Three Stooges," Green said. "I just knew the handwriting was on the wall for me."

Before classes began Green got his transcripts and brought them to Dunbar High School, which was closer to his home. He transferred and played football there. "It was the best decision I ever made," Green said. "If I had stayed at McKinley, I don't think anybody would have ever heard of me."

Soon, anyone who followed high school football in the D.C. area heard of him. He took over the starting quarterback job during his sophomore year and was rolling by his junior year in 1970. A 23-year-old sportswriter from *The Washington Post* who had just moved to prep sports coverage, Leonard Shapiro, covered a Dunbar game on November 7, 1970. Shapiro would go on to a five-decade career at *The Post* that included covering the NFL, writing several books, and a stint as sports editor. But on this night, he would nickname 16-year-old Cornelius Green. "The first time I saw him play, he was wearing red wristbands, which you didn't see too much back then," Shapiro said. "He had red shoelaces on white shoes, which was about the same time Joe Namath was wearing white shoes. And the laces had little tassels on them. And he was cool. He looked great. They ran the option offense, and he carried the ball a lot, of course, and he could throw like hell, and he was just a great, great, great, great athlete. I was just really impressed, and he put on a show, and I talked to him afterward, and he was a great kid, really nice, not a braggart."

Green led Dunbar to a 22–6 win against Bell High School, running for one touchdown and throwing for two others. Shapiro's story in *The Post* began, "Cornelius Green, a young man with a flair for the flamboyant." And a nickname was born. Over the next five years through the end of his career at Ohio State, *The Post* sportswriters would use the word "flamboyant" to describe Green in at least 15 different stories. Green was all about it. When Shapiro covered a Dunbar game in September 1971, Green had the word "flamboyant" taped across the front of his helmet.

Soon after, Shapiro called Green "the flamboyant flim-flam man," and the "Flam" name followed Green to Ohio State, later making its way onto his car's license plate. "This was an era of wishbone offenses and some razzle-dazzle stuff," Shapiro said. "And Cornelius was a magician. He could fake a handoff, sucker guys, they'd tackle the wrong guy, and he'd go around the end. He was just a great player."

Bob Headen, who would go on to become the winningest high school football coach in D.C. history, prepared to face Dunbar and Green in a conference championship game in November 1970 and called him the best quarterback in the city. "Every time I pick up a newspaper, I see Green," Cardozo said.

Who was reading those papers, using his subscriptions to keep tabs on Washington high school happenings? Hubbard did while working his territory. "You go to the high schools and then, as you go to the high school, you ask the other coaches, 'Who do you have?'" Hubbard said. "'Who have you played against that might be Ohio State caliber?' And that's the way we got started. But I have to tell you, Cornelius Green, when I went to see him play, guys couldn't touch him, man. He'd shake them loose in a phone booth. He was just that quick. Now, we had success with Rex Kern who was that kind of quarterback as well. And Rex, being as quick as he was and elusive, could fake people out. When I saw Cornelius, he reminded me of Rex, but he seemed to be quicker. Now he was small. He was probably at the time 150 pounds. But he could throw it and then he would light the crowd up."

After his junior season, Green said he was surprised to get some scholarship offers, mostly from Historically Black Colleges such as North Carolina Central and Howard. While he had a handful of scholarships in hand at the start of his senior season, Hubbard and Ohio State made their move. "Once people find out Ohio State wants you, everybody is going to want you," Green said. "I thought that was a recruiting line. But once people found out about Ohio State, it boosted from about eight to 80 football scholarships."

Hubbard was the backfield coach while George Chaump, who was also hired in 1968, coached the quarterbacks. It wasn't difficult to get Chaump on board with Hubbard's interest in Green. "George Chaump was really excited about what he saw on the film because all of Corny's films—they were great," Hubbard said. "People had difficulty touching him! What could you not see? He was fast. He had that gift."

Hubbard was discovering his gifts as a recruiter. As a player he had been regularly asked by Hayes to host players on their recruiting visits. "They kind of liked what I was doing back then," Hubbard said. "Most of the guys I talked with, we ended up getting them if we really wanted them."

If he was that effective recruiting as a player, Hayes must have figured, he could do it as a coach. Hubbard's relationships in Washington were already paying off. "It was because of Ohio State's popularity, and then my first year as a coach, you go undefeated. So I think I was a hit because of Ohio State," Hubbard said. "I was a hit with those coaches and I ended up being good friends with some of the people who were not coaches but had influence on some of the guys. I had people down there. If they had an athlete, they were calling me. They wanted me to have the first look at him. So I just always thought we were the front-runners with Corny."

Ohio State's first Black assistant was recruiting what everyone expected to be the first Black starting quarterback at Ohio State. But there was another Black assistant in the Big Ten with a deeper knowledge of what Green's college career might be like. Jimmy Raye II was a quarterback from North Carolina who became the second Black quarterback ever to win a national championship, doing so with the 1966 Michigan State Spartans. After a few years in the NFL, he returned to Michigan State as a coach in 1971, as Green was preparing for his senior season. "Jimmy Raye was the first African American quarterback I saw," Green said. "And I couldn't believe that he was recruiting me."

Green also had three uncles who lived in Flint, Michigan, which was 45 miles from Michigan State's campus in East Lansing, and Green had spent several summers with that side of the family. "When Michigan State came in," Green said, "that was a godsend because I thought my relatives could come see me play."

"I thought I had a chance to get him, to convince him to come to Michigan State," Raye said. "He was a tremendous athlete, a great football player as he proved…When I saw him play, I said, 'We gotta get this guy. He has Big Ten all over him.'"

Green specifically had Michigan State all over him. Willie Thrower, who would become the first Black athlete to exclusively play quarterback in the NFL, had served as a Michigan State backup quarterback in 1952. Then came Raye. And after Raye graduated in 1967, Bill Triplett was another Black quarterback for the Spartans from 1968 to 1970. "We'd had a history, and Michigan State was Black quarterback-friendly back in that time," Raye said. "Not many schools were playing Black quarterbacks, and I remember trying to get Cornelius to come to Michigan State because I had plowed that ground. I knew some of the challenges he would face playing quarterback at Michigan State or in the Big Ten. And I was talking about something I knew, not something somebody had told me. So we developed a pretty close relationship."

Raye was 25 years old in the fall of 1971, just embarking on a coaching career that would extend until 2013. He stayed at Michigan State through the 1975 season and then made his first NFL jump to the San Francisco 49ers in 1977. Over the next 36 years, he made 15 NFL stops, including serving as the offensive coordinator for seven different teams for a total of 19 years. His longest stretch was running the offense for the Kansas City Chiefs from 1992 to 2000.

Hubbard was also 25, in his fourth year coaching the Buckeyes, and just three years away from taking over his own college football program at Florida A&M well before his 30th birthday. They were after the same player, someone who was just eight years younger than both of them. "I ran into Rudy quite a bit," Raye said. "We were on the same kids. We bumped heads quite a lot. Rudy and I were good friends, but we battled a lot on the recruiting trail."

Then it came time for the visits, which is where it went wrong for the Spartans. But the Ohio State visit came first that winter after Green's senior football season. "When I went to Columbus, Ohio, and I got off that plane and my ride from the airport to the campus, it was an overwhelming feeling, like a spiritual feeling of this is where I belong," Green said.

When Green asked to see Ohio Stadium, Hayes sent him to the business school to learn about his anticipated major for three hours. Hayes met with Green for 45 minutes and thought the quarterback had a skinny neck. "He thought I might get hurt," Green said.

But Hayes said Hubbard had vouched for him, and Hayes also promised that if he was good enough, Green would play. Then Hayes asked what Green wanted to do with his life. Green had a good time with his player host and he finally did get to see the stadium, but when he got home, he told his mother he wasn't sure Ohio State wanted him because they'd barely talked football. That made Jinny Green Floyd perk up. She liked the academic focus.

Despite the feeling that washed over Green on his drive to Ohio State's campus, he would visit Michigan State next, and as things stood, the Spartans had a real chance. The family pull was there, and Raye made a compelling case for Green to continue what had already been started by the Spartans. But then…"I just had the worst recruiting trip at Michigan State," Green said. "The player who recruited me, he was a third-string tailback and he hated Michigan State. He said, 'If I were you, I wouldn't come here.' And what topped it off: I'm a 12th grader, and he takes me to a college party and he leaves me there at the party. So here I am: a 12th grader posing as a college guy, and everyone knew I was a high school guy. So I'm at this party, and he leaves me and I had to find my way back home to the hotel, which was two blocks away. And I was terrified. I couldn't wait to get out of there."

Green's meeting with Michigan State coach Duffy Daugherty didn't go much better. Daugherty had famously and aggressively recruited Black players in his 1963 recruiting class, bringing Black players from the South, who were denied the chance to play at their home state colleges, to East Lansing. Dubbed the Underground Railroad, the class formed the heart of Michigan State's 1966 national championship team, of which half its starters were Black. There was a history but no personal connection for Green. "I met with Duffy Daugherty, and it was like a two- or three-minute conversation," Green said. "When he talked to me, it was like he had to be somewhere."

All that ruined Michigan State's chances, when Green had been ready to be a Spartan. "If I had a good visit and a good host, I'm at Michigan State," Green said, "no doubt about it."

He never told Raye nor Hubbard any of it. Raye never knew about the visit gone bad, and Hubbard never knew how close Green was to going to Michigan State. "I never told Jimmy Raye. You just don't snitch," Green said. "You just keep that to yourself. So when he said, 'How was your visit?' I said, 'Oh, it was great, I had a great time, the guys are great here,' just lying."

"That would have been on me," Raye said, "because I would have been responsible for his hosts that weekend, and I thought I put him with the best of what we had. That was an error. That was an error by me putting him with some of our players so that he didn't have a good time, a good feeling for it. But I enjoyed the time I spent with him. I guess I spent almost every Thursday and Friday in Washington trying to convince him to come to Michigan State."

"Wow," Hubbard said in response to hearing the whole story. "I never knew that. This is crazy. Jimmy was a great recruiter now. But I didn't think anybody else was even in on him. This is all news to me—all these years later talking about Jimmy Raye."

As Green planned to sign in February 1972, Hubbard thought the Buckeyes were in the clear, and meanwhile Raye was still in pursuit. *The Washington Post* in February still mentioned Ohio State, Illinois, and UCLA as possible destinations. Hubbard had promised that Green would get a fair shake at quarterback in Columbus at a time when a lot of Black quarterbacks didn't. "In the early '70s, it was typical for a school to get an African American quarterback, and once he got to that school, they would change his position to defensive back or receiver," Green said. "So I wanted to be reassured that wouldn't happen to me no matter what. So Rudy Hubbard promised me, 'We're going to keep you at quarterback. That's why we recruited you.'"

Green said Raye feared that wouldn't be the case. "He said, 'Woody's not going to play an African American quarterback, never have, and I don't think he ever will. But if you come here, you know you'll play here at Michigan State,'" Green said.

The Spartans stayed in the game right up until Green signed, still unaware that anything had gone wrong on Green's visit. "He still thinks I'm coming to Michigan State because he didn't know I had an awful trip," Green said. "So when signing time comes around, he calls me, and I say I'm going to Ohio State. And he was almost in tears."

Raye thought Green was making the wrong decision. "I didn't want to tell him how much I loved Rudy Hubbard," Green said, "just as much as I loved him,"

Helped by fate and a Spartan who stranded Green at a party, Hubbard had won over Ohio State's future quarterback. Green would soon meet his future teammate, backfield mate, and roommate that Hubbard was also securing—Columbus Eastmoor High School's Griffin, who didn't officially announce his Ohio State choice until late March after looking like a Northwestern lean well into February. Hubbard did his student teaching under Eastmoor coach Bob Stuart and fought to make Griffin a Buckeye, while he said other assistants preferred Pennsylvania running back Dave Mazeroski. Ohio State wound up taking both.

With an NCAA rule change that made freshmen eligible to play, Griffin won a starting job the last nine games of their freshmen seasons in 1972. Green broke out during spring practice leading into their sophomore seasons, and in 1973, 1974, and 1975, they started together and combined to rush for 6,802 yards, an average of 194 yards per game. The Buckeyes went 31–3–1 in those three seasons, as they ran for 52 combined touchdowns, while Green threw for 2,348 yards and 17 scores. Griffin was named first-team All-Big Ten in 1973, '74, and '75, while Green was named first-team All-Big Ten in '74 and '75. Griffin, of course, won back-to-back Heisman Trophies in 1974 and 1975. He was named the team MVP and earned *Chicago Tribune* Silver Football Award as the Big Ten MVP in 1973 and 1974. But in 1975 Green won both awards—team MVP and league MVP—over Griffin.

That's a pretty good recruiting combo from his two assigned areas for a 25-year-old assistant coach. "I had a great recruiting year, to be honest," Hubbard said. "It's evident now that it was, but even then I was so busy running to get these guys, I knew it was gonna be a great year, but I never knew it would turn out like it did. I'm so proud of these guys, not just as players, but they turned out to be big-time Ohio State people."

Hubbard brought in two trailblazers—college's football's only two-time Heisman winner and Ohio State's first Black starting quarterback. "I owe so much to Rudy," Green said. "And I put so much trust in Rudy that it would be okay."

It wasn't easy. Once on campus Green said Chaump became a father figure to him, but no one could stop the hateful letters and the death threats he got over the phone from racists who didn't want a Black quarterback at Ohio State. "Nobody prepared me for that," Green said.

Green also gradually learned to not take Hayes' criticisms of his play personally and to try to learn from the advice regardless of how it was delivered. "I guess he always loved me," Green said, "but I didn't love him until I was able to do that."

And at Michigan State, Raye watched and wondered what might have been but appreciated what was. "Even up to the last minute, I thought we had won the battle," Raye said. "I was pretty convinced I was going to get him to Michigan State. He could have started for us as a freshman, but he was a delightful guy. I kind of followed his career and kept up with him. But we still had a relationship that lasted for a long time, and I have a lot of respect for him and like him a lot. But I long regretted missing out on him because he was a tremendous player. He was a great example of leadership and maturity. I knew he would fare well. I think if we had gotten him, we would have been in the market for a national championship. But this one is a success. This one is a happy ending because he turned out to be a good player and had a great career. He did well, and we went on to do okay. So it was a win-win. I'm just sorry we didn't happen to get him."

## CHAPTER 5

# Kirk Herbstreit, Class of 1988

The clock ticked to zero with a final, desperate Michigan incompletion, and as the Ohio State Buckeyes lifted coach Earle Bruce onto their shoulders, a young fan in the crowd raced from his seat to celebrate this victory with the football family he'd been born into. The Buckeyes made Michigan Stadium their own on that late November Saturday, and Bruce pumped his fists in the air, as the 23–20 win against the Wolverines in the last game of the 1987 season sent Bruce out on a literal and figurative high. The job no longer was his, but this victory would stay with him. Uncertainty lay ahead for the Buckeyes after Ohio State president Edward Jennings had fired Bruce on the Monday before this Michigan game. In 81 days a new coach would sign a recruiting class of 21 players as a tentative first step in a new era of Ohio State football.

But this day belonged to Bruce. This day belonged to Buckeyes such as freshman running back Carlos Snow, who had carried the ball 21 times for 67 yards and weaved past three Michigan defenders while turning a five-yard catch into a 70-yard touchdown that injected life into the Buckeyes and gave them a 14–13 lead on their first drive of the second half. This day belonged to OSU die-hards such as 18-year-old Kirk Herbstreit, that fan in the stands who now found himself in the midst of scarlet and gray elation. "I'm sprinting down, trying to get down on the field. I don't even know what I'm trying to do," Herbstreit said. "But I'm just trying to go down there to celebrate with the team like a fan would. And my buddy's with me, and we get down onto the field somehow because it's really easy to jump over that fence. So we're down on the field, and I'm jumping on top of some of the players, and Carlos Snow sees me. He looked me in the eye, and everyone's just bowing down to him at that point. He's being pushed. I mean, imagine just pandemonium. Everyone's being pushed side to side, and somehow Carlos Snow and I get eye to eye. And he points to me right in the chest and he's like, 'We'll see you in Columbus next year.' And I was like, 'Are you kidding me?' In my head I was like, *Of course you are.*"

Before Snow delivered his message to Herbstreit, who was one of the best high school quarterbacks in Ohio, the running back caught sight of the nametag on Herbstreit's chest. It identified what Herbstreit was that day—a guest of the Wolverines as a visiting Michigan recruit.

He was Michigan on the outside at that moment. But as always, Herbstreit was Ohio State on the inside.

Decades before he was the voice of college football on ESPN and ABC primetime telecasts and on ESPN's Saturday morning *College GameDay*, Herbstreit was famously a Buckeyes legacy. His status as the son of former Ohio State captain Jim Herbstreit didn't just gain him access to Ohio State's postgame locker rooms as an elementary schooler in the mid-70s; it landed him a spot on Woody Hayes' lap. "You didn't get to watch every game on TV then. But at a very young age, I was just tuned into the sport and just in love with the Buckeyes," Herbstreit said. "Archie Griffin and Corny Green and the Buckeyes, they were as high up in my mind as Batman and Superman. I mean, they were mythical gods in my mind."

In his 60s and coaching through what would be his final few seasons in Columbus, Hayes lived in Herbstreit's imagination during the week and then presented himself in person on home fall Saturdays. The magic became real. "I'd look through his glasses, and with his white shirt and his tie, it was like Santa Claus," Herbstreit said. "It was just mythical to me to be six, seven, eight years old and do that."

This was Herbstreit's introduction to the sport that would become his profession. His first moments on a football field were in his backyard, and his first moments as a Buckeye came while pretending he was Griffin or Green. "That just tells you where I was my whole life," Herbstreit said. "I knew the fight song from the time I was three. I knew 'Carmen Ohio.' We used to do Script Ohio in the yard. That was a big part of me."

The allegiance had been earned by his father, who played defensive back and halfback for Hayes from 1958 to 1960, starting his final two seasons. Jim Herbstreit told the *Dayton Daily News* in 1988 that he'd played some 60-minute games as a junior in 1959 and a few 55-minute games as a senior captain in 1960. "Woody was very fond of my dad," said Kirk, who continued to see Hayes at times over the years until Hayes' death in March 1987 during

Herbstreit's junior year of high school. "Every time I would see him, he would pull me in and tell me something about my dad, tell me, 'Pound for pound, Jimmy Herbstreit was the toughest son of a bitch I ever coached,' stuff like that. And I would just beam with pride."

A graduate of Reading High School just outside Cincinnati, the elder Herbstreit had become a Buckeye only after an initial commitment to Miami (Ohio), where he believed he had a better chance to get on the field. In the spring of his senior year of high school in 1957, Herbstreit simultaneously played shortstop for his baseball team and sprinted for his track team in state championships held on the Ohio State campus. The baseball team won, and Herbstreit finished fifth in the 100-yard dash and third in the 220-yard dash. "Two assistant coaches, Gene Fekete and Clive Rush, were waiting for me at the finish line of the 220," Jim said, as he spun his recruiting tale in that *Dayton Daily News* story in 1988. "I ran a 21.4, and that was sufficient enough for them. We set up a meeting for the next weekend, and I didn't hesitate. There wasn't a lot of nonsense. I was the last recruit for Woody."

"Woody didn't even know much about him," Kirk said. "Just based on that alone, he offered my dad a scholarship to go to Ohio State."

Thirty years later that Hayes offer led Jim and his son to the intersection of two Hayes disciples—Bo Schembechler and Earle Bruce. The intersection occurred in Schembechler's postgame office after that 1987 game, a room occupied by four people—two Herbstreits and the two coaching friends and rivals.

By then, Kirk had established himself as one of the best high school quarterbacks in Ohio. He'd progressed into the position slowly—from a junior high that didn't have football as a seventh grader, to playing on the offensive line as an eighth grader, to serving as a backup quarterback as a ninth grader. As a sophomore he saw the field for Centerville High School outside Dayton and then he won the starting job as a junior in 1986. Herbstreit threw for more than 1,200 yards and ran for more than 500 while making first-team All-State in Class AAA at 6'3" and 186 pounds. He accounted for 28 touchdowns, and Centerville won a state title.

He made his mark from his first start. In the opener against rival powerhouse Cincinnati Princeton High School, Centerville scored with 1:07 to play to cut the Princeton lead to one, and Centerville coach Bob Gregg asked the players what they wanted to do. They wanted to go for two and the win. "I kept it on a triple option and dove into the end zone," Herbstreit said. "It was a really a holy cow moment for our team."

It was almost immediately followed by a holy cow moment for Herbstreit personally. His first recruiting letter arrived, and it came from Bob McNea, the Buckeyes' recruiting coordinator. "The very next Monday I got a letter from Ohio State that one of my teammates taped onto my locker," Herbstreit said. "It was just to congratulate me, and he had the score of the game, and 'We're watching you, that was an impressive win, you're on our radar, you're one of our guys.' And I could not believe that after one start I got a letter from Ohio State."

The magic was becoming real. "After all the dreams in the backyard and growing up and thinking about it, that's when it became a reality," Herbstreit said.

This was the reality at Ohio State: two days before Centerville's opener, the Buckeyes had lost their opener in 1986 on a Wednesday to Alabama in the Kickoff Classic in New Jersey 16–10. Ohio State started 0–2 after a 40–7 loss to Washington the next week. They recovered to win nine straight before falling to Michigan 26–24 and then beating Texas A&M in the Cotton Bowl 28–12 to finish out the season at 10–3. But the Wolverines went to the Rose Bowl that season, where a loss to Arizona State dropped them to 11–2.

As Herbstreit played his last season of high school football in 1987, both the Wolverines and Buckeyes struggled in their own ways. Michigan lost three of its first seven; Ohio State lost four of its last six. Bruce was fired in November; Schembechler underwent quadruple bypass surgery in December. Herbstreit had been introduced to college football when the Buckeyes and Wolverines were battling atop the college football world. During the four seasons from 1973 to 1975 when Herbstreit was aged four to seven, both the Buckeyes and Wolverines finished in the top eight of the final Associated Press poll each season. A decade later, the ground under the rivalry wasn't quite as stable.

Despite that opening OSU recruiting letter, Schembechler would shoot his shot. There was perhaps a slight opening. Jim had briefly served as an assistant coach under Hayes and alongside Schembechler. In 1962 Herbstreit was a second-year OSU assistant assigned to the offensive backfield, while Schembechler was a fifth-year assistant in charge of the offensive tackles and guards. When Schembechler took the Miami (Ohio) head coaching job in 1963, Herbstreit followed for several seasons.

So when Jim took Kirk and two friends from Dayton to Michigan's Upper Peninsula for a fishing trip in the summer of 1987 before Kirk's senior year, the return trip included a swing through Ann Arbor, Michigan. "Bo asked my dad if we would stop by," Herbstreit said. "So we stopped by, and Bo pulled me into his office. And he was just the way he looked on the sideline. He's got his glasses on, and my dad's in there, and he asked if he could talk to me by himself. My dad said, 'Sure, of course,' then he walked out. Because we were just kind of glad-handing up to that point, just kind of BS-ing, and then he just was very honest. He was like, 'Just talk to me. Am I wasting my time here? Can I recruit you? Are you open? I know your ties to Ohio State. I understand it more than anybody. But we really love you, you fit perfectly with what we do, we'd love to recruit you. But I don't want to waste my time if there's no point in doing it.' I appreciated his honesty, but I couldn't bring myself to say, 'Yeah, don't bother recruiting me.' So I just said, 'No, no, no, no, it's great, I'm open, I really appreciate it.'"

So Schembechler put assistant Jerry Hanlon on the case. Hanlon grew up in North Bend, Ohio, a small town outside Cincinnati near both Kentucky and Indiana. He played at Miami (Ohio), coached high school football around Ohio for almost a decade, and then coached at the University of Dayton before landing back at Miami on Schembechler's staff. He then followed the boss to Michigan and coached under Schembechler for 23 years, including every one of Schembechler's 21 seasons. Hanlon coached offensive line and quarterbacks, but one of his specialties was turning Ohio high school football players into Michigan Wolverines. "If I hadn't had kids from Ohio," Hanlon said, "we wouldn't have had a football team. I wouldn't have had a job."

Hanlon was far from the only Michigan assistant working Ohio, but he may have been the most tireless. His home turf was the southwest corner of Ohio. "I had to have that," Hanlon said, "so I could go home and see my mom once in a while."

A quarterback from Dayton would naturally fall under his purview. "Jerry recruited me like crazy," Herbstreit said.

"We worked the areas very hard," Hanlon said. "It was a year-round situation. You just didn't go there a couple of days a year. You worked those areas, you got to know the coaches. You did what you could do to help them with their football programs. And you certainly invited them up here to see what you could do to help them. You had to let them know that you were interested in them, not just for their players, but for their overall programs and for the coaches themselves."

With that kind of focused plan for getting Ohio high schoolers to enroll one state north, everything about Herbstreit to Michigan made sense—except for the Buckeyes blood in him. Geographically, culturally, and in style of play, Herbstreit was everything Schembechler wanted. He was a big kid and a Big Ten kid who played a lot like the Michigan quarterback who had just graduated after the 1986 season—Jim Harbaugh. "The reason I wore No. 4 was because of Jim Harbaugh," Herbstreit said. "I loved Jim Harbaugh's style of play and the offense that he ran in Ann Arbor. If I would have gone to Michigan, it would have been, 'Hey, this is your wheelhouse. This is what you've been doing your whole life.'"

The 92-year-old Hanlon, who worked in Michigan radio after retiring as a coach and still lives in the same house in Ann Arbor he lived in while coaching there, has no doubts that Herbstreit would have fit right into Michigan's plans. "I'm sure he would have. We did things with our quarterbacks back in those days that I thought were innovative," Hanlon said. "They had to learn the game of football. They just didn't have to know how to throw the ball or catch it or run with it. They had to learn the whole game of football, and that's what made us a little bit better in a lot of situations. He was a heck of a nice kid, and it was a good family. He's the kind of kid you want to have in your program, that was for sure."

That potential fit and that Schembechler conversation in the summer led Herbstreit back to Ann Arbor on November 21, 1987. But being there in a Michigan nametag only made that Buckeyes fervor more intense. Herbstreit was reminded of that before the game, as he gathered with other prospective Wolverines on the biggest Michigan recruiting weekend of the season, knowing he was a Buckeye in Wolverine clothing. "I'm listening to Bo and listening to all the talk before the game," Herbstreit said. "And as much as I'm a high school recruit, I'm a 1,000 percent fan. So it's like a fan getting access to this. I'm sitting here, listening to all this Michigan stuff, and in the back of my mind, I'm thinking, *This is BS.* I was taught to respect Michigan my whole life—except one day out of the year we want to kill them. That's the way I was taught. And so that one day, man, my blood was boiling."

Herbstreit's Buckeyes lean was literal. When the recruits took the field to watch warmups, Herbstreit stood on the OSU side of the 50 while the rest of the recruits huddled near the maize and blue pregame rituals.

Then came the game and the OSU win and celebration…and yet Herbstreit found himself back in Schembechler's office once again after the game. "My dad wanted to say good-bye to Bo, just basically say thank you for your hospitality," Herbstreit said. "So we waited until his press conference was over and we're standing right outside the Michigan locker room. Bo asked us to come in. So we came in. All the players are getting undressed, they're dejected from the loss, and we go right by all the players and right into Bo's office. And he sits down, he's rubbing the top of his head, and he starts telling my dad about the game, 'What the hell, son of a bitch, we should have done this.' They're just talking football. And I'm sitting on a couch. It's a small office, but there's a little couch in there. I'm just kind of sitting in there, just listening, and they're just going on for 10 or 15 minutes, just talking ball and talking about the game, and out of nowhere, the door slams open, and it's Earle. Still in his fedora, his tie all sideways, and he does that bulldog face and he just starts laying into Bo about the Ohio State president and how he felt like he was railroaded."

This was the other side of the Ohio State–Michigan rivalry. Bruce's team had just gone helmet to helmet and heart to heart with Schembechler's team for three hours, and Bruce had been lifted in celebration on Schembechler's field. Now not even an hour after a three-point upset win, Bruce stormed in not as a foe—but a friend. He was there to commiserate, to get something off his chest, to explain the hurt of having to leave this rivalry to the only other person who could understand it. "He's yelling and yelling, almost like confiding in Bo," Herbstreit said. "It's so weird. I'm 18, I'm thinking, *These guys don't know each other; they hate each other*, but now he's like bulldog Earle Bruce, and Bo's like, 'I hear you, I know, I know,' just trying to calm him down, and Earle's yelling and yelling and he realizes there's other people in the room. And with that bulldog face, he looks over and he sees my dad and he sees me and he goes, 'And what the hell are you doing in here?' I was terrified."

Herbstreit didn't know if Bruce was surprised that anyone else was in Schembechler's office, or whether he was angry that an Ohio high school quarterback that Bruce and the Buckeyes had been recruiting so relentlessly was visiting Michigan. Regardless, it was enough. Herbstreit wouldn't have had an answer either way because he was supposed to be a Buckeye. Bruce wouldn't be in Columbus the next season, but regardless of who replaced Bruce, Herbstreit would be there. Bruce's quarterbacks coach, Tom Lichtenberg (who died at age 72 in 2013), had led Ohio State's recruitment of Herbstreit and he wouldn't remain on staff. But the specifics didn't matter. Herbstreit's relationship was with Ohio State.

Other schools had checked on Herbstreit as well. He had wanted to experience being recruited, and beyond Ohio State and Michigan, schools such as Notre Dame, Penn State, Florida State, USC, and Tennessee had obliged. Craig Cirbus, a 10-year Joe Paterno assistant who later became the head coach at Buffalo, recruited him for Penn State. A young Tennessee assistant named Kevin Steele, who was still coaching in the SEC more than three decades later, made an enthusiastic pitch.

But this could only end one way.

After two years of it, Herbstreit was weary of the recruiting process. Nothing had changed him from the days of playing Griffin and Green in the yard. He was a Buckeye at his house, he was a Buckeye at Bo's house, and he'd be a Buckeye in Woody's house. His father called former longtime Ohio State assistant coach Bill Myles, now an assistant athletic director, who had been tasked with holding together the recruiting operation between Bruce's firing and the hiring of the next coach and let it be known: Kirk is ready to be a Buckeye.

John Cooper was introduced as Ohio State's next head football coach on December 31, 1987. Five minutes after he left his introductory news conference, the phone rang in the Herbstreit house. "Kirk, this is John Cooper," the new coach said. "I heard you're ready to become a Buckeye."

As a coach without Ohio roots arrived from Arizona State to take over a program that had started the season with national championship hopes and ended it at 6–4–1 with a controversial coaching change, Cooper needed a first step as the new Ohio State coach. The son of a Buckeye whose father had been recruited by Hayes at the last minute had provided one. "He's the easiest recruit probably I ever had," Cooper said. "All I had to do was make a call. He was coming to Ohio State. All I had to do was confirm that we wanted him."

They wanted him, and Herbstreit wanted the Buckeyes. "I didn't really know John Cooper," Herbsteit said, "other than I had watched some of his games on TV. But I didn't really know a lot about his offense. It was such a different world in 1987. You just didn't think that way. Today? My youngest son, Chase, is a quarterback. If he went through that, the first thing we'd be interested in is what kind of system is he going to bring in? Who's his offensive coordinator, and what is he about? For us, that was like an afterthought. It was more about I'm going to Ohio State, and that's all I know. I'll learn more about him on the back end. That's kind of how I felt."

Hired six weeks before National Signing Day, Cooper was behind in assembling the 1988 recruiting class before he started. In the end the Buckeyes rallied to finish with what recruiting analyst Tom Lemming at the time considered the No. 2 or No. 3 class in the conference behind Michigan. Despite Schembechler's heart procedure, the Wolverines locked down 27 recruits on Signing Day, including seven from Ohio. Two of them were teammates from Cleveland St. Joseph—future three-year starting quarterback Elvis Grbac and future Heisman Trophy winner Desmond Howard. The Buckeyes signed 21 players. Seventeen of those were from Ohio, including Herbstreit, one of three OSU signees on Lemming's list of top 100 national prospects. Cooper felt Herbstreit helped make that happen. "You gotta have a quarterback and to get a guy like Kirk committed," Cooper said. "Once you get a guy like that committed, he's like having another coach."

In the scramble after the hiring and then while playing through a program transition, the 1988 recruiting class fell short of the star power that would follow in future Cooper classes. Though right where he wanted to be, Herbstreit found that the fit wasn't ideal. He redshirted in 1988 and discovered that the West Coast Offense favored by offensive coordinator Jim Colletto didn't match his strengths as a quarterback. Accustomed to a physical run aspect as part of his quarterback play, Herbstreit compared it to learning football in French. Add in the personal expectations built over a lifetime, and the reality had a hard time living up to the magic, at least on the field. "If I had been a normal recruit, it probably would have been different," Herbstreit said. "Nothing against Ohio State or John Cooper, but if I had been looking at where do I fit, where does my style fit, it either would have been Lou Holtz and Notre Dame or Michigan. Those were much better fits for my style. But that was not even a thought in my head back in that time."

Herbstreit did start in his fifth season in Columbus in 1992 and helped lead the Buckeyes to an 8–3–1 record. He was named a captain, and he and his father became the second father-son captain duo in Ohio State history, following James and Jeff Davidson. Whatever dreams didn't come true on the field were carried over to the booth, where he has been one of college football's leading voices for 25 years. "Whatever he did, he was going to be successful," Cooper said. "It wouldn't have surprised me at all if he had been a coach, and he would have been a great one. But he's the best in the business in my opinion. There's some of these guys when I watch games I turn the volume down. They talk too much. But Kirk Herbstreit is the best."

And he just had to be a Buckeye. Twins Jake and Tye, the oldest of the four sons of Kirk and Allison Herbstreit, were invited to join the Clemson football team as preferred walk-ons. Their next son, Zak, accepted a preferred walk-on spot to play quarterback at Ohio State. Their fourth son, Chase, plays quarterback in high school.

That generation of Herbstreits made their choices—just like their dad made his choice and his dad made his. Jim Herbstreit died in 2016 at age 77, always a Buckeye. Frankly, he may have had a hard time imagining his son being anything else, especially a Wolverine. Kirk described his father as jolly with an upbeat and sunny personality—except when crossed on the wrong day of the year.

It's a lesson that a friend of Kirk's, a Michigan fan who came to the house on that one Saturday in November, learned in high school. "I thought it would be okay. I didn't think it was that big of a deal," Herbstreit said. "And then he cheered for Michigan, and my dad didn't even know the kid and he laid into him and told him, 'Get the hell out of my house.' Any day other than that day, that never would have happened. But on that day, there was an intensity in him he never lost."

So if Jim Herbstreit's son had gone to Michigan? "Man, he and Bo were so tight. He eventually would have gotten there. So it's his son. It's Bo. And I think eventually he would have been okay," Herbstreit said. "But it would have been really, really tough for my whole family. Not to mention me."

CHAPTER 6

# Damon Webb,
# Class of 2014

Soon after his arrival as Ohio State's head coach for the 2012 football season, Urban Meyer looked at the roster numbers and offered a challenge. He had to direct the challenge toward the correct assistant coach. And then the assistant coach had to find the right recruit to start solving this problem. Because to Meyer, it was a problem.

Ohio players were all over the football roster of the University of Michigan. But Michigan players barely made a dent on the roster of the Ohio State Buckeyes. For the 2012 season, 23 players who played high school football in Ohio were wearing the maize and blue. Conversely, only two Michigan natives wore scarlet and gray for the 2012 season—defensive tackle Johnathan Hankins and offensive tackle Reid Fragel. Wrapped in that reality was a talent opportunity and a strategy adjustment. By going into Michigan more ferociously, the Buckeyes wondered if they could win some battles that would strengthen their program. But they also knew they could win in the long run—even if they lost recruiting battles in the short run.

A big part of recruiting is selecting the geographic areas in which to engage. At a winning, traditional power like Ohio State, defending the recruiting ground in Ohio is a must, but beyond that the Buckeyes could pick their battles. Where would they go? And which opponents would they fight for great high school players? It was time to go into Michigan and time to make the Wolverines play a little defense on their home turf.

For this task Meyer sent cornerbacks coach Kerry Coombs. Then, Coombs found a top 50 national recruit named Damon Webb. "We were having this meeting," Coombs said, "and Urban was saying, 'I don't understand how they can come in here and get these Ohio kids.'"

From his 24 years coaching high school football in Ohio, including 16 seasons as the successful head coach at Colerain High School in Cincinnati, where his team made regular playoff appearances and won a state title in 2004, Coombs knew. "[Michigan] recruited my school really hard when I was coaching high school football," Coombs said. "So I said, 'Well, Coach, they get all the players they want from their state. They don't have to do any work at home. And because of that, they can spend all of their time in Ohio.' And remember the Big Ten was very regional with recruiting at that time. So I said, 'We've got to make them work at home. I don't know if I'll ever get a player out of there, but I'll go up there and at the very least I'll make them work to keep their own guys and try to keep them out of our state and hopefully turn that tide a little bit.'"

If the Buckeyes were going, they had to mean it. Coombs' personal motto, the one he spoke to his children before their games growing up, is "Fearlessly be yourself." Coombs wears his passion on his sleeve, then he rips off those sleeves and waves them over his head.

Powered by coffee, faith, and a love of football, Coombs is fiery with a smile, and if he was going to Michigan on behalf of the Ohio State Buckeyes, everyone would realize it. "I knew Kerry," Meyer said. "You challenge a guy like Kerry Coombs, especially with that big block M up there...he was relentless."

At the time the Buckeyes made their move, two truths were at play. One was that Michigan, which always coveted and acquired Ohio school players, was really leaning into that plan under head coach Brady Hoke, and the Wolverines had been headed that way late in the tenure of Rich Rodriguez as well. Meyer's first full recruiting class at Ohio State was in 2013, as he arrived after the Michigan game in 2011 and made some late additions to the 2012 class.

In the 10 recruiting classes from 2003 to 2012, this was the breakdown of Ohio high school players and Michigan high school players signed by each school.

**Ohio State:** 117 Ohio players, six Michigan players.

**Michigan:** 51 Michigan players, 47 Ohio players.

The Buckeyes signed nearly 20 in-state players for every player plucked from the state of their rival. The Wolverines were at nearly a 1-to-1 ratio.

In the last five years, from 2008 to 2012, Michigan's Ohio lean had increased.

**Ohio State:** 59 Ohio players, three Michigan players.

**Michigan:** 25 Michigan players, 37 Ohio players.

Those were the numbers that overwhelmed Meyer as he thought about his head coaching debut in The Game, the rivalry between the Buckeyes and Wolverines that is unmatched in college football.

Meyer didn't want to replicate those cross-state numbers; the Buckeyes didn't need 20 players from Michigan to succeed. But if Ohio State could take a couple players from Michigan and keep a couple Ohio players out of Ann Arbor, Michigan, it could show up on the last Saturday in November, when Ohio State had beaten Michigan nine times out of 10 under Jim Tressel before the Wolverines prevailed in a one-score game in 2011 during Ohio State's transitional year under Luke Fickell. Ohio-born and steeped in Buckeye history, Meyer fervently wanted to keep Ohio State's recent dominance in the rivalry rolling. He didn't need much from Michigan to beat Michigan, but he needed more than what the Buckeyes had. "There are good players there," Meyer said of Michigan. "There's not quantity. The quality is incredible, though."

The other factor was that Meyer and his new staff arrived in the midst of Michigan's greatest downturn. The Wolverines' streak of 33 consecutive bowl games had ended in 2008 with a 3–9 record in the first year of Rodriguez. He lasted just three years, and though Hoke had gone 11–2 in 2011 in his first season, the Wolverines weren't what they usually were. The rivalry had flipped after Michigan's 10–2–1 record against Ohio State in the John Cooper era. While the Buckeyes had just hired a two-time national championship coach and Ashtabula, Ohio, native in Meyer, Michigan was relying on Hoke, a Dayton, Ohio, native and loyal Michigan man who had gone from a Wolverines assistant under Lloyd Carr to the head coach at Ball State and San Diego State. In Hoke's second season in 2012, the Wolverines slipped back to 8–5. At the same time, Ohio State went 12–0 in Meyer's first year, though the Buckeyes were banned from the postseason for one year stemming from the end of the Tressel era.

For so long an equal to Ohio State under Bo Schembechler and for so long a tormentor of Ohio State under Gary Moeller and Carr, Michigan had slipped behind the Buckeyes as Tressel dominated the decade. Meyer wanted to capitalize on that in recruiting. "There was a big challenge from Urban to Kerry, like, hey, 'They're down right now. They're a wounded animal. Let's go and get some guys from there,'" said Mark Pantoni, Ohio State's recruiting director who had arrived with Meyer. "Kerry, being the guy he is and the energy he brings, being a former high school coach, he was able to connect with those guys."

Coombs carried his energy onto social media, where on Twitter he created a hashtag that followed him across the country. Coombs tweeted about "planting the flag" wherever he went on a recruiting trip. There was no better spot to plant that Ohio State flag than a talent-laden high school in Detroit coached by a former Wolverine who had been stacking the Michigan roster with players for years. "It was really about Cass Tech to start," Meyer said. "That's where most of the good players are. There are about three or four schools in that Detroit area, and Cass Tech was No. 1."

"Kerry joked about planting the flag in Detroit," Pantoni said. "And he sort of did."

Ohio State had been to Cass Technical High School in midtown Detroit before. Among the six Michigan players to sign with Ohio State between 2003 and 2012, two stood out, and one was a Cass Tech player. In 2006 and 2007, the Buckeyes signed two players from Orchard Lake St. Mary's Prep outside of Detroit—safety Aaron Gant and receiver Taurian Washington. They played mostly as backups in Columbus. In 2009 the Buckeyes won a major recruiting battle for receiver James Jackson from Grand Ledge High School in the

Lansing, Michigan, area. He stayed two years before transferring. Also in 2009 the Buckeyes signed tight end Fragel from Grosse Pointe South High School in the Detroit suburbs, and after a move to tackle, he started in 2012 as a senior.

Of course, the Buckeyes had won their most recent national title prior to Meyer with Michigan quarterback Craig Krenzel, a recruit in the Class of 1999 from Ford High School in Sterling Heights, Michigan. But in the last 10 years, the real Michigan prizes had been Hankins, a defensive tackle in the Class of 2010 from Detroit Southeastern High School, and 2004 Cass Tech recruit Vernon Gholston. Hankins filled a need for the Buckeyes as they targeted more athletic defenders on the interior of the defensive line and, as a 320-pounder with quick feet, Hankins turned into a star with the Buckeyes and a second-round NFL draft pick in 2013.

And then there was Gholston, who was pulled onto the Cass Tech team as a sophomore after head coach Thomas Wilcher had seen him walking the halls as a freshman and thought he was a parent. A sculpted late bloomer, the 6'3", 240-pound pass rusher had picked the Buckeyes over Michigan and Michigan State. In 2007 he set what was then Ohio State's single-season sack record with 14, setting up his selection as the No. 6 pick in the 2008 NFL Draft by the New York Jets.

That was just a taste of the talent at Cass Tech, where Michigan had been going for seconds and thirds at the talent buffet. In the 2013 recruiting class, four Cass Tech players were ranked as four-star recruits. Three went to Michigan, and one went to Michigan State. In 2012 both Cass Tech four-stars landed at Michigan, as did the best Cass Tech player in 2011.

At times during the 2014 season, three Cass Tech grads started on Michigan's defense: cornerbacks Jourdan Lewis and Delano Hill and linebacker Royce Jenkins-Stone. Two more, defensive backs Terry Richardson and Delonte Hollowell, were backups, and three-year starting safety Thomas Gordon had graduated after the 2013 season. "A lot of the top dudes that went to Cass were going to Michigan, especially in the 2011, 2012, and 2013 classes," Webb said. "So I feel like everybody at the time was having me as a Michigan lock. A lot of articles were saying I was going to Michigan."

It wouldn't have been a shock. Much like Glenville High School in Cleveland, Cass Tech was a program that attracted talent in a metropolitan area and then established a pipeline to the primary state football program. That pipeline was aided by the presence of Wilcher, a winning coach who had been a track national champion and running back for the Wolverines in the '80s.

"That's the magnitude of what Cass has done for Michigan," Wilcher said. "But in being a coach and just talking about that situation, at some point in time, you have to encourage kids not to follow each other. The reason why is they're all competing against each other for the same school, but you can go someplace else and be a superstar. That's what it came to as a reality for me as a coach. You can't follow your boys. You've gotta break up."

Enter Coombs. And cue a young defensive back establishing himself as almost a five-star recruit in the Class of 2014. Webb started his high school career at the University of Detroit Jesuit High School, but after his freshman year, he transferred to Cass Tech. There, he found competitors in practice whom he knew from summer leagues, including Lewis, a corner who was a year older and headed toward an All-American career at Michigan. "They were great friends already,"

Damon Webb Sr. said. "So now you've got a chance to compete with Jourdan every day in practice."

Would Webb Jr. be covered by Lewis in practice or play alongside him? With hands he had shown off by catching footballs in the basement with his father as a kindergartner, Webb had developed skills and ideas as a receiver. He imagined himself scoring touchdowns, not stopping them. "I always felt like I had the potential to play big-time college football if I kept developing and kept progressing," said Webb, whose initial belief was reinforced while starting at receiver as a freshman. "I didn't know I was gonna play safety and corner, but I knew I could play."

His father saw the same potential and held the same belief. College football was ahead. But so maybe was another change. It was time for some fatherly advice. "I said, 'Damon, you're a good receiver. You're probably a MAC guy from a receiver standpoint at this point, a MAC guy, a mid-major guy. There's nothing wrong with that,'" Webb Sr. said. "'But if you want to go to the bigger schools like Michigan, Ohio State, those type of programs, you should play defense.'"

From the first time he saw Webb after his transfer, Wilcher agreed. After one workout, Wilcher told Webb, "Son, you're gonna be a helluva DB." "He had great coordination, he had great body posture. He had great feet and great hands and great eye contact," Wilcher said. "Upon watching those things and watching them develop, a young man like that, who was that focused, you can get them to do what you need a DB to do."

Webb went to work under Jermain Crowell, the Cass Tech defensive coordinator at the time who Webb said was one of the best coaches he ever had. Add that instruction to the defensive back talent around him, and Webb was in an ideal developmental situation. "The talent was just crazy," Webb said. "Some dudes that you probably never even heard about should have made it to the NFL."

Webb, who had grown to 5'11", had the feet and hips for corner and he soon acquired the proof. At an IMG seven-on-seven camp in Detroit in May 2012, the spring of his sophomore year of high school, Webb locked up five-star receiver Laquon Treadwell, an Illinois native in the Class of 2013 who would commit to Ole Miss, make first-team All-SEC, and go in the first round of the 2016 NFL Draft. The camp organizers told Webb early on he'd be on Treadwell all day. Despite being new to the position, Webb stuck by Treadwell's hip and fought him for passes in the air as observers shouted, "That's it, Webb," from the sideline.

"That's when I realized I could really play corner," Webb said. "When I first started playing, it was really just raw talent out there, really no technique, just going out there and just covering. When Crowell started teaching me the techniques and different things, that's when I realized I'm a defensive back."

At the same time, Coombs was realizing he could make inroads in Detroit. The Buckeyes were one of the finalists for offensive lineman David Dawson, a Cass Tech player and top 100 recruit in the Class of 2013 who committed to and then decommitted from Michigan. Dawson ended up back with the Wolverines in the end, but Ohio State had been in the mix. With Webb they'd have more success. "I went up there and I didn't know a thing about the high schools at the time," Coombs said. "All I did was go to the ones that were winning the most games and I started at Cass Tech. That was the first school that I went to, and I became friends with Coach Wilcher and a guy named Jermain Crowell."

While Coombs developed relationships, Meyer committed to speak at a well-known Detroit football camp called "Sound Mind, Sound Body" that attracted the best players in the Midwest. Coombs said Meyer's pledge to visit opened eyes. "As a result," Coombs said, "it was game on. And that was a lot of fun. It really was. It was an incredible amount of fun. To me, that's kind of what college football is about besides the Saturdays. I think people shouldn't undervalue the recruiting competition of this because it's really pretty cool, and it's a lot of fun. Because all of us are in this to win, right? And this is another form of competition. You ride an emotional ebb and flow as much as you do in games on Saturdays. I mean, I can have a tweet or a text just make me sick to my stomach as much as somebody catching a pass on Saturday. That's really the reality. Especially because they're people, and you develop a closeness and a fondness and an affinity for a kid that you really like. You become very close to the family and you know them very well, and then they don't pick you. That's like being jilted by the pretty girl down the road. What could be worse than that? You've invested an unbelievable amount of emotional energy into a relationship, and then they pick somebody else. That's devastating to me when that happens. And to me, that's the good and the bad of it. That's the thrill of the competition, and I enjoy making those relationships and I maintain them even if they pick another place. It's one of the beautiful things about college football."

Coombs was ready to put that emotional investment on the line in Michigan territory with Webb. Despite a lack of cornerback experience, Webb started putting on shows at camps across the Midwest in the summer of 2012. By June of that year, Michigan, Ohio State, and Michigan had all offered. Damon's mother, Stephanie, was from Baton Rouge, Louisiana, and still had family members near LSU's campus, so the Tigers had an inside track as well. Webb camped at LSU in July and earned an offer. "Now we got to a point of: okay, this is serious," Webb Sr. said.

UCLA and Alabama offered later in the process, but they were never really in the mix. Even with cousins nearby, LSU ended up being too far away. So the choice for Webb, like so many of the best Cass Tech players, came down to Michigan or Michigan State and a late push from Ohio State. "It was like a no-brainer to come get him," Wilcher said. "His parents—they liked Michigan and all those other schools, but Ohio State just recruited him very, very hard. Ohio State showed the interest and showed the love."

"Coach Coombs used to always come up to Cass Tech," Webb Jr. said. "When I met Coach Coombs, from the jump he just automatically felt like family. He treated me like one of his players already. I was just super comfortable with Coach Coombs, and that played a big part in me going to Ohio State."

Webb Sr. said Coach Coombs was tireless. He would be the last guy to leave the Cass Tech weight room. "That's what put it over the top," he said. "It could be Brady Hoke and Mark Dantonio in that room recruiting Damon and the other guys, and Coach Coombs would be the last one to leave. Coach Coombs was steady and he would just stay. Damon liked the sincerity about Coach Coombs, the honesty, that he said he was going to coach you hard."

Coombs also made it clear he was targeting the best corners in the country and he couldn't take all of them. Coombs told Webb and those recruits something he often repeated since: "I only recruit first-round draft picks."

According to 247Sports.com, Webb was the No. 5 cornerback and No. 36 overall player in the Class of 2014. Glenville High School's

Marshon Lattimore was the No. 6 corner and No. 55 player, and the Buckeyes wanted them both. They got them both. And Tony Brown, the No. 2 corner who committed to Alabama, was among the other top corners who made an official visit to Ohio State.

Webb considered his other options, primarily Michigan State, where he built a strong relationship with defensive backs coach Harlon Barnett and with head coach Dantonio. He didn't feel the same about Michigan, where a connection never developed with Hoke and his staff. And all those Cass Tech players on the Michigan roster, according to Webb, weren't recruiting him for the Wolverines. "A lot of the former Cass Tech players were telling me not to come," Webb said. "I guess they didn't like Brady Hoke's program. I don't know the inside details, but some dudes that didn't even go to Cass Tech told me not to come there."

Despite all of Wilcher's Michigan connections, Webb said his Cass coach never tried to push him toward Michigan either. "He's going to let kids make the decision that's best for them," Webb said. "Just because Coach Wilcher went to Michigan doesn't mean all his best players—he's going to lean them toward Michigan. Coach Wilcher knew that Ohio State was the best school for me. He told me, 'I'm happy you went to Ohio State. You didn't need to go to Michigan.' He doesn't work for the University of Michigan. Michigan doesn't control Coach Wilcher."

And Michigan didn't control Webb. It took the right player with an open mind, the right situation, and the right assistant to get the Buckeyes back in play in Michigan. It helped that the Wolverines were down. It helped that Webb was a defensive back, and Coombs coached defensive backs. It helped that Coombs could make friends with a tree stump. "When you meet Coach Coombs, after he walks out the door, you feel like you've known him for a long time," Wilcher said. "The way he talks and his manners and the way he smiles and greets you and talks to you, he makes you feel comfortable. He understands what he has to do as a coach and he understands what a young man wants as a coach. It's an easy transition because almost everyone who meets Coach Coombs, you fall in love with him."

Meyer remembered walking into Cass Tech with Coombs and the greetings he received from the principal and others in the building. Meyer could tell a connection had been made. "You know right away when you're with a great recruiter," Meyer said. "He used to say, 'I'm planting a flag,' and boy, did he. That was all Kerry."

And it helped that the second-best player in the state of Michigan that year was the type of person who would even consider playing for the other side of the rivalry. "He had real courage," Coombs said. "He wasn't afraid to entertain the conversation. Up until that point other than [Hankins], I don't know who we had even gotten out of that state."

And it helped that the new Ohio State head coach looked at recruiting with the same competitive fire as Coombs and was always ready to close a deal. "You can't undervalue Urban's part of the process," Coombs said. "Once he got his teeth into it, it became like *the* thing. So every available recruiting moment by rule, every time I was allowed to be in the State Up North, then that's where I was. We were canvassing the state and doing clinics at the high schools and anything and everything we could do."

It worked. And it was the start of something. Webb Jr. called it "shocking" to the whole state of Michigan. His father agreed. "It was big for the Buckeyes," Webb Sr. said. "Traditionally, Cass Tech is a Michigan spot. I think what hurt Michigan is they didn't recruit him like Coach Coombs did. I think they thought they had him in the bag. Damon didn't have that kind of great relationship with the [Michigan] DB coach at that time. He was a good guy, but there was just something about Coach Coombs that lit his fire."

That spark helped lead to two more Cass Tech players in the Class of 2015 picking Ohio State—running back Mike Weber and lineman Josh Alabi. In 2016 the Buckeyes added offensive lineman Michael Jordan from Canton, Michigan, 30 miles outside Detroit. And in 2017 they went hard after receiver Donovan Peoples-Jones, a five-star from Cass Tech. The Buckeyes offered Peoples-Jones as a freshman. It was the first offer he received, and his recruitment went down to the wire. When the Wolverines won out, Meyer viewed it as one of the toughest recruiting losses of his OSU tenure. Michigan worked overtime to win over Peoples-Jones, playing a lot of home state defense. Fulfilling the objective of Ohio State's recruiting strategy, Michigan signed only three Ohio players in the Class of 2017 and none in the Class of 2018. Perhaps it was because the Wolverines had to spend so much time playing defense in their home state.

Win or lose, it was clear that the Buckeyes were in Michigan, thanks to the Webbs. "It was like, hey, maybe we could start a pipeline here," Pantoni said of Cass Tech. "His dad was a great ambassador for our program. He knew everybody around that area and he could help us figure out which kids were serious about Ohio State... So he was a great advocate. And every time Damon went back to school to work out or during his vacation breaks, he's an ambassador for us and he's telling them how much he loves it down here. And so those guys who have great experiences down here, that really helps. If Josh or Mike came down for a game, they knew they could crash with Damon, and he could show them a good time, they could hang out with other guys on the team. And that's how you start to feel that chemistry."

As a freshman in 2014, Webb was part of the Buckeyes' national championship team and then started as a safety in 2016 and 2017, playing his best football at the end of his senior season. He had three interceptions in his final five games and went out as the Defensive MVP of the Cotton Bowl in his last game, as he had five tackles against USC, a fumble recovery, and a 23-yard interception return for a touchdown off future first-round pick Sam Darnold. Webb wasn't selected in the NFL draft, but he did sign as an undrafted free agent, spending the 2018 season on the practice squad of the Tennessee Titans, where—not coincidentally—the defensive backs coach was Coombs.

Coombs had left Ohio State for the NFL for two seasons in 2018 and 2019, and—also not coincidentally—the Buckeyes lacked any Michigan players in their 2017, 2018, or 2019 classes. When Coombs returned to Ohio State as the defensive coordinator for the 2020 season, one of his first orders of business was securing the commitment of a Michigan defensive back who had committed to the Buckeyes but then put off signing in December after the departure of previous secondary coach Jeff Hafley. Cam Martinez, a high school quarterback from Muskegon, Michigan, 200 miles northwest of Michigan, was twice named the Michigan High School Player of the Year. He was going to play defensive back in college, and his uncertainty was natural since Hafley had been his primary recruiter. On the first day Coombs came to Michigan in January 2020, the two formed an "O-H" on social media together. A week later Martinez confirmed he'd be a Buckeye. In announcing his decision, he noted Coombs' energy level and his own comfort level.

Coombs looked back at the decisions to leave Michigan for Ohio State made by Webb, Weber, and Alabi. "It wasn't easy for them," he said. "But over time it got easier. So that when you get to Cam Martinez, it's not even really a big deal." He was just a Michigan player comfortable at Ohio State. And Ohio State was comfortable in Michigan.

## CHAPTER 7

# Michael Jenkins, Class of 2000

Over the course of his senior season of football in 1999 at Leto High School in Tampa, Florida, Michael Jenkins played quarterback, running back, receiver, linebacker, safety, and cornerback while returning kicks for a school that won a playoff game for the first time in its 34-year history. Jenkins had longed to play for one of the powerhouse programs in the area, but his father, also named Michael, told his son that he would enroll at the school in their district and make the best of it. "You just have to *be* the team," he said. "It's on you."

So he *was* the team, as Leto won a combined 15 games his junior and senior years, the best pair of seasons Leto ever experienced. Jenkins lifted the program and fascinated recruiters. Years later, Jenkins would save an Ohio State national championship season. In the moment he was wooed by a future national championship head coach, a future No. 1 pick in the NFL draft…and a cold and mostly empty Big Ten campus.

Jenkins was both a rare prospect and a do-it-all prospect, a 6'5" receiver who also made 77 tackles at linebacker as a senior.

He wasn't viewed quite like the best players at the biggest Tampa programs, but entering his senior season, he was ranked as the No. 22 prospect in the state of Florida by *SuperPrep* Magazine. A week after Leto's season-ending loss in the second round of the playoffs in late November 1999, Jenkins and his father started a recruiting tour that would determine his future. His final four college choices came down to Georgia Tech, Virginia Tech, Notre Dame, and Ohio State because the options in Florida were slow to come around. Jenkins said Florida Gators coach Steve Spurrier offered him as a defensive player, but he knew he wanted to catch the ball in college, so he turned them down. Then the Gators played Michigan State in the Citrus Bowl on New Year's Day to end that season, and 6'6" receiver Plaxico Burress lit up Florida for 13 catches, 185 yards, and three touchdowns in a 37–34 MSU win. "Literally the day after that game, Florida called back and was like, 'Hey, we're thinking about getting big receivers,'" Jenkins said. "At the time they had smaller, shiftier guys."

"One of the recruiters called and said, 'You know we had him as an athlete because he didn't play a lot of receiver, but Coach Spurrier is now committed to focusing on the big receiver,'" said Jenkins' father.

The message relayed from Spurrier? We can't let Michael Jenkins get out of Florida.

Jenkins' answer? Too late.

The tour started with back-to-back visits to Notre Dame and Virginia Tech. Friday, December 3 opened a mammoth weekend of official visits for the Fighting Irish. Of the 18 high school seniors listed by the *South Bend Tribune* as planning to visit, eight signed with the Irish, including a 6'5" receiver named Ronnie Rodamer, who battled injuries while catching three passes during his Notre Dame career before transferring to Montana.

Jenkins' father remembered them attending a banquet and soaking in the historic nature of the program. But there were also rumblings about the job status of head coach Bob Davie since Notre Dame was coming off a 5–7 season. This was a wounded traditional college football power—much like Ohio State, which was coming off a 6–6 season. But the Irish did have an enthusiastic 35-year-old receivers coach who made an impression on the Jenkins family— Urban Meyer. "He was on me hard to come to Notre Dame," Jenkins said. "And I really liked it up there."

"What a classy guy," Meyer said. "Incredible kid. That was a Notre Dame kid. I thought I had him."

"Urban Meyer and I were having a lot of great conversations," Jenkins' father said. "He would call me anytime he saw anything or heard anything about Michael. He would fly down to Tampa to talk to Michael, to meet him at basketball games. So he was really engaged with trying to make sure Michael committed to Notre Dame."

"I had a great time," Jenkins said, "but I just didn't feel it deep down in my soul."

"I lost him right at the end," Meyer said.

Years later, Jenkins was visiting Ohio State and was reintroduced after Meyer had taken over as the Buckeyes' head coach (and by then had three national titles to his credit). "It had been basically 14 or 15 years since I'd spoken with him," Jenkins said. "I kind of introduced myself like, 'Hey, Coach, Michael Jenkins,' and he shoves me with two hands and says, 'I know who the heck you are. I tried to get you to come to Notre Dame.' And he goes back through the whole story. I thought it was something he wouldn't remember because he's been recruiting so long and recruited so many kids, but he remembered. So that was pretty cool."

"Like anything in life, you develop relationships where you're just so like-minded and you appreciate that," Meyer said. "Michael Jenkins, I'll never forget him. I thought he was the epitome of class, and those are the kind of guys you want to coach."

After the Notre Dame trip, Jenkins flew on alone to his next visit to Virginia Tech as his father got back to his job as a military recruiter. The fact that the elder Jenkins spent much of his professional life talking to young people about potentially joining the military was an undercurrent of the entire process for his son. One thing was known in that household—you do not make life decisions hastily. "I had this protective layer as a parent in place," Jenkins' father said, "trying to teach him how to look a man in the eye, kind of listen to what's being said, make a decision based on your head, not just necessarily on your heart. I have young men and young women that come to me, and when they get themselves into the military, I want them to be prepared for what they're going to experience and not be in a situation where their lives were ruined because they just didn't know what they're getting themselves into. So I shared with him that we're going to ask the hard questions. I had a list of like 25, 30, 40, 50 questions, and we're going to ask each one of these individuals the same questions, so that you can hear exactly what their responses are, so that you will kind of know what you're getting yourself into as you prepare for the challenges that you're going to face."

Yeah…but Michael Vick was the coolest player in college football.

The Hokies had just wrapped an 11–0 regular season on the shoulders of their spectacular redshirt freshman quarterback. Vick had carried Virginia Tech into the BCS National Championship

Game, a showdown with Florida State looming in a month, and Jenkins' father recalled Vick getting the call that he was a Heisman Trophy finalist while he was hosting Jenkins. If someone could relate to Jenkins' do-everything exploits in Tampa, it was Vick, whose passing and running talents changed the game in Blacksburg, Virginia. "Back then, of course, you'd want to play with Michael Vick as a receiver," Jenkins said. "So he drove me all around Blacksburg and took me all around campus and the facility. And you knew he was just a star. We would go around campus, and guys and girls would just look at him in awe, like he was Michael Jordan or Michael Jackson or somebody."

Jenkins' father remembers that Hokies assistant Rickey Bustle, the offensive coordinator and quarterbacks coach, was at their Tampa home and ready for a commitment soon after the visit ended, and his father felt like his son was ready to do it. The dad wanted to stick by the plan. The son was maybe getting a little tired of looking around. "This is about being able to hold firm to the things we set in place to have the best possible outcome," Jenkins' father said. "He's like, 'Okay, Dad, okay,' but he was really kind of upset. The next school was going to be Ohio State, and at that point in time, he was like, 'I don't know if I really want to go to Ohio State, I kind of really want to go to Virginia Tech.' I said, 'Son, you already made a commitment to Ohio State that you're going to go there and visit them. When we make commitments, we follow through.'"

The future overall No. 1 pick in the 2001 NFL Draft to the Atlanta Falcons was no match for a military man with a plan. Virginia Tech had Vick. Ohio State had the cold but also a little taste of home. Jenkins' dad wanted that official visit to Ohio State so they could see old friends in Ohio, where Michael had first picked up a football.

Jenkins was born in South Carolina, moved to Germany, and then to Cincinnati around age five, as the family moved with his father's military duties. He moved to Kentucky for a year at age 11, then on to Tampa, but his football introduction was an Ohio one. He started playing at age eight, but he asked before then. His parents said no, and when Jenkins responded with tears, his father came up with a plan. "The only thing I could think of was to come up with a list of things that was going to make it impossible for him to play so that it would be on him and not me," his father said with a chuckle.

Earn straight A's. Take out the trash. Clean your room. Make your bed—military style. Don't get in trouble. Check. Check. Check. Check. Check. Jenkins hit every benchmark, so a football career began. Jenkins scored in his first game, but his father remembered him walking off the field in tears. "There were fans everywhere because you know Ohio," the elder Jenkins said. "So I said, 'Oh my goodness, you had a fantastic game,' and he was walking and he had his head down and I said, 'What's wrong?' and he said, 'Dad, I thought there was gonna be fans all around in the stands.' He thought he was going to be playing in a stadium."

Give it a decade, Michael.

Soon after, Jenkins started playing a lot of quarterback. He also kept growing and started playing a lot of basketball as a result. His mother, Geri, never loved the idea of her son playing football, and with his father often on the road for work, football slipped a bit. During Jenkins' freshman year of high school at Leto, his father suggested he take a year off from the sport to give his body a break. And then football almost got away. "Sophomore year came up, and football season started, and I wasn't even really interested in playing," Jenkins said. "They went through training camp and then they had gone through a game or two, and my dad was like, 'You want to get back out and play?'"

He did. So they watched a game and saw that Leto had a quarterback but could use help at receiver. Even though he had never played the position, he said he could play wide receiver.

So he did, and he did it well. He caught a touchdown pass in his first game back. "It kind of just took off in high school after that," Jenkins said.

At the time Leto was competing in the highest classification of Florida high school football based on the school's size, but the varsity roster was lucky to crack 30 players. So he really did it all (along with senior running back Ricky Sailor, who would play at Texas Tech), which can simultaneously get a player noticed and hide him in plain sight. Facing off against local powers, Jenkins helped keep Leto competitive. In a preseason matchup against a favored opponent, Jenkins scored on a 92-yard interception and then recovered a fumble to set up his own go-ahead touchdown, a nine-yard catch off a fake field goal. In a Week 4 win, Jenkins carried the ball six times for 103 yards and caught two passes for 56 yards and a touchdown. By Week 5 he had 21 carries for 180 yards, nine catches for 215 yards and four touchdowns, and had been named Leto High School's September student of the month with a 3.8 GPA. After a 7–3 regular season that ended with a loss in Leto's playoff opener, Jenkins had 26 catches for 480 yards and eight touchdowns, 51 carries for 313 yards, 80 tackles, three interceptions, five forced fumbles, and a 90-yard punt return for a score.

It was the kind of season that opened eyes, even if it was difficult to decipher exactly what you were seeing. Jenkins was worth figuring out. "Back then recruiting was a lot different. You went to an area and you kind of bounced around that particular area. I had Tampa at that time," former Ohio State defensive line coach Jim Heacock said. "So I went to that area and then I would try and hit all the schools. It's not like it is today…Back then it was you scout around and see if you can find somebody that we could get that would end up being a good player for us. With Michael, to be honest, he was kind of a hard recruit. He was playing weird positions. He was a linebacker. I think he played some quarterback in high school. And so he was a little bit hard to evaluate."

Into his senior season, Jenkins continued to do everything and more, including playing some quarterback as Leto wanted to take some pressure off another young passer being eased into the position. But the idea for Leto, one way or another, was to get Jenkins the ball. And the idea for Ohio State, one way or another, was to discern just how Jenkins might fit as a Buckeye. As part of that pursuit, Heacock brought OSU running backs coach Tim Spencer to a game to aid the evaluation. "I really liked him," Heacock said. "From the time I met him at the school and watched him practice and got to know him, I just really thought he was a special kid. But I guess I needed help on it because we were evaluating for a different position."

So Heacock and Spencer together watched a game where Jenkins played mostly quarterback and linebacker and tried to figure out if he could be a receiver. "He was all over the field, he was tough, he was aggressive, he looked like a good athlete, and he had the skills and the height," Heacock said. "The thing that sells you on all recruits is if you really think he's a winner. And he was such a great kid, and his dad and mom were just great people. He was really a pretty easy recruit from the standpoint of there were no flaws. The only flaw was we really didn't see him play a whole lot at wide receiver. But a lot of times, how a kid envisions himself, that's what he is or what he's going to be. So all along I don't think we looked at him as a defensive player." The Buckeyes were in. Now Heacock had to get Jenkins and his father to Columbus. They arrived in mid-December with Ohio Stadium under construction, the campus practically empty, and the team mostly gone because for the first time in a decade the Buckeyes weren't going to a bowl, which meant no bowl practice. The Buckeyes had finished a 6–6 season with three straight losses, and the players had mostly scattered. "I couldn't see the stadium. Nobody was on campus. Kid from Florida, it's freezing, and there's only five or six players around just to host recruits who are coming in," Jenkins said.

"He was like the kid who didn't want to be there," his father said. "He was kind of sulking a little bit and not saying much and he's a quiet guy anyway. So they worked him over to try to get him to open up a little bit."

Center LeCharles Bentley served as his host. Defensive lineman Ryan Pickett, also a Tampa native, was around. And Jenkins slowly started to warm up. The coaches got him on the blackboard and started diagramming plays and talking football. Jenkins started absorbing the Ohio State history prevalent in the football building. And maybe the connection for a kid who first played football in Ohio started to take hold. "Just before lunch," Jenkins' father said, "it was starting to get to a point of: oh my God, this is Ohio State. I want to go to Ohio State. He said, 'Dad, I love it. I love it.' My heart almost melted because you've got to know my son. He doesn't talk much. So he walked ahead of me, and I said, 'Remember now, you can't commit,' and he said, 'Oh Dad,' and we went to lunch, and Coach Heacock said, 'Mike, Coach Cooper wants you to have lunch at his table.'"

John Cooper wanted a commitment with his meal. Michael Jenkins, once again, seemed ready to give one. "I want to commit," Jenkins said, "but my dad said I can't commit yet."

The plan wasn't finished. One more trip remained to a school that by that point had clearly established itself as a viable option: Georgia Tech, which was the favorite of Geri Jenkins. "My mom fell in love with Georgia Tech. George O'Leary, who was the coach then, sat in our living room and just won over my mom," Michael said. "She was all in with Georgia Tech just because of Coach O'Leary." (Having heard this, Cooper flew to Tampa to talk to Geri before the Georgia Tech official visit, and Cooper's words made a difference.)

She also didn't like to fly, which made the 450-mile drive to Atlanta even more attractive. It was the closest option of her son's finalists compared to Virginia Tech (750 miles), Ohio State (1,000 miles), and Notre Dame (1,150 miles). But she didn't want that to be a deciding factor, though she did put the brakes on a proposed official visit to UCLA. California wasn't happening.

Dez White, a bigger receiver and soon-to-be third-round pick in the 2000 NFL Draft, had put up big numbers at Georgia Tech for two seasons, and Georgia Tech quarterback Joe Hamilton finished second in the Heisman Trophy voting that season behind Wisconsin running back Ron Dayne and one spot ahead of Vick. The Yellow Jackets were a legitimate football force. "Georgia Tech was right in the heart of Atlanta, and playing in the ACC, there was just something that intrigued me about it," Jenkins said. "I was big on education and I didn't know if I wanted to be an engineer, but that intrigued me as well. So there was strong interest there, and I had a great visit. But I just knew it was kind of too busy and kind of too city for me at the time."

His visits completed in December, Jenkins thought about his choice until mid-January. Ten years earlier, Jenkins' father had laid out a plan for him to be able to start playing football—grades, trash, bedroom cleaning, behavior—and now they had followed the plan for where he'd play football next—visit, visit, visit, visit. Jenklins committed to Ohio State on January 10, the 20th member of what would be Cooper's final class with the Buckeyes. "It's like buying a house," Jenkins said. "You go and see so many houses and you like some things and you don't like some things, but then you get to the house where you walk in and you just kind of know. And that's how I felt when I got to Ohio State. It was just a feeling. It just felt right."

Jenkins looked past what may have pushed him away. He looked past an empty campus on a cold December visit. And he looked past a 6–6 record because he remembered the 11–1 team of 1998 and figured better days were ahead. He instead focused on the details that helped draw him to the Buckeyes. "Jim Heacock was my guy. I loved Heacock," Jenkins said. "He flew down to Tampa. He came to my spring practices. He stayed in constant contact with handwritten notes, which you kind of take notice of who's doing a handwritten note and who was just sending you something that's a copy of 500 other letters. So just little things like that. And then getting up here and meeting the staff and, of course, it was Cooper's staff at the time. It was a great feeling. They made you feel like they really wanted you."

"My wife and I just thought [Heacock] was fantastic," Jenkins' father said. "He was very personable. He was a people person. It was a little bit odd that he was not the wide receiver coach, but he was such a natural recruiter, such a nice guy, very forthright, very honest. Once again, with the string of questions that I had for all the people that we spoke to during that recruiting process with all the different coaches, he never gave us any sort of feeling of not being transparent because I had a lot of tough questions."

At every other school, Jenkins questioned whether what he saw in recruiting would actually be there to greet him as a freshman in the fall of 2000. He wondered about the coaching staff at Notre Dame, and Davie lasted two more seasons through 2001. However, Meyer left after the 2000 season to become the head coach at Bowling Green, so Jenkins would have been coached by Meyer for only a single season.

At Georgia Tech he would have played for O'Leary, so loved by his mother, for only two seasons. O'Leary left after the 2001 season to replace Davie as the Notre Dame head coach—a deal that lasted for less than a week because of inaccuracies on O'Leary's resume. But that "too busy" feeling Jenkins initially got from Atlanta? He spent the first seven years of a nine-year NFL career in Atlanta after the Falcons picked him in the first round of 2004 NFL Draft. He even stayed in the Atlanta area after his playing days.

At Virginia Tech, Jenkins would have played with Vick for a single season. Vick turned pro after his redshirt sophomore season in 2000, which Jenkins sensed while visiting Virginia Tech. Regardless, Jenkins' father still believes his son would have picked the Hokies in the moment if he had been permitted to. "He would have committed to Virginia Tech," his father said. "They were the most talked about story in college football during that time. They've got Michael Vick, they're competing for a national championship, they're exciting, they're electrifying, and they did a really good job of selling him."

So Jenkins missed Vick that time around, but he caught him (literally) in the NFL. Three years before they picked Jenkins, the Falcons picked Vick, who was then Jenkins' quarterback for his first three years in professional football.

He eventually re-connected to the aspects of the other three programs he considered. But it was at Ohio State where he settled in... and where Cooper was fired after his freshman year. Jenkins then had to go through the evaluation process again. Another coach would have to figure him out. When Jim Tressel was hired, he brought on several new assistants but retained three from Cooper's staff. Those three were recruiting coordinator and tight ends coach Bill Conley and the two coaches that had watched Jenkins play in Tampa and decided he would fit on the Buckeyes—Heacock and Spencer. Still, this was a new start. "There's an unknown," Jenkins said. "You don't know how everybody's going to handle it and you don't know his coaching style and how he's going to be because you hadn't really spoken with him during the recruiting process."

While he was being recruited, Jenkins hadn't been aware of Cooper's rough record against Michigan—2–10–1 when he was fired—so he hadn't feared an imminent coaching change. Now that it had happened, Jenkins said the transition was seamless, but while he got to know Tressel, Tressel also was getting to know the roster. As a freshman Jenkins had seen just 22 minutes of game action and hadn't caught a pass. "When you get to a place, everyone wants to tell you who's going to be a good player and who's not," Tressel said. "I don't care if it's the equipment people, the trainers, the assistant coaches that were on the staff before, the strength coaches that are still on the staff, whatever. And I kept telling everyone, 'I think you guys have got to relax and let us have spring practice. Let us make decisions.' Sometimes when there's change, kids change. Sometimes kids mature."

Tressel had been taught by Jim Dennison, the head coach at Akron when Tressel was an assistant there, that there are two times you don't evaluate a player. One is when he's hurt, and the other is when he's a freshman. Then Tressel heard someone around the program suggest there were two players just off their freshmen seasons who might not be good enough to make it as Buckeyes: defensive back Will Allen (a future All-American safety) and Jenkins (a future first-round draft pick). "We're going to let this play out," Tressel said.

Soon enough, the new coach was walking off the field with quarterbacks/receivers coach Joe Daniels after the first day of spring practice in 2001. "I said, 'Joe, No. 12, that guy can play. I don't know what people around here are talking about. This guy's gonna be special,'" Tressel said.

Daniels agreed. "Oh my gosh, this guy is gonna be the best," he said, according to Tressel.

Tressel hadn't seen Jenkins in Tampa. But the next spring after Jenkins had led the Buckeyes with 41 catches for 836 yards in Tressel's first season, Tressel was recruiting in Tampa and stopped by Leto High School. "I'm talking to the coach," Tressel said. "And I said, 'We've got Michael Jenkins. We think the world of him. I just want you to know: he's doing a great job.'"

The coach responded by telling stories of everything Jenkins did in high school, all the positions he played, all the games he helped them win, as Tressel was now experiencing everything Jenkins would do in Ohio.

The next season in 2002, the Buckeyes won the national title in Tressel's second year, a 14–0 season for the ages. Ohio State wouldn't have done it without Jenkins, who caught 61 passes for 1,076 yards, which was double the number of receiving yards of any other Buckeye. And they wouldn't have done it without Holy Buckeye.

Brent Musburger had always been the favorite announcer of Jenkins' father, so when Michael Jenkins (his middle name is Evel, while his son's is Gerard, so they are not Sr. and Jr.) settled in at his Tampa home to watch the 10–0 Buckeyes against 4–5 Purdue on November 9, 2002, he was thrilled that Musburger was broadcasting the game for ABC. "All I want to do is hear him call Michael's name one time when he makes a catch. If he can just call his name one time, that'll make my day," Jenkins' father said.

It happened a few times, as Jenkins had four catches for 50 yards entering the final minutes of the game with the Buckeyes trailing 6–3. Facing a fourth and 1 from the Purdue 37-yard line, the Buckeyes called a pass play, and quarterback Craig Krenzel stepped up in the pocket and let fly what would become one of the most famous plays in Ohio State football history. Matched in single coverage against Boilermakers cornerback Antwaun Rogers and with both of them wearing No. 12, Jenkins had raced deep. The game was in West Lafayette, Indiana, but the play took Jenkins back to his football roots in Ohio. "Antwaun Rogers and Michael came up in Cincinnati playing together as a one-two punch when they were nine, 10 years old," the elder Jenkins said. "It was the Antwaun Rogers and Michael Jenkins show with them playing every position that could be played."

The ball was in the air with national championship hopes on the line for the No. 2 team in the country, and a big receiver, who had come up doing it all, determined the fate of this game, this season, and this team. As the clock ticked down to 1:38, Jenkins cradled the ball over his shoulder at the goal line, and Musburger shouted out the result to Tampa, Columbus, and everywhere OSU fans were counting on a third-year Buckeye that a few short years earlier had some schools questioning whether he was a receiver. "Touchdown, touchdown, Michael Jenkins!" Musberger said. "On fourth and 1, would you believe it? Craig Krenzel strikes with a minute and a half left. Holy Buckeye."

Michael Jenkins' son and his favorite announcer had combined for a call no one would ever forget. It happened because years earlier Jenkins had looked past a cold, empty campus to choose Ohio State. Something just felt right. The do-it-all player from Tampa came back to Ohio and he came back home to do this.

## CHAPTER 8

# Eddie George,
# Class of 1992

John Cooper learned early in his coaching career to find the athletes and then let them decide where they wanted to play. He tried it while wooing a quarterback to Tulsa, his first head coaching stop, in the early '80s. He applied what he learned to a future Ohio State Heisman Trophy winner a decade later. "We got a good quarterback at Tulsa and beat Oklahoma on him," Cooper said. "Oklahoma wanted him to play safety. I told him, 'You come to Tulsa, you can play whatever position you want to play out here.' He wanted to play quarterback and he turned into a heck of a football player for us."

Steve Gage was a four-year quarterback for the Golden Hurricane from 1983 to 1986. Cooper moved on to coach Arizona State in 1985. By the time Gage was finishing a brief NFL career—as a safety—in 1988, Cooper was coaching Ohio State.

Finding the talent first and figuring out the rest later had served Cooper well. It would soon help the Buckeyes land Eddie George, the only Ohio State Heisman Trophy winner who didn't play high school football in Ohio.

That's a fitting benchmark for Cooper, who branched out in his search for the best football talent he could find—25 years before Urban Meyer took Ohio State recruiting around the country. "We were gonna go as far as we need to go to recruit the best players," Cooper said. "Some people don't go back far enough, and some people say that Coach Meyer started recruiting out of state. [We] started recruiting out of state and we got David Boston and Joe Germaine and Eddie George and Will Smith and Shawn Springs and guys out of Florida, guys out of Texas. We said we're gonna go as far as we need to go to get the top 20 or 25 players we can recruit a year. Michael Wiley was from California, Na'il Diggs from California. I didn't care where they're from."

Meyer certainly earned and received a lot of praise for the level to which he took Ohio State recruiting after his arrival in 2012. But Cooper's accumulation of talent from around the country is one of the defining characteristics of his tenure from 1988 to 2000. In the 1989 NFL Draft, the spring after Cooper's first year in Columbus, the Buckeyes had four players drafted. They were taken in the fifth, fifth, ninth, and 12th rounds. Thirteen other Big Ten players were drafted in 1989 before offensive lineman Jeff Uhlenhake was the first Buckeye off the board at pick No. 121 overall. "I said, 'The heck with this,'" Cooper said. "I was very disappointed with the talent level."

That's why he went around the country seeking more talent. But he had also been disappointed that a delay in his hiring left the Buckeyes behind for his first recruiting class in 1988. Earle Bruce was fired before the Michigan game in 1987, but Cooper wasn't hired away from Arizona State until December 31. "We got six weeks in there where there's absolutely no recruiting," Cooper said. "And there were some great high school players in the state of Ohio—O.J. McDuffie,

Desmond Howard. Not only did we not get those players, we had to play against them."

McDuffie, a receiver, and John Gerak, a fullback-turned-offensive lineman, were two Ohio players in the late 1980s who played at Penn State. Howard, the Heisman Trophy-winning receiver and return man, and quarterback Elvis Grbac were Ohio players who picked Michigan that year. Cooper told his staff he didn't want that to happen again. "We don't want to overlook an in-state player," Cooper said. "We don't want to have to play against a guy who can play for us, and he's from the state of Ohio."

Although Cooper, who was born in 1937 and was remembering these recruiting stories at the age of 83, said that he didn't want to brag, there is no argument that he raised the talent level with his recruiting at Ohio State. After joining the first full Cooper class in 1989 and establishing himself in three years, defensive end Alonzo Spellman was the first Cooper recruit to be drafted. The Chicago Bears selected him in the first round in 1992.

Cooper coached Ohio State for 13 years and during that time recruited 21 players who became first-round draft picks between 1992 and 2004. In the previous 13 NFL drafts before he arrived, only six Ohio State players had been picked in the first round. (Three Buckeyes were taken in the first round in 2004: Cooper recruits Smith and Michael Jenkins and Chris Gamble, a recruit from the Class of 2001 that Jim Tressel finished off after Cooper was fired.)

Through his recruiting Cooper nearly tripled Ohio State's first-round talent. The majority of that was from Ohio, as 11 of those first rounders—Robert Smith, Dan Wilkinson, Joey Galloway, Korey Stringer, Craig Powell, Terry Glenn, Orlando Pace, Antoine Winfield,

Andy Katzenmoyer, Ahmed Plummer, and Nate Clements—played high school football in-state.

None was a bigger get than Pace, a high school All-American in the Class of 1994 who became the first freshman to start on Ohio State's offensive line, a two-time consensus first-team All-American, and a two-time winner of the Lombardi Award as the nation's best lineman or linebacker. The left tackle also won the Outland Trophy and finished fourth in the 1996 Heisman Trophy voting. He was the No. 1 pick in the 1997 NFL Draft, a seven-time Pro Bowler, and a 2016 inductee into the Pro Football Hall of Fame. "Orlando was a great, great player in high school and he could have gone anywhere," Cooper said of the 6'8" star from Sandusky High School. "I think the major competition on him was Michigan. But there is not an offensive tackle that ever played the game better in college than Orlando Pace. We knew he was gonna be a great player."

Another eight first rounders recruited under Cooper came from outside Ohio. Spellman arrived from New Jersey. Tight end Rickey Dudley was recruited out of Texas by basketball coach Randy Ayers but joined the football team as a junior and turned into a first rounder after a huge senior season in 1995. Cornerback Shawn Springs out of Maryland was the son of former Buckeyes player Ron Springs. Defensive lineman Ryan Pickett and Jenkins, a receiver, arrived from Florida. Boston, a receiver came from Texas. Smith, a defensive end, was out of New York.

And from Philadelphia, Pennsylvania—by way of Fork Union Military Academy in Virginia—came running back Eddie George. "Eddie was born with a football in his hand," said his mother, Donna George. "That's the kind of child that goes to bed with a football. That's the kind of child that goes to family reunions with a football.

When he goes to his grandmother's, he plays in the backyard with the football. He would get in the mirror and say, 'This is my Heisman Trophy speech.' So as a child, he had this big dream. So I just wanted to make his dreams come true. He said he wanted to be an architect. He said he wanted to go to college. He said he wanted to win the Heisman Trophy. And he said he wanted to go to the NFL."

To make those dreams possible, Donna decided her son needed a change in high school. After his sophomore year at Abington High School just outside Philadelphia, he was enrolled at Fork Union, a move he fought at the time but now credits for shaping the rest of his life. "He started acting up, he didn't want to do his homework," Donna said. "You think you're the big man on campus, you think you can run that school? I'm not taking something away from you *at* Abington, I'm taking you away *from* Abington."

Her brother had attended Fork Union, which is about 50 miles west of Richmond, so Donna was familiar with the program and believed in what it could do for her son. He, in that moment, did not. "He didn't like it at first," she said. "He wouldn't talk to me for a whole year because I messed up his career at Abington. But then one day he turned around and he said, 'Thank you, Mom, for making the decision. It's something how one person's decision has changed another person's life.'"

Fork Union gave George the structure he needed, but he also had to find his football outlet. His future coach, Micky Sullivan, clearly remembers the first day he met George. It was the summer before his junior year. "I looked up the hall, and here's this kid and a mom," Sullivan said. "And I just went up and started talking to them, and we started walking down the hall, and Eddie asked me about a jersey number, and I looked at him, and at that time, Eddie weighed about

175 pounds. He wasn't the Eddie George that you know. He was a nice-looking kid but a skinny kid, and I said, 'You show you can play, you can get a jersey.'"

Years before he'd make his college choice, this choice had been made for him. George would have to prove himself to a new team in a new place and hope that would lead to the opportunity to do it again for a college team on a college campus. Donna would later help him make that decision among the myriad choices. But for this move, she felt there was no choice. If she'd let her son stay in Philadelphia, he wouldn't have become the person and player she knew he could be. "It was the education," Donna said. "I told him, 'If you can't read, how in the world can you get out there and play football?'"

He wasn't yet 16 years old when he arrived at Fork Union, but George was taking his first steps toward becoming a new man. "I had to send my baby away," Donna said. "It was the best thing."

During his inaugural season at Fork Union as a junior, George was a backup on the junior varsity, but he came to Sullivan and asked what he needed to do to play college football. They worked on his academic plan and did work on the track and in the weight room. He excelled in track; Sullivan still holds a memory of watching George win a 300-meter hurdles race through a light snow. "He came out of the turn and he might have been one of the uglier 300-meter hurdle runners that you ever saw," Sullivan said. "There were hurdles going everywhere. But he came out of the turn and he was leading. He won that race and never lost another race in high school, and I remember thinking that day, *This kid could be pretty damn good.*"

Yet during his senior year, George held a single football offer— from Division II Edinboro University outside Erie, Pennsylvania. Sullivan said he called coaches he knew and tried to get them interested in George. He asked for even partial scholarships, insisting to friends in the business that George was a talent. Sullivan had grown up in Huntington, West Virginia, so he was particularly insistent to a friend on the coaching staff at Marshall. No go. A few years later, that Marshall coach was with some other coaches visiting Ohio State to watch spring practice. George saw him, recognized him, and came over to say hello. After George left, the coaches turned to the Marshall coach and asked, "How do you know that guy?"

"You don't even want to know," he replied.

Marshall had passed, but that was because no one had yet seen the potential in George. So he took advantage of the opportunity at Fork Union to play a postgraduate year. The postgrad football program is what Fork Union is most known for. Players with college football goals take a year between graduating from their hometown high school and enrolling at college to get their academics in order and/ or get more football exposure. Ohio State receiver Michael Thomas and quarterback Cardale Jones both played for the Fork Union postgrad team in the fall of 2011. Vinny Testaverde spent a postgrad year at Fork Union before going to Miami, where he won the Heisman Trophy in 1986. Receiver Plaxico Burress did the same before enrolling at Michigan State and developing into a top 10 pick in the 2000 NFL Draft. More than 100 players from Fork Union have found their way onto NFL rosters, according to the school.

What George went through in actually attending high school at Fork Union isn't quite as common for players hoping to play college football. But after those two high school years, George stuck around for that extra year. Sullivan said a ruling about whether a Fork Union undergrad could play postgrad at Fork Union led to confusion about

George's eligibility and shortened his last season. But he had enough time to change the arc of his career—with a little help.

The student body at Fork Union is divided into companies, and each has a company commander who is a student. According to Sullivan, Dan Osman, George's company commander from his senior year, enrolled at Ohio State and worked as an undergrad in the football training room. There, Osman floated George's name. Bill Conley, an OSU assistant and the recruiting coordinator at the time, gave Osman the same credit in his book, *Buckeye Bumper Crops*. "Danny would call me every week and ask how Eddie was doing," Sullivan said.

George was now playing for coach John Shuman on the postgrad team, but Sullivan knew everything that George could do and was doing. Osman would pass the Sullivan updates on to Conley until Conley called Fork Union and asked for some film. And then Ohio State got very interested. "Once one school started to recruit him," Sullivan said, "then he had a number of people that wanted to recruit him."

Donna had supported the extra year at Fork Union, but as offers rolled in during the fall of 1991, she told her son, "I am not going to [visit] 25 different colleges."

She wanted to narrow the list of schools and would do so with education in mind, remembering the dreams of that young boy who gave Heisman speeches in the mirror. He had wanted to go to college, win the Heisman, play in the NFL...and be an architect. "Your education is architecture," she said. "So we have to find a college that is going to have these courses because I knew my son at that time. If he had gone for another major and he doesn't want to do that, he would have been kicked out. So he wanted to study architecture, and Ohio State had an architecture program."

She agreed to three visits in December: Virginia, Ohio State, and Penn State. Virginia was fine. Ohio State was different. "Their presentation was so exciting," Donna said, "I felt like putting on a helmet and carrying the football."

Donna was sold, calling Ohio State "a welcoming school" and she was pleasantly surprised when Eddie told her how often Ohio State was on TV. She'd be able to watch him play. She hadn't been able to do that while he was at Fork Union. But she knew this had to be Eddie's choice. Then, during part of the Ohio State presentation, she saw that her son was crying. "He said, 'This is it, Mom. This is it.'"

"Once he came to visit the campus and saw how things were going and how we treated players, we had a good chance to get him," Cooper said.

After George flew back to Fork Union from Columbus, Sullivan picked George up at the airport. Sullivan always encouraged players to visit multiple schools to get a feel for all their options. George knew Sullivan wanted him to take his time. "Coach, I've got something to tell you," George said, and suddenly Sullivan was fearing something had gone wrong. "I committed to Ohio State."

"Okay," Sullivan said. "Why?"

"Coach, they showed me the Buckeye Grove."

"What's the Buckeye Grove?"

"They've got buckeye trees for everybody that makes All-American at Ohio State. Coach, I want a buckeye tree."

When Sullivan first met George two-and-a-half years earlier, the running back had wanted a jersey number. Now he wanted the honor bestowed upon the greatest players in Ohio State history. "Guess what?" Sullivan said. "He got his buckeye tree."

The Georges then canceled what was supposed to be their third visit to Penn State, the school that Eddie as a child had envisioned himself playing for. He had visited Penn State unofficially in November when the No. 8 Nittany Lions beat No. 12 Notre Dame 35–13. But something stuck with George from that visit that he couldn't shake decades later. After the game he said he saw head coach Joe Paterno and defensive assistant Tom Bradley talking. "I'm like, oh God, there's Joe Paterno," George told ESPN in 2019. "He walks to the side and pulls his assistant aside and whispers something in his ear. Tom Bradley comes over and says, 'Hey, we want to talk to you next week about coming up for a visit.' And I was like, oh, my God, the moment has come. I want to be a Penn State Nittany Lion. And he says to me, 'Yeah, we're going to bring you for a visit and we want you to get with the linebacker coach.'"

George's heart sank. "Joe Paterno, God bless his soul, wanted to change his position," Donna said. "I said, 'No way.' I spent all this money on going to camps for running backs ever since he was 12 years old. So I wasn't too keen on Penn State. But I think it was because of his height and his build. He was built like a linebacker. But we made the right choice."

Sullivan said other schools also looked at the 6'0", 195-pound George for defense. Some believed he wasn't fast enough or quick enough to play running back. But for Penn State, this was also part of the cycle of recruiting. In the Class of 1991, the year before, Cooper and the Buckeyes had a rough time, losing arguably the four best players in Ohio—two to Michigan and two to Penn State. On Signing Day in 1991, Cooper said it had been the roughest recruiting year of his life. "The thing we're doing here I don't think is right," Cooper said at his Signing Day news conference. "I don't think we should continually have to defend our program, and that's what we do. We weren't as much selling our program as we are defending it."

Three seasons into his OSU tenure, Cooper was 19–14–2 and he was 0–2 in bowl games and 0–3 against Michigan. Meanwhile, Penn State had signed one of the best classes in the country in 1991, including three of the top running backs in Mike Archie of Pennsylvania, Stephen Pitts of New Jersey, and Ki-Jana Carter from the Columbus suburb of Westerville. Carter had eliminated Notre Dame and Michigan in the final week before Signing Day and then surprised some by picking the Nittany Lions over the Buckeyes.

As a result, Penn State was loaded in the backfield and wasn't sure how George would fit. But Cooper was in the business of providing opportunities. Decades later, George could still tick off the names of Archie, Pitts, and Carter as providing the running back depth in State College that may have blocked him. For George's freshman season at Ohio State in 1992, the Buckeyes would have stiff competition with Robert Smith, Raymont Harris, and Butler B'ynote' at running back, but Cooper wouldn't let that be an issue. "I considered myself a good recruiter," Cooper said. "And I told a kid, 'We want you to come to Ohio State. You play what position you wanna play. Some schools, some coaches, recruited Eddie George as a linebacker. You come here, you play wherever you want to play. If you wanna play running back, play running back. If you wanna play quarterback, play quarterback. If you can't play that position or somebody's better than you, come in and talk to me, and we'll work it out.' But you can lose a player otherwise. So we let the kid play the position he wanted to play. And, of course, Eddie wanted to play running back. And you couldn't have a better work ethic than Eddie George."

As always, a part of recruiting is what you already have on your team that might prevent a recruit from becoming all he wants to become. Every great high school player wants to play. Penn State had too many running backs then. Aware that he's remembered by George as the guy who delivered him the linebacker news, Bradley laughed as he recalled those days, though Bradley never directly recruited George himself. "Eddie tells the story that I came in to tell him he was going to be a linebacker," Bradley said. "And I remember he was a helluva high school football player. But the problem was we had all the backs at the time. So Joe said, 'Well, just tell him he's a linebacker.' That didn't go over big."

Bradley laughed again. "We were just figuring a way to get him on campus," Bradley said. "Once we got him there, we'd go figure it out from there."

Paterno and the Nittany Lions won their fair share of recruiting battles through the years. A major one was for Carter, who in 1994 rushed for 1,539 yards and 23 touchdowns, finishing second in the Heisman Trophy race. The Ohio kid in blue and white went on to become the No. 1 pick in the 1995 NFL Draft.

In the fall of 1995, the Pennsylvania kid who had dreamed of wearing blue and white raced to the Heisman Trophy in scarlet and gray, rushing for 1,927 yards and 24 touchdowns. Based on class schedules, George's architecture goals shifted to landscape architecture once he got to Ohio State. He later founded a landscape architecture firm. He won the Heisman and earned additional landscaping—his All-American tree in Buckeye Grove. He was the No. 14 pick in the 1996 NFL Draft and played for nine years in the league, rushing for more than 10,000 yards. He earned his master's degree in business and even performed the role of Billy Flynn in the

Broadway show *Chicago* and later in the national touring company. And in April of 2021, he was named the head football coach at Tennessee State University, meaning he now will be the one doing the recruiting.

He has never stopped chasing dreams. "I think God for making the right decisions for my son," Donna George said.

The first was choosing Fork Union. The second was choosing Ohio State.

CHAPTER 9

# Kenny Guiton, Class of 2009

High school quarterback Kenny Guiton was at home sick, Ohio State assistant coach John Peterson was heading to the airport, and that should have been the end of their story. But because Peterson was in this city (Houston), on this day (January 28, 2009), under these extreme and unexpected circumstances (quarterback recruiting desperation), Guiton was going to need to get off the couch, get to Aldine Eisenhower High School, and change the rest of his life.

Guiton was on the couch. His Eisenhower teammate Greg Timmons was on the other end of the phone. The 6'3" receiver, a four-star recruit and one of the best receivers in the state, had been committed to the University of Texas for almost a year. Fellow receiver Jazz Reynolds would sign with Oklahoma, and Craig Loston, a five-star safety ranked as one of the 10 best recruits in the country by the 247Sports.com composite rankings, was headed to LSU. Eisenhower was stacked with talent, but the quarterback of the Eagles was still uncommitted—confusingly, but crucially, uncommitted in the recruiting process. "Hey, man, I'm not feeling good," Guiton said when he finally picked up his cell.

"He was like, 'Nah, you need to get over here, man,'" Guiton said. "'You got a big Ohio State coach with a trench coat on who just came in. Man, he's got a trench coat on and he said he's looking for you, man.'" Guiton hung up. "I think he's joking," Guiton said. "I'm thinking my [recruiting] process is kind of messed up now and I'm hurt, and the next thing you know, my dad's calling. And when my dad starts calling, I'm like, 'Maybe he's not playing.' And my dad's on it. He's like, 'I know you're not feeling good. I don't care if you need to stop 10 times before you get here. But I need you to get here to school. You've got Ohio State here wanting to talk to you. They want to meet with you.' I said, 'I'm on my way. I'll find a way.' And I did have to make one stop. I stopped at a corner store real quick, about 10 to 15 minutes, jumped right back in the car. I made it there, and coach John Peterson was the guy that came in, and yes, he had on a big trench coat."

"It was amazing to me," said Kenneth Guiton Sr., an Eisenhower assistant coach, "because we had just watched Texas play Ohio State in a bowl game and we were rooting for Texas. And all of a sudden Ohio State comes in and is asking about my son. And we're going, 'This is one of the five top schools for football—not in the nation but in history.' And it was amazing how things had flipped so fast."

Peterson was in the car. The Ohio State assistant was in his sixth year as the Buckeyes' tight ends coach and recruiting coordinator under Jim Tressel, and a week before National Signing Day for the 2009 class, he was in Houston, one of his peripheral areas as a recruiter. Primarily, Peterson worked sections of Ohio—just like, primarily, Ohio State worked sections of Ohio. The Buckeyes were preparing to sign 24 other players in a week: 14 from Ohio, six from states that touched Ohio, three from Florida, and one from Maryland.

In the first seven full recruiting classes pulled together by Tressel's staff since 2002, the Buckeyes had signed two Texas players: defensive back Ashton Youboty in 2003 and offensive tackle J.B. Shugarts in 2008. Both were from Klein High School, also in the Houston area. But this was rare. "That was a secondary area," Peterson said. "So you pick bits and pieces because you can't recruit the whole area because it's too big. So you may spend a day or two at most, looking for specific needs per year. But we really had very little knowledge until we ran across a need."

When he arrived in Houston, Peterson wasn't aware of a quarterback need. But after making other rounds in Houston on this Wednesday, he prepared to head toward the airport for his flight back to Columbus, when he, too, got a call. This one was from Ohio State football headquarters. Something had happened at quarterback. There's an uncommitted quarterback in Houston they wanted him to check out. "If you know Houston, it's quite a large city," Peterson said. "And I believe Eisenhower High School was opposite from where the airport was and where I was. So I drove about an hour across Houston to get there and I found out he wasn't there."

Peterson was at the end of a long recruiting grind on the road. He was thinking about whether he could still make the last flight out of Houston to get back home. Signing Day was almost here. So how long would he wait on this kid? "I was holding my breath. And when I first walked in and he wasn't there, I was like, okay, do I wait and miss my flight or sit here for however long it takes him to get over here?" Peterson said. "And I opted to wait, and if I had to get a morning flight to see this young man, I was going to do it. I'm definitely glad I waited that extra time to see Kenny." (Peterson did then make the last flight out that night.)

Ohio State had a Terrelle Pryor problem. Specifically, Pryor was so talented and playing so soon that he was scaring off other quarterbacks. The No. 1 recruit in the class of 2008, Pryor had ascended to the starting job in the fourth game of the 2008 season as a true freshman, following Art Schlichter in 1978 as the only true freshmen to start at quarterback in Columbus. The 6'6" Pryor ate up ground with long strides as a runner and was dangerous, if a little raw, as a passer. But the Big Ten Freshman of the Year was talented and he wasn't going anywhere. His recruitment had transformed the football program, and that meant the starting quarterback job was locked down for at least 2009 and 2010 (unless something went wrong) and possibly into 2011 if Pryor stayed at Ohio State for four seasons. That made it difficult to recruit a quarterback in the class behind him because the pecking order was obvious: Pryor first, anyone else next. "Strategically, when you think about what you need, Terrelle had just gotten there," Tressel said. "And he was playing. So I felt we needed someone who would come and develop. We needed someone who would fall in love with the school. And I didn't need to go and bring someone in who was going to transfer or whatever."

Still, the Buckeyes shot high with their major quarterback target in the 2009 class. Tajh Boyd of Virginia was a five-star quarterback who was choosing between Ohio State, Clemson, and Oregon on January 27. He said Troy Smith was his favorite quarterback, and on his OSU visit, Tressel offered him the chance to wear No. 10, just like Smith. But Boyd wanted to go where he could play the earliest. He chose Clemson, where he redshirted in 2009, saw limited action as a backup in 2010, and started in 2011, 2012, and 2013. The Buckeyes didn't see him again until the Orange Bowl after the 2013 season. In the last game of his career, Boyd threw for 378 yards and five touchdowns in a 40–35 win against the Buckeyes.

But Boyd's timing and decision also cost the Buckeyes their first backup plan. Austin Boucher, a Dayton-area quarterback, was told by Ohio State he was next if Boyd didn't pick Ohio State. But during that week, Boucher heard rumors that Boyd would choose the Buckeyes. So Boucher committed to Miami (Ohio) to play with his twin brother. When Boyd went with Clemson, the Buckeyes told Boucher on Tuesday evening that he was up. The Archbishop Alter High School standout, a three-star prospect, slept on it. On Wednesday afternoon he told the Buckeyes he was out. He was sticking with Miami. That's when the call went out to Peterson. "They had to go and get Kenny Guiton right after I committed to Clemson," Boyd said four years later in a pregame news conference for the Orange Bowl.

They didn't have to get *this* Kenny Guiton. They had to get *a* Kenny Guiton from wherever one of their assistant coaches was on that Wednesday. If Peterson had been in another Texas city, he would have been looking for a quarterback there. "Part of the story was me being in that specific location and a match that showed a young man with some skillsets that we liked on tape that was still available," Peterson said. "If I had been in Dallas, they wouldn't have looked at the rosters in Houston. They would have looked at the rosters in Dallas back in the office."

So when he got the call, Guiton got to school however he had to. (There is some dispute about the severity of Guiton's illness and his exact whereabouts that day. His mother, Veronica, believes he was at Popeyes when the call came. "Who is sick enough to go eat spicy food at Popeyes?" she said with a laugh.)

But there is no disputing this fact: Guiton was still uncommitted, though he never should have been. That's because Guiton was playing with and against some of the best talent in Houston, in Texas, and in the nation and holding his own. During his junior year at Eisenhower in 2007, Guiton faced Stratford High School quarterbacked by Andrew Luck, a top 50 recruit in the Class of 2008 who committed to play quarterback at Stanford and went on to be the No. 1 pick in the 2012 NFL Draft. Going into their matchup in the sixth game of the season, Luck had 1,034 passing yards, nine touchdowns, and seven interceptions; Guiton had 1,234 passing yards, eight touchdowns, and five interceptions. Eisenhower and Guiton won the game 19–14. "There was a lot of hype about Andrew Luck," said Marlon Taplin-McMillan, Eisenhower's offensive coordinator for Guiton's freshman through junior seasons. "Kenny was this sleeper guy who was No. 2 in the area and No. 5 in the state in passing, and everyone was trying to figure where this kid came from."

Guiton threw for more than 200 yards with two touchdowns and no interceptions in one of the first games where Taplin-McMillan gave him three plays to choose from when he got to the line of scrimmage. "Kenny was the only quarterback I ever had that could do that," Taplin-McMillan said.

Then came Aldine High School quarterbacked by Darron Thomas, a top 300 recruit in the Class of 2008 who committed to play quarterback at Oregon. "That was the last game before we got into the playoffs, and he took that real personal as far as Darron Thomas," Taplin-McMillan said. Eisenhower won 49–14.

Throw in Nimitz High School quarterback Michael Thomas, who went on to play safety at Stanford, and Guiton called the competition that season "the district of quarterbacks. But I got my chance."

Knowing that he was surrounded by great talent on his team, Guiton led Eisenhower to wins over all of them. In the playoffs Eisenhower ran into Cypress Ridge quarterbacked by Russell Shepard, a five-star player who would be the No. 3 overall recruit in the nation in the class of 2009. Shepard ran for 191 yards, while Guiton threw for 186 yards and three touchdowns. Trailing by seven points, Eisenhower got the ball back with 1:37 to play, and Guiton led a 10-play, 75-yard drive—only to be stopped on a run from the 1-yard line on the final play of the game. But it took a junior who would be the best quarterback in the country the following year to knock Guiton and his team out.

So where did that leave Guiton on the recruiting trail? "It was a crazy story," Guiton said. "I knew I was doing some good things. I was leading the city in passing yards, but I always felt like I was a small guy. I hit a growth spurt when I got into my sophomore year, I was 6'1" or 6'2", but I was skinny, I was skinny. I graduated high school probably at 165 when I was 6'3". I was a stick figure. So I always felt like, *Man, I'm just too small, I'm not strong enough, I'm not fast enough.* Everyone has those certain doubts about themselves, but I always felt like colleges aren't going to want me because of that. I'm out to prove them wrong, but colleges aren't gonna want me because of all these things I keep making up in my head."

Colleges sent mail, but Guiton didn't think anything was serious. Then one day something arrived from the University of Kansas that was more substantial. This was an actual scholarship offer, and it raised Guiton's confidence in himself. Soon, more followed. Iowa State and Kansas State were big offers. Texas Tech showed a lot of interest. The University of Houston was involved, and Guiton really liked head coach Kevin Sumlin. He was right in the mix, going to camps the summer between his junior and senior year, taking unofficial visits, enjoying the process, picking favorites. One coach he liked the most was Tom Herman, who started recruiting him as the Rice offensive coordinator in 2007 and then kept in touch when he moved to Iowa State after the 2008 season to become the Cyclones offensive coordinator. He even came to watch Guiton practice at Eisenhower one day. "Loved him," Guiton said. "He was just so honest throughout the entire process with me."

Everything was lining up. Guiton played with talent and played against talent. Schools were showing interest in the returning starter who had good film. His parents really liked the option of Rice, an excellent academic institution in Houston with a high graduation rate for football players. But entering his senior season, Guiton figured Iowa State, Kansas, and Houston were his top three choices. And then Guiton found out what happens when recruiting goes wrong.

Houston told Guiton they weren't as interested in him as a quarterback. A great high school basketball player, he actually had scholarship offers in both sports to Houston. But the Cougars had Case Keenum at quarterback, and Keenum would throw for more than 5,000 yards in 2008 as a sophomore and would be a junior in 2009 when Guiton arrived. So Guiton was told he'd start out as a receiver or cornerback. Guiton, who was willing to redshirt and then compete, knew that a position switch wouldn't work. "I literally told them on the phone, 'Coach, I love you to death, but if you put me out there at corner, you're gonna throw me on the back burner and say, 'Why did y'all recruit him?'"

Kansas was Guiton's first offer and therefore his first love. Guiton knew Johnathan Wilson, a freshman from Houston who was at Kansas, and the Jayhawks went 12–1 in 2007, won the Orange Bowl, and finished in the top 10 in the country. Guiton was also a big fan of head coach Mark Mangino. "There were so many connections there. I was like, yeah, this is probably where I'm going to end up," Guiton said.

But the process got him. "What happened is I lost out on offers waiting too long," Guiton said. "I'm kind of waiting to go do my official visit my senior year because I want to visit Kansas and Iowa State. And I just waited too long. And next thing you know even after my visit, I actually called Kansas to commit, and they said, 'We just had a guy commit last week. We're out of business for a quarterback.'"

Quinn Mecham, a junior college quarterback from Utah, committed to Kansas in mid-December. So Guiton moved on to Iowa State, but the same thing happened. The Cyclones were set with Jared Barnett, a quarterback from the Dallas area who had committed in May and made his official visit in December to reaffirm his choice. Guiton had waited that long to take his official visit without ever accepting an offer. "This is just me not getting the process," Guiton said. "These are my two schools, they both tell me they're filled, and I don't know what to do next because I hadn't been talking to the rest of them."

Enter a coach who lived one mile from Eisenhower High School and who would go for walks around the track at the school and occasionally catch glimpses at football practice of a quarterback with an intriguing arm. Prairie View A&M assistant coach Prince Pearson was very interested in Guiton. In the Southwestern Athletic Conference, a historic league made up of Historically Black Colleges, Prairie View A&M had been a powerhouse in the 1950s and '60s. Then the program fell on hard times, losing 28 straight in the early 1980s and 80 straight games in the 1990s. But by the late 2000s, the Panthers were rolling under head coach Henry Frazier. They went 9–1 in 2008 playing FCS-level football and they liked Guiton. "I saw him develop, and his senior year, he had some big schools offer. So when I went into the school to recruit some other players, I didn't think I had a shot at him," said Pearson, the Panthers' offensive line coach for 11 seasons. "The coach said, 'Hey, what about Kenny?' So that's how that connection started. I knew the head coach very well. And I didn't think we'd get him on a visit, and, man, this kid came and he was very receptive."

"I loved the visit, had a great time, loved the coaches, had an awesome coach recruiting me," Guiton said of Prairie View. "You could tell they wanted me. They showed me the love."

"It was getting closer to Signing Day, and nobody was making a call, and then Prairie View called," Veronica Guiton said. "I guess they heard Eisenhower's quarterback hadn't committed to anybody. So he went down there, and I said, 'Look son, whatever you decide to do, your mother is going to be there. At least Prairie View is close enough that I can come to the practices, too. So we're gonna be all right.'"

Located 38 miles northwest of Eisenhower High School, Prairie View knew it had a chance at something special with Guiton. "I remember getting excited," Frazier said. "I was like, 'This is like a joke. This kid, he's a major player.' We came down to the end. I know we offered, I know we said, "Hey, we'd love to have you.' But I never thought we were going to get him. I always thought it was a dream. And then we got closer, and I was like, *Wow, we're getting ready to steal one. We're gonna win a championship with this kid.*"

That's where it was heading. With Signing Day coming on February 4, 2009, Guiton had his eyes on Prairie View well into January. His older sister graduated from Prairie View with a nursing degree. So he knew a bit about the school and he was ready. "I'm all in for it," Guiton said. "Two weeks before Signing Day, I'm literally telling Prairie View, 'I'm coming, I'm coming.'"

He just hadn't made his commitment official or public. But his plans were in place, and Kenneth Guiton Sr. and Veronica Guiton were going to be able to drive less than an hour to watch their son play college football. Guiton Sr. ran track and cross country and then became a football coach. Veronica was a volleyball star. So Kenny was always around sports, and growing up around football, he started thinking like a typical coach's kid. "I was a smart guy who always understood the game because I grew up in it," Guiton said. "I'd just be there for high school practices and in second or third grade I was getting coaching from the high school coaches."

He was a small kid with a big arm and a coach's mind. And all he wanted to do was one day play quarterback for Eisenhower High School. "Coming from inner-city Houston, everybody wants to go to college, but guys don't know if it's really going to happen or not," Guiton said. "So that was my dream. One day I wanted to lead Eisenhower High School to a state championship."

Then it was time for another dream because Peterson was at his school. Guiton Sr. remembers what Peterson told him that day: "Coach Tressel told me not to come back without a quarterback."

"All the things people said in my short time there was that he was nothing but a first-class person and leader," Peterson said. "And then when he walked in, I saw 6'3", skinny, the big smile of Kenny Guiton."

Ohio State got a quarterback. And Guiton got a story to tell for the rest of time. He tells the Pryor part. He tells the Boyd part. He tells the Boucher part. "They said they scoured the Earth for a quarterback," Guiton said, "And they saw a guy down in Houston that's not committed."

It was, in its own way, a football miracle. Ohio State had to lose Boyd and Boucher. Guiton had to lose Houston, Kansas, and Iowa State. Peterson had to be in Houston on that very day when Boucher told Ohio State. And Guiton had to have kept what he thought was his decision about Prairie View to himself because Ohio State in the final scramble was only looking for uncommitted quarterbacks. "We weren't poaching," Peterson said. "We weren't trying to go and turn a kid."

All those things had to line up to lead Guiton to Ohio State and Ohio State to Guiton. "It's definitely fate," Guiton said. "It's just meant to be. That's the only thing I could put it on because how would all those things fall into place like that?"

"It's God-given," said his father. "I've told people, and once they hear the story, they say, 'Something extra was working here.'"

Peterson was in Eisenhower on Wednesday, and Guiton and his father were in Columbus that weekend. The visit was a formality; Guiton was the guy. But they were greeted by a layer of snow. "We come and touch down, and everything's white," Guiton said. "So me and my dad are like, okay, this is already different."

Veronica was back in Houston, waiting to hear every word. She was a sports mom and she craved every detail. She went to church while she waited for that word, and when Kenny called to tell her he'd officially accepted Ohio State's offer, Veronica announced it to the church. "Everybody was so happy," she said. "They love him. At the end of the day, I said, 'This is where God wants you to be. There's too many things that could have happened that didn't happen. It happened for you right here in Houston at that time on that day.'"

Ohio State's gain was Prairie View A&M's loss, but no one viewed what transpired as anything other than a celebration. "I was kind of tuned into his recruitment. So I didn't want to get head over heels over a cat that I might not get," Pearson said. "And hey, he was honest with me, his dad was honest with me, and I lived in the neighborhood. So they didn't want to lead me on in a way to hurt me. So the family was up-front with me, and that's all you can ask.

You remember the ones that were good and that treat you right. He did everything you were supposed to do in the whole recruitment process. I tell guys about him all the time. He was probably one of the best players I ever recruited that I got to visit Prairie View."

"When we lost him, I got mad at the coach, 'You got me all excited; now he's gone,'" Frazier said with a laugh. "But I'm very proud of him."

That's because what Guiton did at Ohio State may be even more remarkable than how he got to Ohio State. He redshirted in 2009 and then played briefly in a handful of games in 2010 as a third-stringer behind Pryor and Joe Bauserman, completing one pass. When Tressel resigned before the 2011 season, Guiton was lost a bit as Bauserman and Braxton Miller shared the quarterback role. And when Urban Meyer arrived for the 2012 season, Guiton was ready to leave. Tressel had wanted a quarterback who wouldn't transfer, but Guiton had considered it before and really thought about it now. "When Coach Meyer first got there, he wasn't thrilled with Kenny," his father said. "Kenny was a step or two away from getting on a plane and coming back to Texas."

Anticipating a possible transfer after a coaching change, other Texas colleges put out feelers that they'd be interested if Guiton left. "I didn't want to bring the T-word up. I just didn't," his mother said. "And then finally one day I broke down and I said, 'What do you want to do? Do you want to transfer? Do you want to leave?'"

By then Guiton had talked it out with some other Buckeyes, including Bauserman, who understood life as a backup, and decided to stay. He believed he wouldn't find another place like Ohio State. And his mother believed that he'd find his purpose at Ohio State because he'd been directed there for a reason. In the eighth game of his fourth season in Columbus in 2012, undefeated Ohio State was trailing Purdue 20–14 when Miller was injured with 21 seconds to play in the third quarter. Guiton was nervous warming up on the sideline, but he also was thinking this was why he'd come to Columbus. He had taken mental reps in practice, standing 10 yards behind Miller and simulating plays and he had cracked jokes in the locker room while becoming a favorite of his teammates.

Now he'd have to save the Buckeyes.

He had thrown just 12 passes in four seasons, but he was a player that a team, which was shocked to be losing, could rally around. Down eight with 47 seconds to play, the OSU offense took the field for a last gasp. Guiton avoided pressure and completed a 39-yard pass to Devin Smith. After another completion and a pass interference call, Guiton rolled out and hit a diving Chris Fields for a two-yard touchdown with three seconds to play. A pass to tight end Jeff Heuerman for the two-point conversion tied it, and the Buckeyes won in overtime 29–22. The win saved what would be an undefeated 2012 season for the Buckeyes, and it established the legend of Kenny G. He was a backup quarterback who became a fan favorite and a backup quarterback who became a leader. Before the 2013 season, Guiton was elected one of the team captains despite being a backup.

When Miller missed games against Cal and Florida A&M in 2013, Guiton started in his place, throwing for 276 yards and four touchdowns against Cal and 215 yards and six touchdowns against FAMU. Nobody was surprised. When Veronica can't sleep at night, she pulls out her computer and watches those three games to relive what her son did in an Ohio State uniform when he got his chance.

The last-minute quarterback from Houston was the ideal backup quarterback in Columbus. That's just what the Buckeyes needed with

Pryor on the roster and Tressel realizing that Miller and Cardale Jones were two Ohio high school quarterbacks who were interested in the Buckeyes and "in the pipeline." "We needed to get the right kind of person," Tressel said. "And there's going to be a moment when you're called on, and he was. And he had the maturity to meet that need. And to the credit of Kenny, what impressed me about him was that he was thinking beyond college. He was thinking, *This was a great place to come and learn, and maybe I can be a coach.*"

Guiton is a coach now. He started his OSU career under Tressel, but he finished it under Meyer, playing for two offensive coordinators who had recruited him in high school—Herman, who always loved him, and Ed Warinner, who was part of the Kansas staff back then. In reconnecting with Herman, Guiton found a mentor, and when Herman took the job as the head coach at the University of Houston for the 2015 season, one of his first moves was to bring Guiton on as a graduate assistant. Guiton did that for two years and then became Houston's receivers coach. He then coached receivers at Louisiana Tech in 2019, Colorado State's receivers in 2020, and for the 2021 season, he was hired to coach the receivers at Arkansas, moving up to the SEC before he turned 30.

It started when Peterson walked into Eisenhower High School, and Guiton got off his couch. His life changed. "It set me up," Guiton said, "to where I am today."

CHAPTER 10

# Keith Byars,
# Class of 1982

In February of 1982, two high school baseball stars made football choices. Both were running backs who could swing a bat—one a 6'2", 215-pound star in Dayton, Ohio, the other a 6'1", 215-pound standout in McCalla, Alabama. Both stayed home for college. Both made it big. Only one played both football and baseball in college. The other wondered what might have been. "When Bo did what he did at Auburn, I wasn't impressed. I was like, man, I could have been doing that at Ohio State if I'd been given an opportunity," Keith Byars said. "I still think that way."

Jackson helped set a modern standard for dual-sport athletes with the exceptional baseball/football package of skills he exhibited at Auburn, which culminated with the 1985 Heisman Trophy. That led Jackson into a two-way career in the NFL and in Major League Baseball and into the annals of legendary American athletes with a "Bo Knows" campaign from Nike that cast Jackson as the epitome of crossover talent and appeal.

As for Byars, he nearly won his own Heisman Trophy, finishing second to Boston College quarterback Doug Flutie in 1984. And he went on to be a first-round NFL draft pick in 1986. The Philadelphia Eagles chose him at No. 10, nine spots behind Jackson. But the baseball never followed.

On a football field, both dominated as big backs who could run by you or run over you, breaking tackles, piling up yards, and carrying offenses. Both Byars and Jackson missed most of a college season due to injury. During his junior season in 1984, Jackson missed time because of his shoulder, and Byars missed time as a senior in 1985 because of his foot. But combining their best two seasons—Jackson in 1983 and 1985 and Byars in 1983 and 1984—leads to this comparison.

**Jackson:** 436 carries, 2,999 rushing yards, 6.9 rushing yard average, 29 touchdowns, 17 catches, 146 yards, 8.6 yards per reception, and two touchdown receptions for 3,145 yards total yards from scrimmage and 31 total touchdowns.

**Byars:** 558 carries, 2,963 rushing yards, 5.3 rushing yard average, 42 touchdowns, 65 catches, 838 yards, 12.9 yards per reception, and three touchdown receptions for 3,801 total yards from scrimmage and 45 total touchdowns.

Jackson existed in rarified air as an '80s superstar. Byars didn't occupy the same airspace nor become a two-sport star in college, but he played four sports at Dayton's Roth High School. He also served as an example of the primary recruiting strategy throughout the history of Ohio State football: secure exceptional in-state Ohio high school athletes and turn them into Buckeyes. And Byars did live a remarkable recruiting journey that featured names Dan Marino, Barry Bonds, Woody Hayes, Bo Schembechler, Archie Griffin, and Dom Capers.

Before Bo Knew, everyone in Ohio knew Byars. "Keith was as good of an all-around athlete as you'll find," Capers said. "With his size and his demeanor and his competitiveness, if he set his mind to it, I think he had a chance to do whatever he wanted to."

As part of his five-decade coaching career that would lead him to be an NFL head coach for the Carolina Panthers and Houston Texans, Capers recruited Byars as a Tennessee assistant. "He was one of those guys that you knew was going to be successful," Capers said, "because he had all the physical qualifications in terms of the height, weight, and speed. But he was driven."

"We knew what we had before he got there," said Glen Mason, Ohio State's offensive coordinator during Byars' career in Columbus from 1982 to 1985. "He's a physical specimen. And there's a lot of guys that are physical specimens, but when they're a running back and they get to the next level, they end up playing linebacker or something like that because they don't have the skills to go with it. But he had everything."

Byars just had to decide how to use those skills. Like many great athletes before and since, Byars' recruiting decision wasn't only about choosing a school; it was also about choosing a sport. As is often the case for high school players but is seldom the reality for college players, the goal was to play both in college. "You could talk to a lot of people in my hometown, and they'd say they don't think I made the wrong decision by playing football," Byars said. "But if I had not played football and played baseball, it would have worked out the same, and I'd have played longer."

While in high school, Byars impressed at an open tryout for the Cincinnati Reds, but he said he told baseball teams not to draft him out of high school because he was certainly going to college. The plan was to delay the time when Byars had to choose one sport over the other, so Byars' entire recruiting process went down two paths. He looked at football and baseball as nearly equal parts of his immediate future. "I had a football/baseball scholarship to Ohio State," Byars said. "A lot of people don't know that. Every college I visited was a two-way scholarship. Football is going to pay so the baseball team can save a scholarship because I'm already on a football scholarship. But the intention was to play baseball in college."

For that reason one of Byars' college visits took him 1,800 miles from Dayton to Tempe, Arizona, and the campus of Arizona State. For the Sun Devils, the pitch was clear. In football Byars would replace another big back with a build and style similar to Byars, as Gerald Riggs was about to be taken in the first round of the 1982 NFL Draft by the Atlanta Falcons. In baseball the Sun Devils had just won the 1981 College World Series under legendary coach Jim Brock and were raking in talent. Byars knew playing baseball there would mean playing with other future stars even if he didn't know exactly who they would be. In that same 1982 recruiting class, the Sun Devils were zeroing in on another outfielder as well. "Barry Bonds went to Arizona State. We would have been in the same out-field," Byars said. "Arizona State wanted me big time for baseball. Big time. So when I visited Arizona State, one day was dedicated to football, and the second day was dedicated to baseball."

Bonds, a second-round pick in the baseball amateur draft out of high school, played three years for the Sun Devils and then was the No. 6 overall selection in the 1985 draft by the Pittsburgh Pirates. He hit 45 home runs in college and another 762 in the major leagues, developing from one of the greatest all-around players in baseball history into a central figure in the steroid era. Byars could have started his professional journey next to Bonds. "They finished third in my recruitment," Byars said. "And it was really almost a tie for second. It was so far away from Dayton. But I had a great visit at Arizona State. They had a good football program and a better baseball program. And I was like, oh my gosh, whew, I love it out here. It was the first time I had been out West in my life. And I just had a great, great, great visit there. And I was like if y'all was just a little bit closer."

While baseball was a draw, Byars knew football would come first for him. So the fit there mattered most. With that in mind, Riggs acted as Byars' host and sold him on what was possible. Under coach Darryl Rogers, Riggs ran for 891 yards, and fellow back Robert Weathers (who was a second-round NFL pick in 1982) ran for 711 yards, leading the Sun Devils to a 9–2 record in 1981 and a top 20 ranking. The Sun Devils had been built into a power by Hall of Fame coach Frank Kush in the '70s, and now Rogers, the former head coach at Michigan State, had continued that. With Riggs and Weathers both headed to the NFL, the Sun Devils offered what a back like Byars wanted: a chance to win and a chance to play. "Gerald was like, 'Man, you're gonna play right away out here,'" Byars said. "He was just leaving, and I'd have been coming."

But the distance was too much. Byars passed, and the Sun Devils signed the best high school athlete in Colorado, a running back named Darryl Clack. He rushed for 606 yards in 1982, becoming the first freshman to lead the Sun Devils in rushing in decades. Arizona State went 10–2, won the Fiesta Bowl, and finished No. 6 in the final Associated Press poll.

Though Arizona State wasn't for Byars, the University of Pittsburgh almost was. Byars had grown up a Pirates fan. Hall of Fame outfielder

Roberto Clemente was his first sports hero. Byars also had extended family in Pittsburgh, and the Panthers had gone 11–1 in both 1980 and 1981 and finished No. 4 in the final AP poll in 1981 after a win against Georgia in the Sugar Bowl. Head coach Jackie Sherrill left for Mississippi State after the 1981 season, and suddenly, Foge Fazio, the assistant who had been recruiting Byars for more than a year, was the head coach.

Plus, the Panthers in 1982 could offer a senior quarterback who would pair perfectly with a freshman running back. Marino had thrown 37 touchdown passes in 1981 and tried to get Byars into the Pitt backfield. "When I visited Pittsburgh, me and Marino, we hung out," Byars said. "He was crying, like, 'I love you man,' and I was like, 'But I'm only going to get to play with you one year, and then you're gone.' But we made up for it when I went to the Dolphins. I said, 'I finally get to play with you.' And me and Dan, we've been friends ever since."

That reunion came in 1993, when Marino was 11 years into a Hall of Fame NFL career as Miami's quarterback and Byars signed as a free agent with the Dolphins after spending his first seven NFL seasons in Philadelphia. Their time together wouldn't happen in college; Marino's Panthers finished second in the race to woo Byars.

There were other attempts, including a strong relationship built by Capers, the Tennessee assistant. And then there was, of course, the visit that was a rite of passage for so many future Buckeyes in Ohio in that era. Coach Schembechler came to town. "They came on as early as Ohio State did," Byars said of the Michigan Wolverines. "They were able to recruit me hard and heavy from the word go, from right after my junior year."

Just before Thanksgiving in 1981 and just after Ohio State beat Michigan 14–9 in Ann Arbor during Byars' senior high school season, Schembechler came to Dayton. "He comes to my house and sits in my living room for two hours," Byars said.

Michigan had been sending letters and calling, and Byars had entertained the dalliance from a distance. But he had no actual interest in the Wolverines and certainly not enough to warrant a visit from the 52-year-old head coach who was coming off his first Rose Bowl win in 1980. "I was like I don't know about Michigan. But Bo Schembechler just came," Byars said. "I can't blow off Bo Schembechler. I'm a Woody Hayes guy, even though he's no longer the coach, and Bo's the bad guy, but I've got to be respectful. So he sits in my living room for two hours, and it wasn't a fair fight. I'm only 17 years old, and he brainwashed me, and I've agreed to come to Michigan for a visit. And my first visit was to Michigan. He had me in the Sunken Place. I was like, *Oh my god, I visited Michigan.*"

Byars left his mark on that visit. He went to Ann Arbor in December as the Wolverines were preparing to play UCLA in the Bluebonnet Bowl. "That's my first visit, and everybody's telling me when you visit these schools, that's the only time in your life they're going to basically treat you like a king," Byars said. "So that Friday night, we go to dinner, and the Michigan coaches ordered everything. That was the first time I ever heard of a porterhouse steak. I'd never heard of a porterhouse. I didn't know what that was. So they said, 'Get the biggest steak on the menu. You want some oysters on the half shell?' And I was like, 'Okay, I've only heard of it, only seen it in the movies.' I didn't know what that was. So some of the coaches and the other recruits, we're on the car ride back to the hotel, and I tell the coach, 'You need to pull over, you need to pull over.'"

Weighed down by too much rich food, Byars was about to throw up on his first official college visit. "My stomach is rejecting all of this," Byars said. "As soon as we get in the parking lot, some of it was in the parking lot, but a great deal of it was in his brand new car. So that was kind of how I felt about Michigan."

The primary recruiter for Michigan's rival on Byars was Fred Zechman, the quarterbacks and receivers coach for the Buckeyes from 1979 to 1982. A former successful coach at Miami Trace High School, he joined Earle Bruce's staff for those four seasons and then left to become the head coach at New Mexico State in 1983, where he lasted three seasons. When Byars signed with the Buckeyes on February 10, 1982, Zechman was there at Dayton's Roth High School with him and he declared Byars the best player in the Dayton area that he and the Bruce staff had seen in their four seasons.

It was an area that the Buckeyes historically owned in recruiting for obvious reasons. "Back in the '50s and the '60s and the '70s, if you were a football player in the state of Ohio, you had to have somebody do something against you in order to not want to be an Ohio State football player," Zechman said. "Woody Hayes made that tradition work. He's the one that made sure that he recruited all the players that were within a nice radius. And then everything that we found in recruiting was that players go to where their parents can see them play. Woody Hayes made sure that happened. And that was the recruiting premise that everybody had."

The expectation carried into the '80s. Zechman admitted to some of the exceptions—players in the Toledo area might have Michigan interest, players in Youngstown might have Penn State or Pitt interest, and players at Catholic high schools may be interested in Notre Dame. "But as a general rule," he said, "Ohio State had to screw up the recruiting process in order for you to not go there."

That was Zechman's approach: don't screw it up. He didn't. "They recruited me the right way," Byars said.

"I just had to show him that we cared about him," Zechman said, "and that we would take care of him and make sure he was part of our family and his parents were part of our family. There is no better place for an Ohio kid to go."

There have been more than enough examples to prove Zechman's point. Byars nearly won the Heisman and he would have joined the other Ohio natives to do it for the Buckeyes. Five of Ohio State's six Heisman winners are from Ohio: Les Horvath, Vic Janowicz, Howard Cassady, Archie Griffin, and Troy Smith. The lone exception is Philadelphia's Eddie George.

The 2020 Ohio State media guide listed profiles of the Heisman Trophy winners and 52 other players under a heading of "All-Time Greats." Of those 52 players, 31 played high school football in Ohio. Add in the Heisman winners, and that's 61 percent of the best Buckeyes ever, as defined by Ohio State, coming from inside the state.

They don't win with Ohio-only talent, but they have won with Ohio-first talent. That can add tension to the smallest hint of a great Ohio high school player even pondering leaving the state. That's what Mason felt as an OSU assistant for eight years from 1978 to 1985. "Both Notre Dame and Michigan recruited the state like it was their own," Mason said. "So it wasn't a foregone conclusion. Maybe for a small-town guy it was. But for the guys who came from cities, no. But you could see these kids as much as possible. So you were bumping into the Michigan and Notre Dame coaches every day."

Coming off the Hayes era, the Buckeyes under Bruce in the 1980s were trying to move into the future while holding tight to the old assumptions. They wanted Ohio high school stars to feel the pull of the Buckeyes, but they couldn't take it for granted. That was true of Byars in 1982 and true again with players like receiver Cris Carter and linebacker Chris Spielman in the 1984 recruiting class. "There was a lot of pressure on all of us," Mason said. "Earle was understanding. Earle was an assistant coach at Ohio State and he knew you're not going to get them all. No state gets them all. But there's pressure to get your in-state players with every school."

At least in Ohio, Mason said, there were plenty of players to choose from. For instance, he felt even more pressure to retain in-state talent when he was the head coach at Minnesota because the state didn't produce the same number of great players. But some recruitments are different. The assistants know, the head coach knows, the fans know, and the recruits know when there is that level of in-state player that the Buckeyes can't do without. Losing that talent is unacceptable, then, now, and always. "When you have certain guys that you really know are difference makers, really difference makers, whether it be an Art Schlichter or a Chris Spielman or a Keith Byars, those types of guys, they're household names," Mason said. "Everybody on the staff knows those guys are difference makers. You've got to get those guys."

Mason felt that most acutely with Spielman, the best high school player he ever saw. "There was a tremendous amount of pressure to get him, and back in those days, recruiting was a lot different," Mason said. "You weren't restricted by all these restrictions you have now on the number of home visits, how many times you can go to school, or how many times you could call him. So literally, when I said I went to Massillon High School every day, I went every day. Not that I spent the whole day there, but every day you were there, and I made sure he saw me literally every day. He was getting highly recruited, and the word coming down the wire was that he might be leaning to of all places—Michigan. And I was really, really nervous."

Mason attended a basketball game that winter where Spielman inspired a furious comeback win, which only increased Mason's admiration for Spielman as an athlete and competitor. But when Mason climbed in his car for the drive back to Columbus, fellow OSU assistant Bob Tucker turned to Mason and said, "He's going to Michigan."

"I about had a heart attack," Mason said.

Spielman next had a flight planned to Florida to visit the University of Miami. Mason wasn't as worried about the Hurricanes, who had just won the national title in 1983. But he still feared Michigan. "So I was checking his flight on the way home, and he was flying through Dayton," Mason said. "I said, 'I know what's gonna happen. Michigan's gonna know it, and that damn Bo is going to be at the Dayton airport to talk to him between flights. I just know that's gonna happen.' I was totally convinced. So I called a bunch of alums in Dayton and I said the flight's coming in, and you've got to get a bunch of people at the airport, and when he gets off that plane, as many people as you can, sing the Buckeye fight song."

They did it. They sang to Spielman. Mason admitted he didn't know if it meant anything, but that was the level it took to secure the best players in Ohio. (Michigan, by the way, never did show up at the airport.) Mason was staying in an Akron hotel the night before Signing Day, and Spielman called around 2:00 AM with a message: "Coach, I'm a Buckeye."

Only then was the pressure off. "Then after we got him at Ohio State, he's telling everybody, 'Oh, I always knew I was going to Ohio State,'" Mason said. "I wanted to kill him."

That's what was on the line with a linebacker like Spielman, a receiver like Carter, a quarterback like Schlichter, and a running back like Byars. That's what it was like with the difference makers.

But Byars wasn't a difference maker initially. As an OSU freshman on a team crowded with running backs, Byars carried just six times for 24 yards in the fall of 1982. As spring football approached in 1983, Byars said that Bruce told him he could play baseball as planned. But Byars said his football coach also told him that if he skipped spring football for baseball, he'd be last on the depth chart for the start of his sophomore football season. "I was like you didn't tell me that when you were recruiting me," Byars said.

Byars said he told baseball coach Dick Finn the situation, hoping that Finn would fight for Byars to play and would talk to Bruce about it. Instead, Byars said Finn acquiesced. Football insisted on him, baseball didn't fight for him, and Byars' dual-sport dream was over before it started. He'd been playing baseball since he was a kid, taking to that sport long before he played football. Growing up in Dayton, Byars wanted to play professional sports and always believed he would, and the only question was whether it would be football or baseball. Along the way, every dream was nurtured by his parents, Reginald and Margaret. Byars remembers his father reprimanding a family friend who suggested to young Keith that becoming a professional athlete was a one-in-a-million proposition. "Don't you ever tell my son what he can and cannot be," said Reginald Byars, who was an associate minister as well as an employee of the county treasury office.

"That was one of those change-your-life moments because I never saw my father in that light," Byars said. "After that if anyone said it's one in a million, all I could think of was, *I'm gonna be that one in a million because my father believes in me, I believe in me, and it's gonna happen. I would never let anybody steal my dreams.*"

The primary dream—beyond playing both football and baseball—was to be a Buckeye. "I always wanted to be a Buckeye," Byars said. "Growing up in Ohio, I loved the scarlet and gray uniforms. I loved the Buckeye leaves on the helmets."

He loved it all. During his recruitment he was taken to Cincinnati Bengals training camp to watch Archie Griffin, another one of his childhood heroes. Griffin invited him to lunch at the training table. The message from the OSU legend was clear: great players in Ohio go to Ohio State. "That was one of the highlights and treats of my life," Byars said. "They say you don't want to meet your idols because a lot of times you get disappointed. That wasn't true, not with Archie. So that left an imprint."

As Signing Day in February approached in 1982, Byars was still in the decision-making process. Schembechler's November visit had been made known to the Buckeyes. So one night in January, the phone at the Byars home rang. A family member shouted for the star recruit: "Keith, he says it's Coach Hayes."

"I picked up the phone," Byars said. "And Woody Hayes basically proceeds to yell at me with a few profanities interlaced in there. And I was just smiling. Who grows up in Ohio and doesn't have Woody Hayes as your hero? And Woody was mad at me. He's like, 'I heard you visited That Team Up North. You know they're the bad guys. Why haven't you committed to Ohio State yet? What are you thinking about? Do you want to be great? Well, all the great players in

Ohio stay in Ohio. They would not even think about going to that school up north. Do you hear me, son?' He was letting me have it. This went on for 10 or 15 minutes. And I was like *Woody Hayes is yelling at me like I've seen him yell at the players.*"

Hayes was three years removed from coaching the Buckeyes, but there was no way he was going to sit by and let Schembechler swipe a player like Byars. Soon after, Byars visited Ohio State and lunched with both Bruce and Hayes. Then came a dinner with his parents. It was the only recruiting trip they made with their son. "For the next four years, every time I saw Woody Hayes," Byars said, "he would ask me how my parents were doing by their first name."

There, though, was another coach who made an impression on Margaret and Reggie Byars as well. Capers went to high school in Byesville, Ohio, about 85 miles east of Columbus, before playing college football at Mount Union College in Alliance. He was a 31-year-old defensive backs coach at Tennessee who knew Ohio football inside and out. Recruiting for the Volunteers, he went after Byars with everything he had, subscribing to the same philosophy as Mason when it came to blanketing a player. "I'd be in my first period class and I'd see Dom Capers walking down the hallway," Byars said. "My parents loved him."

Capers was the only reason the Volunteers were in the picture for Byars and the reason why he visited Knoxville, Tennessee. Capers recruited another must-get player for the Buckeyes, offensive lineman Jim Lachey, on behalf of Tennessee the year before Byars. Ohio State won both those battles, but Capers did all he could. "There was no question that it was an uphill battle, that you were gonna have to have something fall in your favor," Capers said. "My approach in recruiting back then was so much different than it is now. I would specifically try to locate my top five or six guys and then I would just try to live with them. I'd try to see them as much as I could to where you become like a member of the family because I felt for an Ohio player to go to the University of Tennessee he had to have a strong personal relationship with somebody that he trusted. So you had to develop that trust by the amount of time that you spent with him and had to try to convince them that this was the best thing for them and their future."

Capers—like Byars—would soon be an Ohio native recruited by the Buckeyes. On December 31, 1981, after a close, 31–28 win against Navy in the Liberty Bowl, Bruce, frustrated by the defense all season, fired three defensive coaches. One of them was the defensive backs coach, a young assistant named Nick Saban. By early January, Bruce was looking for replacements while Capers was doing his usual recruiting in Ohio. A defensive backs coach with Ohio roots who recruited the state was just what Bruce was searching for. After a stop in Canton to visit a recruit, Capers had the private plane he'd flown on drop him off in Columbus for an interview. "Obviously, being an Ohio boy, growing up around there, I'd followed Woody and Ohio State football from the time I was old enough to," Capers said. "So I was excited about the opportunity to go there to be a part of Coach Bruce's staff. When I was in college football, that was always one of my goals: to come back home and coach at Ohio State."

Fresh off that Tennessee visit engineered by Capers, Keith was visiting Columbus again in January shortly after with his parents, when Margaret saw one of her favorites. "Isn't that Coach Capers?" she asked her son.

It was indeed. Capers had traded in his Tennessee orange for the Ohio State scarlet and gray. It was an introduction to Byars about the pull of the Buckeyes and business of college football. Capers wanted Byars and Lachey, and in an unexpected way, they all wound up together. "It worked out great because I got to be with my two top guys with the Buckeyes," Capers said.

Capers then was able to sell Ohio players on staying, not leaving, a plan that would work during his recruitment of Carter, the talented receiver from Middletown, Ohio. Once Capers started recruiting for Ohio State, which he did for two seasons before leaving for professional football for good, he finally had a full picture of what he had been up against recruiting in the state against Ohio State. Unless there was a reason to leave, few did. "And they've probably taken it to another level now," Capers said.

## CHAPTER 11

# James Laurinaitis, Class of 2005

While he coached the Ohio State football program for 10 years from 2001 through 2010, Jim Tressel implemented a rule about OSU fans and the high school football players in their lives they believed could become Buckeyes: follow up.

If someone contacted the football program with a suggestion about a player that Tressel and his staff should recruit, the coach knew almost certainly the answer would be no. But he thought the effort on their part deserved an effort on his part. That was the rule when a teacher named Leanna Garlinger Nelson from Wayzata High School in the western Minneapolis suburbs sent a handwritten letter to Ohio State in 2004. She had a suggestion about one of her students: James Laurinaitis should play for the Buckeyes. "Back in those days, it wasn't quite as much email and social media and all that. So I would get stacks of letters every day about players," Tressel said. "And I used to always tell my staff that everyone in Ohio wants us to take the best player from their high school. They say, 'It's the best player this town's ever had,' and so forth. And, you know what?

We can only take so many kids. And we're going to get letters from all over the country. So I said, 'You'll get criticized for your decisions, which, that's part of life. You make decisions. But I never want to be criticized for not following up. So I don't care if it's from the high school coach in the smallest 'burb in Ohio. If he says they've got a player who can play, we're gonna look at the film and we're going to give them an evaluation. It's going to take time. But we're going to do the same thing. Anybody that writes us, we're going to write back.'

"So I got this letter from maybe a ninth-grade English teacher, and in the letter she wrote that James came to school many times with an Andy Katzenmoyer jersey on, and we ought to recruit this kid. Well, of course, we get letters that people wear jerseys all the time. And so we're at the staff table, and you know who's in charge of Minnesota? It's Doc. So I gave the letter to my brother, and he said it was a good school because he had been up there 23 years, and he knew the coach, and so he followed up like we pledged to do."

That's how Ohio State running backs coach Dick "Doc" Tressel, the former longtime head football coach at Division III Hamline University in St. Paul, Minnesota, just 23 miles from Wayzata High School, started recruiting future three-time All-American Laurinaitis. "Miss Nelson was from Columbus, a big Ohio State fan. I remember she had an Ohio State pennant in her classroom," Laurinaitis said. "It was just the chance that they opened that letter and actually took it seriously."

Until that letter, the three-star linebacker in the Class of 2005 was all Gopher. The son of Joe and Julie Laurinaitis, James grew up with a professional wrestler for a dad. His father often hit the road as part of the tag-team champion Road Warriors, wearing the spikes and face paint of Road Warrior Animal. He lived in the same neighborhood as Dominique Barber, the son of Marion Barber Jr., who by the time he finished at the University of Minnesota in 1981 was the school's all-time leading rusher. Barber Jr. went on to a seven-year NFL career with the New York Jets.

James and Dom started a friendship on a playground while their older brothers were at football practice and they started it with an argument over whose dad was cooler. "He's like, 'My dad's a professional wrestler,' and I go, 'My dad was a professional football player,'" Barber said.

And for the next decade, the two of them had that argument while planning to play college football together for the Minnesota Golden Gophers. "We were best friends," Laurinaitis said, "since I can remember."

James was all-Minnesota since he could remember as well, a kid in a sports family that was all about the home teams. While her husband was on the road, Julie Laurinaitis, a former powerlifter and a huge football fan, watched every Minnesota Vikings game with James. They watched every NFL draft together. And they thought of his future in football. "Growing up, I never thought about Ohio State," James said. "I was a Minnesota homer for everything. Whether it was the Vikings—I remember my uncle painted their logo on my wall—Timberwolves, Twins, North Stars, then they left; it broke our hearts. It was everything Minnesota, and that included the Gophers."

Beyond his father, James had what he called another real-life sports hero in Marion Barber III, Dom's older brother. He was an all-state running back who committed to Minnesota and gained 742 rushing yards as a true freshman in 2001. Playing for the Golden Gophers became even more real. Dom, a year older than James, would follow his father and older brother and join Minnesota's 2004 recruiting class, and a year later, the idea was that Laurinaitis would be next. "It was like, wow, how cool would it be to be Gophers?" Laurinaitis said. "And we always dreamed about being Gophers together—me and Dominique."

"He's always had that loyalty," Julie Laurinaitis said. "That's kind of what he always thought, and with being close family friends with the Barbers, it was just kind of one of those deals, one of those natural things."

It was also his best option. Wayzata was a large high school with a football coach who leaned toward seniors and a varsity roster that went 100 deep. Laurinaitis played on the freshman team. Then he played on the sophomore team while getting some action with the junior varsity as a blocking tight end. During his junior year, he was part of a three-man rotation with two seniors through two linebacker spots. In a two-year span, Laurinaitis would go from a part-time starter in high school to getting thrown into the Ohio State–Michigan game—as his mother was a nervous wreck in the stands. But at that point in the fall of 2003, his football ambitions seemed outsized and unrealistic. At Halloween as a kid, he either donned a mini-Road Warrior costume and went as his dad or he rotated among NFL teams over the years—from the Vikings to the Dallas Cowboys to the San Francisco 49ers to the Chicago Bears. That costume one day a year reflected the reality he still envisioned daily as a teenager.

He even remembered a high school friend who asked what he was going to do after college. "I was so naive about it," Laurinaitis said. "I said, 'I hope to play in the NFL,' and I can distinctly remember her laugh. She was like, 'What's Plan B?' and I remember saying, 'I don't have a Plan B.' But it wasn't arrogance. It wasn't, 'Oh, I'm gonna play in the league.' I was a three-star in Minnesota. I wasn't even at college yet. It was just this idea that since I was a little boy I dreamed about playing pro football. I just loved football."

As for the football programs that loved him, North Dakota State did. Some Ivy League schools did, too. And then, eventually, Minnesota. His road to the NFL would go through one of those options. "That was North Dakota State before it was a cool thing, before Carson Wentz," Laurinaitis said of the quarterback taken from that FCS-level school with the No. 2 pick in the 2016 NFL Draft. "Most of my recruiting stuff was Columbia, Brown, North Dakota State."

So when Laurinaitis attended Minnesota's spring football game in April 2004 after his junior high school football season, he was ready for everything the Gophers could offer. He committed soon after the spring game—as the second recruit pledged to Minnesota's 2005 class. He was more worried that the Gophers would change their minds about him rather than thinking about changing his mind about them. "I always hoped and dreamed I could be a part of renaissance for that program. So that was obvious. That was a slam dunk," Laurinaitis said. "It was such a rare occurrence that I would have sprinted to sign if they had the paper to sign that day because it was almost like an insecurity thing that they might take it away. I was so thrilled with the offer and the opportunity, I would have signed in Sharpie."

The Golden Gophers were peaking, coming off a 10–3 record in 2003 in coach Glen Mason's seventh year that represented Minnesota's first double-digit win season since 1905. Dominique Barber was signed and ready to enroll as a freshman in the fall of 2004, and Laurinaitis would play his senior season at Wayzata without worry. He also, however, would play his senior season as a different player. Laurinaitis implemented a running program to get faster. He was handed opponents' preferred plays each Monday by his coaches and then spent the week diagramming them. He broke down game film with both his father and his mother. What the Gophers would be getting changed from a solid high school linebacker into one of the better defensive players in the state. What a win for Minnesota. "He was rock solid," Mason said, remembering Laurinaitis from Gophers summer football camps. "His dad, 'The Animal,' used to wear a Gopher jacket around."

Of course, there were experiences still to be had. Joe Laurinaitis wanted to explore every avenue for his son. He'd grown a bit frustrated when James hadn't played more often earlier in his high school career, thinking James deserved more time. Joe put together highlight DVDs of his son and sent them to Big Ten schools and to Notre Dame, but he was against James attending the recruiting camps that were becoming more popular. He believed the game film would—and should—tell his son's story. And though Joe had gone to high school in Minnesota and played some small college football at Golden Valley Lutheran College just outside Minneapolis, he wasn't a Gophers die-hard. He loved college football as a whole and watched everyone—Oklahoma, Nebraska, Ohio State—though he had a particular affinity for Katzenmoyer, the imposing Ohio State linebacker who won the Butkus Award as the nation's best linebacker in 1997, when James was in fifth grade. "My dad probably believed in his mind if he had kept playing football, he would have been Big Kat," James said.

So the summer between his junior and senior years, James and his dad did drive to a Notre Dame camp, where among those checking him out was Notre Dame strength coach Mickey Marotti, later

Urban Meyer's right-hand man at Florida and Ohio State. Marotti has been in charge of Ohio State's offseason conditioning and strength program since 2012 and he later relayed to Laurinaitis the evaluation he gave Notre Dame coaches then: "There's no way this kid's playing college football."

So it was set. Minnesota was both the dream and in many ways the only choice. "In my mind he was gonna be a Gopher," Barber, his best friend, said. "I personally didn't take any other visits. But that's what you do. You go see other places. But in my mind, there was no way he was not going to be a Gopher, no matter where he went or what he saw. In my mind, he's a Gopher. And I was telling that to the staff. I was so confident. I was so confident in my relationship with James and everything."

Then Ohio State received that letter. It wasn't just one letter that did it. But if the Minnesota connections on staff were the tinder, the letter was the spark. Tasked with recruiting Minnesota, Dick Tressel knew the people in that area as well as anyone, and that helped move things along. And in his first season as defensive coordinator in 2004 after three years coaching linebackers for the Buckeyes, Mark Snyder had come to Ohio State from Minnesota and knew the state as well. "He played at a quality high school from a quality football program," said Dick, who was good friends with former Wayzata coach Roger Lipelt. "[Lipelt] said, 'This is a real-deal guy.' So we got involved. People weren't spending quite as much time labeling how many stars people were, and he did not go out and do any of those camps that get you the stars. He just didn't do that. He was just a good player and a good person."

The Buckeyes asked for the high school transcript and some film on Laurinaitis and came away impressed. "You know what? This guy's not bad. He's a pretty good player," Jim Tressel said. "And then it turned out we thought, *Man, he's a really good player.* And so we started recruiting him."

Dick flew up and watched Laurinaitis play against state power Cretin-Derham Hall in a state 5A playoff quarterfinal on Friday, November 12. "I just happened to have the best game of my high school career that day without even knowing that Ohio State was there," Laurinaitis said of his play in Wayzata's 34–27 win. "In my mind I was already at Minnesota."

In his first year coaching the linebackers, Luke Fickell was an Ohio State assistant with an eye for under-the-radar recruits. So he was open to this type of player. "We had a guy on our staff who said, 'You don't want any Minnesota kids. He's probably Minnesota soft,'" Fickell said. "And I'm like, 'I don't know. Doc likes him.'"

And Fickell liked the environment in which Laurinaitis was raised. "You can't grow up around what he grew up around with the confidence and being around elite, high-level athletes and not have a lot of that soak in," Fickell said. "I'm like, 'There's something about this kid.' I know he's a good football player, but for us to go to Minnesota and say we're gonna go all out on this guy, there was something about that whole life situation with the wrestling background. So I was kind of excited about him."

As for the Gophers, they had followed their 10–3 season in 2003 with a 5–0 start in 2004. A 27–24 loss at Michigan, in which the Wolverines scored the go-ahead touchdown with 2:10 to play, started a slide that led to the Gophers losing five of their last six in the regular season to finish 6–5 before a bowl win against Alabama. Along the way, Laurinaitis was getting a little more interest from some other schools. And Julie Laurinaitis felt maybe Minnesota took the commitment of the home state linebacker a bit for granted. The door started to crack open. And there was Ohio State. "It was just the quality of the program and the opportunity maybe to go a little further than other people think you can," Dick said. "And it helps to have a father that wants to make sure that you don't have any limitations placed on you."

Laurinaitis said his family heard that Dick tried to express Ohio State's interest after he watched that Cretin-Derham Hall game and was told by the Wayzata High School coaches that Laurinaitis was committed to Minnesota. Word got to Joe Laurinaitis. "You can imagine my dad's response to that," James said.

"His dad is really the one that said, 'Hey, this kid is not committed to Minnesota. They're making it sound like he is. But I appreciate you guys continuing to follow through on this recruitment,'" Dick said. "The high school coach said, 'Get out of here,' and Dad said, 'No, don't get out of here.'"

Wayzata lost in the 5A state title game on Friday, November 26. Two weeks later, Laurinaitis was in Columbus for an official visit. "Right toward the end of recruiting, I started to hear a rumor," Mason said. "I've always been one of those guys: where there's smoke, there's fire."

Mason checked with Gordy Shaw, the assistant coach who successfully recruited so many in-state players for the Gophers. "I said, 'Gordy, I'm hearing rumors.' He said, 'No way, he's rock solid. I talk to him all the time. I'm in the school, I talk to his coach, there's nothing to it.' So a day or two later, I brought it up again," Mason said. "He said, 'Coach, I'm telling you, there's nothing to it.' I said, 'Gordy, don't stick your head in the sand now.' And a day later, Gordy called me and said, 'Coach, he's on a plane, he's on his way to Columbus, but there's no way he'll go there.'"

Mason is an Ohio State alum. He'd played linebacker for the Buckeyes and graduated in 1972. In 1978 he returned as an assistant under Woody Hayes in Hayes' final season as head coach, and Mason stayed on when Earle Bruce took over, serving as the offensive coordinator from 1980 to 1985. When Tressel was hired as the head coach in early 2001, Mason was the other finalist for the job. Mason knew Ohio State as well as anyone not playing or coaching at the school at that moment. Mason told Shaw three words: "Gordy, he's gone." "For him to make a visit this late in recruiting, he's got second thoughts, or there's an appeal there that's really got him going," Mason said. "He wouldn't jeopardize everything, taking a visit this late, unless he was seriously considering going there."

Laurinaitis was serious. Scott Leius, a family friend who played Major League Baseball and won a World Series ring with the Twins, knew some people who knew some people around Ohio State football and he vouched for Laurinaitis. "I knew the type of young man he was and I knew nothing affected him and nothing fazed him, and as a professional athlete, those things are big," Leius said.

Julie said even Barber Jr., the former Gophers running back who played in the NFL, told the family if the chance at Ohio State was there, James had to take it.

Mason predicted that once Laurinaitis set foot in the OSU football headquarters at the Woody Hayes Athletic Center, he'd be hooked. "That was true. Once I did that, there was no way I couldn't go," Laurinaitis said. "It was so daring. It was also so exciting. And I can't emphasize enough how surprised I am looking back that that 18-year-old kid actually made that decision."

Julie was home while her son and husband made the trip. When James called her while standing in Ohio Stadium, she knew. "I could tell in his voice that Ohio State was where he was going," she said.

James had looked at and read about Ohio State's history and he then felt it standing in the Shoe. He'd known about the Michigan game and Katzenmoyer and little else. It wasn't until the visit that he realized receiver Cris Carter, a star for his beloved Vikings his entire childhood, had played at Ohio State. "As I went through it, I had to really learn the history of this place, and obviously Jim Tressel did that better than anybody, teaching us the history of Ohio State, especially for the out-of-state kids," Laurinaitis said. "But I just remember in that moment: once I was here and talking to Coach Tressel, it just felt right. It was hard to explain."

In November, a month before Laurinaitis visited, former OSU running back Maurice Clarett alleged that Ohio State committed NCAA violations while recruiting him and while he was enrolled at Ohio State in 2002. (The NCAA investigated, Clarett refused to be interviewed, and the NCAA never leveled sanctions against Ohio State directly related to Clarett.) "What really kind of turned it was: when I talked to Coach Tressel, he always spoke so glowingly about the job Glen Mason was doing at Minnesota and how he's proud. 'He's a former Buckeye, Glen will always be a Buckeye, look at the job he's doing up there, isn't it awesome?'" Laurinaitis said. "And there were some hints out of the Minnesota program of: 'You don't even know if you guys are going to be eligible for a bowl.' It was almost that spin of: are you sure you want to go there or even think about there? Ultimately, it was like, I'm gonna go with Coach Tressel. It just felt better. Coach Tressel and that little savvy optimism he has really won me over."

"I think we got out-recruited," Dom Barber said. "I just think maybe the Gophers fell short. Whatever Ohio State did, they did it to the point that he fell in love."

The Buckeyes quickly followed up with a home visit that included Jim Tressel and the co-defensive coordinators, Fickell and Jim Heacock. Tressel swung by the school to thank Nelson. Fickell watched Laurinaitis play hockey, a first for him on a recruiting trip. He liked the linebacker's lateral quickness on skates. "They were just so down to earth," Julie said. "It just made everyone feel super comfortable. That's the most important thing. You're leaving home. You want to feel comfortable."

Now all Laurinaitis had to do was tell his dream school that his dream had changed. He had to call Mason. "Some guys in those situations get really upset and mad," Mason said. "I never have. You're dealing with young guys that are put in this situation to make probably the first important decision they've got to make in their life. At the end of the day, I thought that we wanted guys that really wanted to be here—not because I pressured them or that they're embarrassed about changing their mind. A lot of us change our minds on things."

Even more difficult than that, Laurinaitis had to tell his best friend. "The hardest phone call I had to make was Dom," Laurinaitis said. "I just remember begging for him to be like, 'Hey, it's all right,' which is what he said. Dom and I are still best friends, and every now and then he'll text, 'Go Bucks,' but I know it still kills him."

"I remember that feeling of being crushed," Barber said. "There goes my best friend, my roommate, and all this good stuff. But at the same time, I was extremely happy for him. It's The Ohio State, so you're happy for him. But in the back of your mind, you're heartbroken because that's your best friend."

Barber recovered and so did the friendship eventually. "I can admit I probably was a little standoffish, but in the end, it really didn't affect us at all. I got over it after a couple weeks," Barber said. "He's still that best friend that I can call at any moment and he's the godfather to my youngest. So in time you get over things like that. I got a lot of crap from the staff, though, at the time because I couldn't reel in my best friend."

Barber played in nine games at Minnesota as a freshman in 2004 while Laurinaitis was making his college decision. He started at safety as a junior and senior in 2006 and 2007 and was a second-team All-Big Ten pick as a senior. The friends met all three seasons they were in college together. Ohio State won all three—at Minnesota 45–31 in 2005, at home 44–0 in 2006, and 30–7 at Minnesota in 2007. Barber was drafted in the sixth round by the Houston Texans in 2008, and the two met again on the field in Laurinaitis' rookie year in the NFL in 2009. "Seeing him on the field after a game, it was like, hey, we're living our dream. It's not the same dream we thought, but we both got to play D-I ball and pro ball," Laurinaitis said. "It's one of those friendships that has lasted and endured."

One thing Mason always believed in was preserving the relationship in case things didn't work out for a recruit at his initial school. That made sense with Laurinaitis because a lot of people weren't sure he could play at Ohio State, including the player himself. He wondered if he'd ever get on the field. "In some ways," Fickell said, "I did, too."

"I'm gonna take a chance to go to Ohio State and figure if I play there, I'll have a chance to live my dream, which is the NFL," Laurinaitis said. "If I don't play there, it won't surprise me because there's a lot of really good players there. And there were a lot of people [at high school] saying, 'You're gonna ride the bench if you go there. You go to Minnesota, you can play right away. If you go to Ohio State, you're gonna sit. They've got talent everywhere.' And I remember my dad getting fired up at those people."

Laurinaitis' older brother, Joey, was stationed at Wright-Patterson Air Force Base during his freshman year, and frequent visits to see him in Dayton, Ohio, is what Laurinaitis said got him through the homesickness of his freshman year. Otherwise, he believes he might have been headed back to Minnesota as a transfer. He was awed and eager to learn from the veteran starting linebackers: A.J. Hawk, Bobby Carpenter, and Anthony Schlegel. But he was intimated by the young backup linebackers like Marcus Freeman and John Kerr with better pedigrees than he possessed. An injury in the 2005 opener ended the season for Freeman and moved Laurinaitis up the depth chart. When Carpenter broke his ankle on the first play of the Michigan game, Fickell called on the freshman. 'I was like, 'Oh, man. You gotta go,'" Fickell said.

"I remember the pit in my stomach," Julie said. "I was just shaking. I was like, oh my God, this is happening. I don't think he really had time to think, which is probably a good thing because I don't know how many seconds I had to think to myself and I was in panic mode. I'm thinking, *My poor little son's gonna get hurt.* I'm looking at these guys that are seniors, and they're big and mature and I'm thinking, *He's gonna get smashed.*"

Fickell, though, was immediately impressed by Laurinaitis' demeanor. "I'll never forget," Fickell said. "He was like, 'Yeah, I'm ready,' like, 'What are you worried about, Coach? I'm good.' And I thought, *Ahh, this kid's got a confidence about him I never knew, even coaching him for three or four months.*"

Laurinaitis' career was off. He filled in for Carpenter during the Michigan win and the bowl win against Notre Dame. As a sophomore in 2006, Laurinaitis moved from strongside linebacker to middle linebacker, a role he'd never leave. Initially cowed by Ohio State's illustrious linebacker history, Laurinaitis became the first OSU linebacker—and eighth Buckeye ever—to be named a first-team All-American three times. He won the Nagurski Award as a sophomore as the nation's best defender and the Butkus Award as a junior as the nation's best linebacker. He led the Buckeyes in tackles each season from 2006 to 2008, as Ohio State played for national titles in both 2006 and 2007 and compiled a 33–6 record over three years with Laurinaitis leading the defense. "I'd be lying to you if I thought he was ever going to be like he was," Fickell said.

Laurinaitis came to Ohio State as a three-star recruit ranked in the 500s in national player ratings. He left as a Buckeyes legend. Laurinaitis was drafted by the St. Louis Rams in the second round of the 2009 NFL Draft. He started every game for the Rams in his seven seasons with the franchise before playing a final season with the New Orleans Saints in 2016. After he retired he joined the Big Ten Network as a football analyst—where Mason is one of his colleagues. Laurinaitis and his wife, Shelly, met at Ohio State, and they live in the Columbus area with their daughters London, Hayden, and Remy. Laurinaitis changed his mind from what he thought he always wanted and found a new version of everything he could ask for. "The whole thing from Day One has been like the perfect storm," Julie said. "It's just been like this perfect storm of doors opening for him. He had to prove himself and take the opportunity and run with it. But I just think it was a perfect storm with great coaches and a great school and great players and having those people surrounding you."

Joe Laurinaitis, who died in 2020 at age 60, was one of those people. Joe and Julie raised their son and then watched him seize moment after moment. They missed only one game in four years. They were as proud and involved as any Ohio State parents you'd ever find.

Another one of those people was Leanna Garlinger Nelson. She was raised in Columbus, attending Ohio State football games with her father, Larry, who was an OSU alum. She chose the University of Minnesota for college, but according to her younger brother, Scott, she was always a Buckeye. And she always loved James Laurinaitis. After he enrolled at Ohio State, Leanna and several family members, many of whom still lived in Ohio, were invited to say hello to James after a practice. Her father still remembers the linebacker standing and sweating all over his daughter, and she loved it. This recruiting tale was one she told. She knew she'd helped her favorite football team land one of her favorite students. "It was a moment of pure joy to know that the tide turned and someone went to Ohio State because of her," Scott Garlinger said. "It made a really wonderful impression on her."

Garlinger Nelson knew Laurinaitis was being recruited by other schools, but the teacher with OSU posters in her classroom knew that the school she rooted for would be missing out on a great player if it didn't pursue Laurinaitis. "[She] wasn't going to go down without a fight," Scott said.

She had maintained her Columbus roots, sometimes driving all night to return for Ohio State games. She'd say that she'd been a Minnesota student, but she was always a Buckeye. "Even though she left, even though she went to Minneapolis, even though she did her master's in history, even though she had done this worldly traveling, that didn't leave her," Scott said. "She was a die-hard ambassador to promote her hometown team."

Leanna Garlinger Nelson died in 2019 at age 49, a mother, a daughter, a sister, a teacher, a letter writer, and a proud Buckeyes fan who made a difference. "I think if Miss Nelson doesn't send that letter, I'm probably a Gopher," Laurinaitis said. "And who knows what happens?"

## CHAPTER 12

# Darron Lee,
# Class of 2013

Starting with the Class of 2013, his first full recruiting class as the coach of the Buckeyes, Urban Meyer turned Ohio State into a national recruiting powerhouse. During his time in the 1990s, John Cooper had taken the Buckeyes national and won big. Jim Tressel built a recruiting wall around Ohio in the 2000s and dominated the Big Ten (and reached three national title games) by locking down and developing the best high school players in the Midwest. But when Meyer was hired after the 2011 season, taking over for one-year coach Luke Fickell after Tressel was forced to resign in May 2011, the Buckeyes elevated to another level when it came to gathering talent.

That meant the Buckeyes had to become even more strategic when it came to managing local talent. In the seven recruiting classes Meyer signed between 2012 and 2018, Ohio State landed 62 players who were ranked among the top 100 recruits in their class in the 247sports.com composite rankings. (Those rankings take the evaluations of all the major recruiting outlets and combine them.) Of those 62 players, 16 were from Ohio, and 46 were from outside the state. That meant the average OSU recruiting class of the Meyer era contained 10 players ranked among the top 100—eight from out of state and two from in-state.

In order to stay connected to the Ohio high school scene while chasing five-stars from Florida, Texas, and Georgia, the Buckeyes had to take some in-state chances—the right chances on the right players. Maybe those prospects were from smaller high schools, were late bloomers, or were players caught between positions. But they all wanted to be Buckeyes and they were willing to work for it.

Darron Lee was one of those players. Fickell, a Columbus native and former Ohio State defensive lineman who started for four seasons from 1993 to 1996 and coached for the Buckeyes from 2002 to 2016 before leaving to become the head coach at Cincinnati, was often the assistant fighting for those Ohio players. "When you're on the fence, it's an educated guess, and when you've got these guys that have this desire and passion," Fickell said, "that kind of pushes me over the top for them."

In that same seven-year stretch of Meyer recruiting classes from 2012 to 2018, Ohio State signed 23 high school position players (not counting kickers, punters, long snappers, or junior college players) who were ranked as the No. 400 recruit or lower in the 247Sports. com composite ratings. Of those 23 players, 11 were from Ohio because those risks are often easier to take since the Ohio State staff has existing relationships with the high school coaches. When Fickell was checking in on Lee, he had a former OSU teammate with a son who played with Lee in the Columbus suburb of New Albany. It was a small extra step of familiarity.

Of those lower-rated players, two of the 13 out-of-state players developed into starters or significant contributors for the Buckeyes:

Florida cornerback Damon Arnette and Utah offensive lineman Branden Bowen. That's a 15 percent success rate. Of the Ohio players, 10 of the 18 developed into starters or significant contributors: safety Tyvis Powell; offensive linemen Jacoby Boren and Pat Elflein; defensive tackles Tracy Sprinkle, Robert Landers, and DaVon Hamilton; tight end Rashod Berry; and linebackers Chris Worley, Malik Harrison, and Lee. That's a 56 percent success rate.

The lesson? Take your risks close to home. The price of a scholarship for some of those players? Extra appearances at Ohio State recruiting camps in the summer to let coaches get eyes on them to confirm what they might be thinking. It certainly didn't work out for every Ohio prospect on the edge of an OSU offer. But it worked for enough of them. "I'm sure there were a few kids that came to two or three camps that we didn't take," Fickell said. "And we were spot on *not* taking them."

But two that will always stand out for Fickell are Elflein and Lee. Elflein was ranked as the No. 998 player in the 2012 recruiting class and went on to be a three-year starter on the offensive line, the Rimington Award winner as the nation's top center in 2016, and a third-round pick in the 2017 NFL Draft. Ranked No. 636 in the 2013 recruiting class, Lee went from a high school quarterback to a first-round NFL draft pick at linebacker in four years. Both started for a national championship team along the way. "Some people would say they were reaches or stretches," Fickell said, "but they really, really paid off. They probably had the intangible things that you can't tell."

Ohio State had to be willing to bank on that and take the risk. Under Tressel, there were more Ohio players in the average recruiting class. Under Meyer, greater national success resulted in fewer

Ohioans. For example: Tressel's first full recruiting class in 2002 was 75 percent Ohio players or 18 of 24 recruits. Tressel's last recruiting class in 2011 was 59 percent Ohio players or 13 of 22.

Meyer's first full class in 2013, which included Lee, was 43 percent Ohio players or 10 of 23. Meyer's last full class in 2018 was 15 percent Ohio players or four of 26. Those numbers also reflected a changing landscape of where the best high school players in the country were located. Some dominant recruiting areas in places such as Ohio and Pennsylvania slowly gave ground to the South and the Sun Belt. "Coach Tress' philosophy was different and based on Ohio kids," Fickell said. "I'm not saying Coach Meyer's wasn't, but the recruiting became bigger and broader and rightfully so. So it's a philosophy, and how do you justify what your philosophy is? It doesn't mean you don't want Ohio kids. It doesn't mean you don't take them. But you might not take as many chances."

Lee was one of the chances the Buckeyes had to take. But before he evaded tacklers during his days at New Albany High School—about 20 miles northeast of Ohio Stadium—he first picked up a football while living in Tennessee. Lee was out-of-state before he was in-state. And he was a soccer player before he thrived on the gridiron. "The first sport I ever tried was soccer," Lee said. "And that didn't really work out because I couldn't touch the ball with my hands."

Lee's mother, Candice, then took him to a football practice at Brainerd High School near where they lived in Chattanooga, Tennessee. "She just let me watch," Lee said. "That's when I fell in love with it."

Enamored with the game, he started playing football in elementary school, once tackling another player repeatedly because he thought that's how the game worked. Soon, he was making plays with the ball in his hands. "I wasn't the biggest, I wasn't the fastest, but I had that knack for it," Lee said. "I was always a quarterback."

That continued when Candice Lee, a former member of the Navy who transitioned to broadcast journalism, moved to Columbus with her son in March 2007 during his sixth-grade school year. The move was tough—he was a Tennessee kid who watched former University of Tennessee quarterback Peyton Manning in the NFL and thought that might be his path—but sports was a way to make new friends. So Lee joined a travel basketball team and a travel baseball team and, of course, also was a quarterback. "There was no question that he knew the game," Candice said.

And there was no question that quarterback was the plan. Then, just before football camp was starting in August before his sophomore season of high school, Lee went up for a rebound at an AAU basketball tryout, landed awkwardly, and tore his meniscus. There went a sophomore football season of quarterback play, the time when he might have been getting on the radar of schools looking for a quarterback who could do it all. "Oh man, I probably would have ended up playing quarterback my whole life if I wouldn't have done that," Lee said. "But, hey, life works in mysterious ways."

During his junior season in 2011, he played quarterback, receiver, and safety at New Albany, and at least one school viewed him as a quarterback option. Boston College hired former Ohio State offensive coordinator Jim Bollman in January 2012, and over Darron's spring break months later, the Lees visited the BC campus in Chestnut Hill, Massachusetts. "They were like, 'We want you to come play quarterback for us,'" Lee said. "They were the first team to recruit me, and they were like, 'This guy can play quarterback, he can sling it.' They knew that's what I wanted and they believed in me to do it."

There was a problem. The Eagles had just completed a 4–8 season in the third year for head coach Frank Spaziani. "We had some friends who were close with a coach there, and they knew that coaching staff was in trouble," Candice said. "So I said, 'There's no guarantee when the next coach comes in that you are going to be the quarterback. And that could frustrate you.' So even though we had the offer, we knew we weren't going to take it."

That meant Lee's recruitment would continue along two paths. There were the schools checking on him at quarterback—Georgia Tech, then running the triple option, also expressed interest—and the schools looking at Lee on defense. Once Ohio State landed a commitment from four-star Texas quarterback J.T. Barrett in April 2012, Lee knew how the Buckeyes viewed him. "I knew what Urban Meyer was trying to build there," he said. "Plus, a quarterback from Texas, you already know how they feel about that. But by then I already had in my mind that I wanted to play for Ohio State."

He was now torn between two things he wanted—playing quarterback or playing for Meyer. "I'm like, he's gonna win a national championship in his second or third year," Lee said. (Spoiler alert: it was year three.)

Still, the dual paths continued. On May 4 Lee attended an Elite 11 Regional quarterback camp in Columbus, one of six regionals around the country. Quarterbacks rotated through drills and threw to receivers for two hours, hoping to earn an invite to the Elite 11 finals in Los Angeles. Lee felt he competed at a level equal to anyone at that camp. The four Columbus quarterbacks who made the finals were Michigan commit Shane Morris, Notre Dame commit Malik Zaire, Purdue commit Danny Etling, and future Florida quarterback Luke Del Rio. Among the other quarterbacks that day who, like Lee, didn't get a finals invite—Mitch Trubisky, the future No. 2 pick in the 2017 NFL Draft.

Lee's quarterback window was closing. "I found as we were going through the process that there was an established kind of pipeline for quarterbacks in college," Candice said. "Because of my job as a news broadcaster, I didn't really have the time to get him to all these quarterback camps and I didn't know who the quarterback gurus were in Central Ohio. But it wasn't that surprising that when it came to his recruitment, he was kind of an athlete. Yes, he can play quarterback. Yes, he can play free safety. But then you look at the kids who've been playing those positions exclusively for years, and you were kind of like, yeah, I don't know where we fit in. He probably could have played quarterback at a lower Division I school like Bowling Green or someplace like that. I think he would have been okay there. But I don't know if he could have been happy there."

Now, everything else began to fall away. The Lees thought Cincinnati was an option because Darron had visited several times, but that offer, which arrived in late April, was slower coming than they expected. They visited Illinois but didn't like the vibe. Among the reasons was that head coach Tim Beckman called him *Da-RON* instead of *DARE-in*. "I walk in, sit down with my mother, and he says my name wrong," Lee said. "The first time I'm sitting down, he's saying my name wrong in front of the woman who gave it to me. Nice."

Both Lees thought the Illini tried to talk down the Buckeyes. "For us, it was pretty much over with Illinois," Candice said, "because I didn't like their attitude."

Twenty miles away Ohio State—with a new coach and entering a new era—was coming more and more into focus for Lee. He just had to make the Buckeyes see him. There were at least two people inside the building at the Woody Hayes Athletic Center who did. The first was Mark Pantoni, the Ohio State recruiting director who had arrived with Meyer. He'd worked for Meyer at Florida and was the new coach's right-hand man when it came to initial player evaluation and overall recruiting strategy. Pantoni liked what he saw from Lee, and that was a foot in the door.

Pantoni always looked through the results of recruiting camps, checking for speed and explosiveness in the times and measurements. Lee's raw numbers jumped out, which led Pantoni to his film. "You see the quarterback, the athlete, and you're like, it's not bad," Pantoni said. "So I bring this up to Luke, and he's intrigued. Not sold but intrigued. So Luke would go visit the school, he watched him run track, and he's more intrigued. And I'm kind of loving Darron the athlete. [I] don't know what he is, but I'm pushing hard to get him here on campus and let him get to know everybody. But he's also a three-star guy whose best offers are Boston College and Illinois. So it's hard to really sell Urban on that."

That meant one thing: camp. Lee had been to one OSU camp the previous summer, but now he was coming back for business, coming back to impress this new staff. Thirty-nine days after he'd been competing with the best quarterbacks in the country, Lee arrived at Ohio State's camp on June 12. This time his charge was to stick with a five-star safety, coincidentally also from the Chattanooga area, named

Vonn Bell. "He and Vonn are just going at it in every drill," Pantoni said. "And that's when you saw it. This kid's a freaky athlete. And Vonn's the five-star guy. So I remember after the camp, Luke and I had Darron and his mom in Urban's office. And for whatever reason, Urban was like, 'You're pretty good, but I need to see you come back again.' I could tell Darron was kind of upset about it. He had worked everything he had that day at camp. And Darron was like, 'You want me to come back? I'll come back every single day if you want me to. I am going to get this offer.'"

Lee said he was both inspired and intimidated during his first-ever meeting with Meyer. Eleven days later, Ohio State held another camp for top recruits. Eleven days later, Lee was back. Eleven days later, Lee again showed Ohio State what he could do. "After that," Pantoni said, "Luke and I were both pretty convinced."

Convincing Pantoni was a crucial element of Ohio State recruiting under Meyer. Lee was part of Meyer's second class, but Pantoni's input was already critical, and that would only continue to grow. "Pantoni is the best evaluator," Meyer said. "I trusted him even more than our coaches. If it was between a coach and Mark Pantoni, I'm going with Mark. That's the only place in the country that's like that. The last five years, we would not take a guy unless Mark approved it. We'd have a healthy debate, but if it came down to it, and Mark said, 'Don't do it,' I didn't do it."

Pantoni and Fickell worked together as a reliable reaffirmation of Lee's talent. Fickell watched with one question: could Lee at around 6'3" and 205 pounds grow into a linebacker? Fickell asked Ohio State strength coach Mickey Marotti for his opinion. "I said, 'Mick, go watch this kid. Do you think he can carry 235 pounds? Because if you don't think he can with his bone structure, I can't justify him being a linebacker,'" Fickell said. "And I remember him saying, 'Yeah, that kid can carry 235.' And I'm like, 'Okay, I'll pound the table for him.'"

Lee left that Saturday camp satisfied he'd held up his end of the bargain, and the Buckeyes told him they would have a staff meeting Monday and discuss his offer. "There's no doubt in my mind that my son has the ability to put his fist in the ground and work hard for something, especially if he has something to prove," Candice said. "So I was proud that he went down there and camped again, and I was like good for you. But I did prepare him. I said, 'You may be a late offer. So you have to prepare yourself that this may not come.' And he was very confident. He was like, 'No, I'm gonna get it.'"

"I had the turning point of letting go of quarterback a little bit," he said. "I was being fair to myself on that. I told my mom, 'I did everything just for an offer to play for Ohio State. I did everything I possibly could.'"

Two days later the offer came. Lee was home after a morning workout at his high school when his cell phone buzzed and he saw Fickell's name. Fickell asked where Candice was. Darron said she was at work. "Go give her a call and talk," Fickell said, "because you have a scholarship offer from us. You earned it."

One day later on June 26, Lee committed.

This was a risk worth taking for both of them. Lee had locked up his college choice in the summer before his senior year, which provided a sense of relief. Ranked only ahead of Sprinkle, a defensive tackle, Lee was the second-lowest-rated recruit of the 23 players that signed with Ohio State in February 2013. If the Buckeyes were taking a risk with Lee, the player was also taking a risk that he could compete with the three other linebackers in the class—Texas' Mike

Mitchell, the No. 54 overall recruit; Georgia's Trey Johnson, the No. 108 overall recruit; and Cleveland's Worley, the No. 505 overall recruit. Mitchell transferred from Ohio State after a season without playing in a game. Johnson played seven games as a true freshman but was forced to end his career after the 2014 because of knee injuries. Between Worley and Lee, the Buckeyes thought they were deciding who was a linebacker and who was a safety. Both stuck at linebacker. Worley backed up Lee for two seasons at outside linebacker and then took over the starting job for two years after Lee left for the NFL after the 2015 season.

Once Lee spent his redshirt season in 2013 putting on weight and learning a new position at linebacker, he sped through his Ohio State career. But the start was slow. "We had daily phone calls, just talking about the struggle he was going through learning this position," Candice said of that 2013 season. "I said, 'Look, if you don't want to be there, give the scholarship back. Stop calling me. Get on the practice squad, learn the position, and go knock some heads. No one's going to give you anything.'"

At one point, Lee said Meyer suggested that maybe the coach should send him to Akron as a transfer to the MAC school. Fellow linebacker Joshua Perry heard it and told Lee about his own first-year struggles the season before. "Shout out to Joshua Perry," Lee said. "So I was like okay, I'm being challenged, and it's not like me to even think about quitting or transferring after all the work I did to get there."

He stayed. The next year on the first day of spring practice in 2014, Lee lined up with the starters. Undersized, quick, physical, and with the instincts and understanding of a quarterback, Lee was everything the Buckeyes wanted at a position that was part linebacker, part safety. The weight was added, the responsibilities were absorbed, and Lee once again was ready to go. He was back on a practice field at Ohio State and out to prove something. The Buckeyes won the national title that season with nine members of the 2013 recruiting class—two five-stars, six four-stars, and Lee as a three-star—playing significant roles. By the time the Buckeyes were in their playoff run, teammates were happily debating whether the invaluable Lee was confident or cocky, and the redshirt freshman ranked second on the team in tackles-for-loss.

Pantoni's favorite recruiting photo is from that 2013 class and shows four of those members—defensive end Joey Bosa, running back Ezekiel Elliott, cornerback Eli Apple, and Lee—on a visit at an OSU game together. All of them started for the 2014 national champs in their second seasons and then were first-round draft picks in April 2016 after their third seasons. Bosa was from Florida, Elliott was from Missouri, Apple was from New Jersey, and Lee was from right down the road, an Ohio kid who kept up with all of them. The New York Jets selected Lee 20th overall in the 2016 draft. "If Darron had lived in St. Louis or in Chattanooga, where he was originally from, this never would have happened," Pantoni said. "Him being local was the big thing because we were able to find out so much about him. You probably take a bigger chance if he's from Ohio."

"When you're a tweener that they are taking, they're getting the risk," Candice said. "Because they're basically extending a scholarship offer to somebody who they think athletically can play a lot of positions. They just don't know what to do with you. And I think that's a credit and a testimony to Ohio State as a football program and to Luke Fickell's prowess as a linebackers coach that they were able to coach him up at a position that he had never played in his entire life. And I've got to give it to Coach Mick for putting the muscle on him because he was just tall and skinny, and we were just all wondering how that was going to work." The only way to find out was to take the risk.

## CHAPTER 13

# Tom Skladany,
# Class of 1973

If Woody Hayes was going to extend a scholarship offer to a punter for the first time, it wouldn't be to this guy. Not at this school. Not after what had happened to the last football player from Bethel Park High School in the suburbs of Pittsburgh that Hayes and Ohio State had recruited. Tom Skladany, a future three-time All-American, was behind before he started. "Dennis Franks is a couple years ahead of me, and he told Woody he was going to Ohio State," Skladany said. "And he turned around and went to Michigan. And Woody lost his mind."

That's why the story of Skladany's recruitment has to begin with the story of Franks' recruitment two years earlier. Franks was one of the best linebackers in the country, which is why the Buckeyes' head coach spent at least three nights in the Franks home while navigating one of the great runs in Ohio State football history. The Buckeyes went 27–2 between 1968 and 1970 as Hayes began his personal battle with protege and new Michigan coach Bo Schembechler in 1969. After a rougher stretch in the mid-1960s, Hayes was again on top and accustomed to winning and he wanted Franks in his 1971 recruiting class. In the Franks household, Hayes exhibited for a rapt audience—Franks' German mother and his Italian father—his knowledge of history. And he represented one of the best football teams in the country.

Flooded with offers, Franks made 13 recruiting trips before settling on three final options of Ohio State, Notre Dame, and the home state Penn State Nittany Lions. The real battle was between Hayes and Penn State's Joe Paterno, and Franks had a stumbling block with the Penn State coach. "You wouldn't believe it," Franks said. "As a high school kid, my challenge was he always wore white socks. Whether he was coaching or wearing a suit, he always had those white socks on. It drove me crazy."

Advantage Hayes.

OSU assistant Earle Bruce was in touch with Franks constantly, and the decision was crystalizing for a player who said he'd heard from more than 100 schools during his recruitment. Skladany, a running back without great speed who was two years younger than Franks and who'd flashed his skills punting a football, was finding his recruitment heating up as well. But first, Franks would make a final decision, and everything was pointing him toward Columbus. "It was great," Franks said. "It was really awesome to be recruited by such a wonderful school."

And then Schembechler called about a week before Franks was prepared to sign with Ohio State. "Bo Schembechler called my mother directly," Franks said. "And he basically said to her that it would be a travesty if your son didn't at least look at the University of Michigan before making a decision where he would attend."

Until that point, Franks had no intention of visiting Michigan. Soon, he was in Ann Arbor, wowed by Michigan Stadium, and challenged by Schembechler. "The deciding factor was when I sat across from Bo, and I was talking with him, and he said to me, 'So you're Denny Franks. I hear you're supposed to be pretty good.' And he looked at me and, unlike any of the other colleges, he said, 'I don't know if you're good enough to play here,'" Franks said. "He said, 'But I'd be willing to take a shot with you and offer you a scholarship.'"

Franks was hooked. He went home, remembered the stadium, appreciated Michigan's academics, and accepted the challenge. He'd be a Wolverine. Now he just had to tell Hayes. "Woody was a legend even then," Franks said. "And he called very much upset when he found out I was going to Michigan."

Schembechler had established that he'd be a worthy rival to his mentor when Michigan upset No. 1 Ohio State in 1969. The Buckeyes got Michigan back in 1970, but now months after an upset loss to Stanford in the Rose Bowl to end the 1970 season had extinguished hopes for another undefeated season, Hayes was hearing about Schembechler besting him in this recruitment. "Ohhhh, he really came back at me about leading him on," Franks said, "that it was not a good thing to lead someone on like that, giving us indications that you're going to come to Ohio State and then to go to Michigan. And he didn't say Michigan. It's just, 'That School Up North. I can't believe you chose that one; Penn State would have been a better choice. I can't believe you did that.' He was very stern in his conversation with me. And he didn't talk to my parents. He talked to me. I was being taught a lesson. Don't be giving indications you're going to do something and then pull out, that kind of thing.

My upbringing was such that my father said if you make a commitment, make sure you follow through with it. But I didn't make the commitment. I was leaning to Ohio State, and then Bo came in and he pressed my buttons. I mean, it was just amazing. If he didn't say, 'I don't know if you're good enough to play here,' I would have gone to Ohio State."

Franks did go to Michigan, where he became an All-Big Ten center as a senior. Into the seething aftermath of that choice stepped Skladany, another Bethel Park kid with his eyes on the Buckeyes and a legend to impress. But Hayes was done with that high school. "Dennis Franks had screwed him," Skladany said.

So began a two-year fight for OSU assistant George Chaump, who inherited the Pittsburgh recruiting area when Bruce left to become the head coach at Tampa for the 1972 season. Chaump first evaluated Skladany as a running back and was often on hand for his sophomore, junior, and senior high school seasons, whether he was playing football, basketball, or baseball. Skladany needed an advocate because he had already been blacklisted by Hayes after Franks' decision. "Woody goes, 'They have no character. You can't want him. He's on the same team. They're probably friends,'" Skladany said, taking on Hayes' voice while reliving this recruiting dispute four decades later.

Skladany and Franks *were* friends. But this friend would become a Buckeye.

Skladany hailed from Western Pennsylvania football stock. His uncle, Joe "Mugsy" Skladany, was an All-American defensive end at Pitt in 1933 and 1934 and was inducted into the College Football Hall of Fame in 1975. His father, Tom Sr., played, as did Skladany's uncles and brothers. But it was a detour out of that football region that set him on his punting path. Skladany's father was transferred to Baltimore while Skladany was in elementary school and junior high. Skladany wasn't playing football at that young age. "It was all soccer. I was kicking the ball 70 yards. It's easy. It's round," Skladany said. "I was kicking and kicking and playing soccer. And then he got transferred back to Pittsburgh, and they didn't have soccer. So that's when I tried out for football. And I love knocking people out, and, of course, my bloodline was football."

Tom Skladany Sr., a fullback, had punted as well. Now he showed his son. And once his son started punting, he never stopped. He was an all-around athlete, playing running back, receiver, and defensive back as well, rarely leaving the field, but once Skladany said he ran a 40 that was too slow to be an Ohio State ball carrier, his offensive possibilities ended. Another local Pittsburgh running back made it difficult to keep up. In a September 1972 high school football preview in the *Pittsburgh Post-Gazette*, Skladany was listed as a player to watch directly under a Hopewell High School running back named Tony Dorsett. "You know who I got to tackle once a year? Tony Dorsett," Skladany said. "Guess what happened? My junior year, I come flying up from the secondary to get him going around the end and I never touched him. I never touched him my junior year. My senior year, I did touch him a little bit, and he ran me over like I was a little baby."

Skladany was witnessing firsthand the evolution of a legend. Four years later Dorsett won the Heisman Trophy and the national championship as a senior running back at Pitt. Skladany wasn't that kind of running back, but when the Buckeyes checked back in at Bethel Park looking for a punter, Skladany's athleticism came back into play. He wasn't enough of an athlete to run the ball for the Buckeyes, but he was more than enough to punt it. He kicked it like a soccer player, but he tackled life with a football attitude. Attracted to Skladany by geography and family, Pitt noticed as well. "They're going after me hard," Skladany said. "People are messing with me at church every Sunday, 'You gotta go to Pitt.' I got a little over-recruited by Pitt. And I liked it."

Pitt director of recruiting Foge Fazio, a former Pitt linebacker 10 years away from becoming the Panthers' head coach, wrote Skladany an introductory letter on May 10, 1972, as Skladany was finishing his junior year in the classroom, and ended with:

"I hope this letter will show our interest in you, and will no doubt stimulate your interest in Pitt. Please let me hear from you as soon as possible."

Months later, head coach Carl DePasqua handwrote a postcard featuring an aerial shot of the stadium at the Air Force Academy in Colorado Springs, Colorado, where the Panthers played on September 23 in the third week of the 1972 season:

"Dear Tom, Squad had excellent flight and are going to field for light workout. The weather is just perfect for game. Looking forward to seeing you at our next home game. Carl DePasqua."

Pitt lost that game 41–13 as part of a 1–10 season, and DePasqua was fired on November 27. On December 19, 38-year-old Iowa State coach Johnny Majors was hired by Pitt, and on December 27, Skladany received this Western Union telegram:

"I WOULD LIKE TO TAKE THIS OPPORTUNITY TO WISH YOU AND YOUR FAMILY A WONDERFUL CHRISTMAS AND HAPPY NEW YEAR. WE ARE ANXIOUSLY AWAITING TO MEET YOU IN PERSON IN THE NEAR FUTURE TO DISCUSS OUR PROGRAM BOTH ACADEMICALLY AND ATHLETICALLY HERE AT THE UNIVERSITY OF PITTSBURGH. WE ARE GOING TO BE A WINNER AND WANT AND NEED YOU TO BE PART OF THIS EXCELLENT PROGRAM. JOHN MAJORS, HEAD FOOTBALL COACH."

The renewed local interest from the school 22 minutes from Skladany's front door flattered, but it was too late. Skladany had been receiving recruiting letters from schools throughout the East and Midwest in response to Bethel Park coaches who had put out the word on their punter. Notre Dame inquired, as did Maryland, Michigan State, and Michigan, among others. Wolverines assistant Larry Smith wrote in a letter on May 31, 1972:

"You have been recommended by your coach as a prospective student-athlete for the University of Michigan. We feel that we have a great school to afford a student-athlete. Michigan is recognized as one of the top four academic universities in the United States. We have won more Big Ten football championships and had more championships in all sports than any other Big Ten school. We play in the largest college stadium (101,001) in America. At the present time, Michigan athletics are on the top under Athletic Director, Don Canham. Our eager, young football staff, under Bo Schembechler, is anxious to continue the winning ways of Michigan."

From Boston College came a letter dated June 6, 1972, from a young coach named Joe Daniels, himself a Pittsburgh native and Bethel Park High School grad. Daniels later would go on to coach Dan Marino at Pitt and Terrelle Pryor at Ohio State in a four-decade career of mentoring quarterbacks. But while recruiting Skladany, he was a 30-year-old working his old stomping grounds.

"I certainly enjoyed having the opportunity to talk with you a few weeks ago about Boston College," Daniels wrote in part. "I hope, after our discussion, you have a little better understanding of the type of school we can offer you...I have enclosed my calling card which has our phone number on it. Please feel free to call collect at any time. All of us here at Boston College want to wish you and your team the best of luck for the coming year. The best way to complete your last year of high school football is to win them all."

On August 9, a Penn State staffer wrote with an invite to a game:

"The Penn State coaching staff cordially invites you and your parents to be our guests at any of our home games... We recommend the early games when the weather is nicer and the campus is really beautiful. However, come when you can."

So Skladany began his visits. One of six children, he knew football was his ticket to college. Without a scholarship his other option was a job in a steel mill. "My father made $32,000 a year with six kids," Skladany said. "And he said, 'Hey, I can't do college. So you're gonna have to get through on your own. Or you're gonna have to go work.' So I knew."

As the process unfolded, Skladany found his final options to be Penn State, Ohio State, or the mill. The offer from Penn State came first, and the letter from Paterno was dated February 16, 1973:

"At Penn State it is our endeavor to carry on an athletic program that befits the reputation of the University as one of the great educational institutions of the country. To accomplish this we must have on our team young men who combine athletic ability with a high standard of moral practice and good academic achievement.

"Careful investigation reveals you are this kind of young man. Consequently, pending your admission, we are pleased to offer you the maximum grant-in-aid permitted under N.C.A.A. rules. This grant covers room, board, books, fees, tuition and $15 a month for incidentals. You will not be required to work for this grant, and it cannot be rescinded in the event of injury or similar reasons. The grant is governed by rules of the N.C.A.A., which fully protects you."

The letter went on for two more paragraphs and expressed hope that Skladany and his parents would soon visit for a weekend. It was signed "Joseph V. Paterno, Head Football Coach," and at the bottom Paterno included a personal note. "P.S. Tell your dad thanks for the clippings. J"

So Skladany visited Penn State and he said every other recruit on a trip that weekend did sign with the Nittany Lions. A photo of that visit—six young men in jackets, ties, and nametags posing with Paterno—hangs on Skladany's office wall. But Skladany didn't commit. "Paterno says, 'You're our No. 1 recruit for punting, we're gonna go ahead and give you a scholarship,'" Skladany said of the Nittany Lions' boss. "I say, 'Coach, it's my second visit.' I'm there on a Saturday. I was gonna leave on Sunday. He says, 'Well, if you don't sign by tomorrow, we're gonna pull it.'"

Skladany, who said he was a C student in high school, said Paterno was concerned about his academics and said as a freshman Skladany would work on his grades and learn from the veteran in front of him. Seven years into what would be a 46-year run as Penn State's head coach, Paterno projected that Skladany would take over as the starting punter as a junior. Again concerned that he'd only visited two schools, Skladany called his father. "He goes, 'He's putting limits on you,'" Skladany remembered. "'He doesn't even know who you are and he's telling you what he thinks is gonna happen?'"

Tom Sr. told Tom Jr. to ask Paterno one question. "My father was a genius," Skladany said.

The question: what if Skladany proved earlier than his junior year that he was clearly the better punter? What if he beat out the veteran? Skladany said Paterno told him it wasn't going to happen. So Skladany said he had another visit to take.

Next was a visit to a school that had never given a scholarship to a punter and a visit to a head coach still holding a grudge. Skladany had initially visited Columbus for the Buckeyes' 14–11 win against Michigan on November, 25, 1972. Now the $44 Allegheny Airlines flight from Pittsburgh to Columbus was booked for March 9, 1973. Chaump had been pushing for Skladany, and finally the chance to break through had arrived. "They finally let me come up, and Woody didn't want me up there," Skladany said.

"Chaump told him, 'You've gotta let him see this campus.' Keep in mind: no one had ever got a scholarship to punt at Ohio State."

Gary Lago punted for the Buckeyes from 1970 to 1972, taking over from Mike Sensibaugh, an All-American safety who doubled as the Buckeyes' punter in 1968 and 1969. As Lago prepared for graduation, Mike Keeton appeared to be next in line if the Buckeyes didn't go out and land their first scholarship punter. "I wasn't really recruited by Ohio State," Keeton said. "Back in the day, if there was such a term as a preferred walk-on, which there wasn't then, that's what I would have been."

Keeton's uncle was the head football coach at Muskingum College and put in a word with the OSU freshman coach. Keeton, a lifelong OSU fan from Caldwell, Ohio, was attending Ohio State no matter what. The only question was whether football would be part of his college life. He found himself as the freshman team punter in 1972 when Lago was a senior. He was eager for 1973. "I thought I was going to slide right into where I needed to be because I was fairly decent at what I did," Keeton said.

That would hinge on Skladany's visit. Skladany remembers Doug Plank and Dave Purdy as his hosts. Instructed by Hayes to show Skladany around, they instead said they had to study for their finals. "They said, 'You were a last-minute guy.' So they studied until 2:00 in the morning, and I sat there in a dorm room," Skladany said. "And when they were all done, you know what we did? We went and played hockey for three hours at the ice rink. Next morning, here's breakfast, here comes the Woods. He goes, 'You have a good time here? Thinking you want to play here?'"

Skladany's flight home was in a few hours. Hayes wanted an answer on Skladany's interest in Ohio State, but the question of whether the punter would be on scholarship or instead be invited to walk on hung in the air. As he'd told Paterno, Skladany told Hayes that he had another visit he needed to take. But this time that wasn't true. "He says, 'Well, we're not going to be able to give you a scholarship.' I said, 'Well, then don't worry about it because if I don't get a scholarship, I'm going to be working in a steel mill.' He said, 'We can't do it.' I said, 'It's the steel mill. See you later,'" Skladany said. "He says, "We don't give scholarships to kickers. We get our kickers from campus. If you think you're that good, why don't you just come up here and show us, and then we'll talk about a scholarship?' I said, 'Coach, I never said I was that good. You called me to come up here.' And now we get in a little bit of a fight. I get on that plane. And I say, 'I just screwed this up.'"

That left Chaump to go to work. Hired by Hayes in 1968, Chaump served as Ohio State's quarterbacks coach and reshaped the OSU offense. A 35-year-old Pennsylvania native, he'd also found ways to both connect with high school football players and influence the 59-year-old Hayes. "Chaump saw me play three sports and he saw the camaraderie, and I was captain, and he saw me catching the ball and running and tackling," Skladany said. "And he goes, 'Woods, he's an athlete. He's not just a punter.'"

Skladany felt Chaump was trying to pull that punting scholarship for 1973 out of Hayes' soul. Hayes' view was no scholarships for that position and no scholarships for that high school. At one point, Skladany said Hayes forbade Chaump from mentioning his name because he was so tired of hearing about that Bethel Park punter. Yet about two weeks after Skladany landed back in Pittsburgh after what he thought had been a disastrous, life-changing visit, a letter arrived from Ohio State. It was dated from the weekend Skladany had been in Columbus:

"Dear Tom: This is to confirm what Coach Chaump has already stated to you. From what I understand you are an outstanding kicker and can step right in and be our extra-point, field goal, kickoff and punt man for this coming season. I am certain with hard work and dedication you can come to Ohio State and be our kicker. Please let me put in writing some of the things we talked about while you were on the campus:

"1. You may regard this letter as a definite offer of an Ohio State athletic scholarship.

2. This scholarship includes room, board, tuition, fees, books and school supplies.

3. We award this scholarship for FOUR years. The only way that you would lose it is by quitting football, which I think you will agree, is very unlikely is your case.

4. If you are injured in any way that you no longer can play football, you will remain on your scholarship for the entire four years, but you must be academically eligible.

"You may feel free to show this letter to anyone whom you wish, for there is nothing "under the table" about it. I hope you will show it to your parents, and then make sure you file it away as a matter of record.

"I hope this finds your dad on the way to recovery from his accident. Like all good ex-football players, I am certain he will bounce back.

"Your friend, W.W. Hayes, Head Football Coach."

It wasn't a letter that Skladany was expecting. It was a letter that Chaump made happen and it was a letter that lifted Skladany straight out of the steel mill. "I was already there," Skladany said, imagining that alternate life. "But Chaumpers kept pushing and pushing. Chaumpers was the best."

Before Chaump's death in 2019 at age 83, his former punter recruit had become a lifelong friend. Soon the word about Skladany's future was out—even if the word was initially wrong. In mid-April *The Pittsburgh Press* reported that the choice was Penn State, which had made that previous offer. "Joe Paterno is not upset that Pitt landed Carson Long, the long-balling place-kicker," Pat Livingston wrote in the April 15, 1973, edition of *The Press*. "Paterno has come up with Tom Skladany of Bethel Park, who boots kickoffs not out of the end zone, but out of the ballpark."

"My father got on the phone," Skladany said, "and said, 'Retract that, he's not done.'"

Answering letters from readers four days later, Livingston worked in this line in response to a Pitt fan complaining about the compliment paid to the new Penn State kicker at the expense of the new Pitt kicker. "If it makes you feel any better," Livingston wrote, "the kicker, Tom Skladany, isn't going to Penn State after all. He signed with Ohio State."

The decision was final, and now the competition for the 1973 season was on. Keeton had been advised by Ed Ferkany, the OSU assistant coach who oversaw the punters, that a challenge might be on the way. "He'd given me a heads up that, 'Hey, we're recruiting this kid out of Bethel Park, Pennsylvania, who's a helluva punter. So just do your job, keep working the way you work, and do your best, and we'll see how it shakes out,'" Keeton said. "But it's kind of stacked a little bit against you. You're a walk-on, and they're bringing in a young man on scholarship."

The young man on scholarship averaged 35.7 yards per punt as a freshman and thought Keeton deserved the scholarship as much as he did. Referring to himself as the worst punter in the Big Ten that season, Skladany would tell his friend as much. "That's not fair, but that's life," Skladany said. "I had it, and they can't give someone a scholarship and have him not play, but Keeton was kicking my butt the whole time."

Then came the Michigan game. The No. 1 Buckeyes and No. 4 Wolverines were both undefeated, and Franks wore maize and blue, and Skladany wore scarlet and gray. Skladany, who was also kicking off, was clipped on a return and broke his ankle in the second quarter. His absence limited some of Hayes' punting decisions the rest of the day, as the teams famously tied at 10. Big Ten athletic directors later voted to send the Buckeyes to the Rose Bowl over the Wolverines. Like many Michigan fans and former players, Franks still thinks the Wolverines deserved that trip. Still friendly with Skladany, he's irritated when Skladany talks of playing in three Rose Bowls, while Franks' only Rose Bowl experience came in 1971 when he was ineligible to play as a freshman. "Tommy rubbed it in quite a bit afterward," Franks said, while reinforcing how much he loved his Michigan experience. "He'd say, 'You just made the wrong pick. Admit it.' Quite frankly, Ohio State is such a great program, but you make your decisions and you make the best out of them. My whole career we went into the Ohio State game undefeated. It was a game of titans. It was amazing. But I'm really proud of Tommy. Tommy really excelled. He did a great job. He was a great athlete. And I tried to get him to go to Michigan, but he wouldn't budge."

With Skladany out for the Rose Bowl, Keeton got his shot. He averaged 41 yards on two punts as the Buckeyes beat USC 42–21. Before Keeton's senior season, Hayes made him stand up in front of the team to make a point to the newest Buckeyes. Hayes asked where Keeton was from and how many students were in his graduating high school class. "Caldwell, Ohio," Keeton replied. "Eighty-eight."

"Sit down," Hayes said. "Now you know the schools you came from. Look at what this kid did, and he played in the Rose Bowl for us and did a great job. In fact, if he wanted to, he could go punt for any other school in the Big Ten."

Keeton never earned a scholarship. But he earned Hayes' trust and he earned his Woody moment. He also acquired the admiration and friendship of Skladany, who embarked on a rehab program that he believes determined the rest of his career after dislocating and breaking his left plant ankle. It started as he walked Ohio State's campus for three months with a full cast on his left leg, which had the effect of strengthening his kicking leg. That's why he calls the injury the best thing that could have happened to him.

After a summer of constant punting, he returned to campus driven by what he viewed as an unsuccessful freshman season while refusing to be sidetracked by an injury suffered against Ohio State's greatest rivalry. He was a new man with a bigger leg. From 35.7 yards per punt as a freshman, he averaged 45.6, 46.7, and 42.4 yards over the next three seasons, becoming Ohio State's sixth three-time All-American. As a junior the punter—and also long-distance field goal kicker—booted a 59-yard field goal against Illinois that still stands as a school record.

At first, Hayes didn't want Skladany. By the end, he was calling Skladany, a captain, to ask if there were any problems with the team. Skladany also slowly expanded a relationship with Hayes that allowed the punter to prod the legend like few ever have. "Woody and me were tight," Skladany said.

On that visit in March 1973, Skladany pushed back so hard on Hayes he thought he'd cost himself a chance at playing for him. That irreverence—coupled with a sly sense of humor and the ability to get a punt to fly like it had wings—turned him into a Hayes favorite. "Tommy had that likability," Franks said. "He was just a good guy. And he performed."

"I had the time of my life, and Skladany was the best guy to hang around with as a punter," Keeton said. "To this day, I've never met someone so damn happy all the time."

Drafted in the second round of the 1977 NFL Draft by the Cleveland Browns, Skladany held out and was traded to the Detroit Lions and then played in the NFL for six seasons and made the Pro Bowl in 1981. He returned to the Columbus area, where he raised four daughters and opened a printing business. His office is filled with Ohio State memorabilia, including multiple photos with Hayes. And framed by the door to his office in a place where Skladany can't help but read it every day, is the letter that started it all. "Dear Tom," it begins. "This is to confirm what Coach Chaump has already stated to you…"

## CHAPTER 14

# Cameron Heyward, Class of 2007

Rivalry history unfolded on November 18, 2006. The crest of Big Ten dominance matched undefeated foes atop the college football landscape. This Ohio State–Michigan game between the No. 1 Buckeyes and No. 2 Wolverines played out in the shadow of the death of Michigan coaching legend Bo Schembechler days earlier and in the spotlight of the Heisman Trophy season of Ohio State quarterback Troy Smith, who would win the award three weeks later in a landslide. This was the best the Buckeyes could offer: a charged home atmosphere around electric talent like Smith, Ted Ginn, Beanie Wells, Anthony Gonzalez, James Laurinaitis, Malcolm Jenkins, and Vernon Gholston. In the Ohio Stadium stands among the 105,708 fans, absorbing it all, was a sick 17-year-old from Georgia and his mom.

Gathering information for his choice in the 2007 recruiting class, defensive lineman Cameron Heyward hadn't taken any recruiting visits before. Heyward had never been to Columbus. Heyward's mother, Charlotte, was intrigued but still a little unsure about the 600-mile distance from their home outside Atlanta to her oldest child's potential college choice. But here they were, unofficially, last-minute, and not even sitting with the other recruits. "We were kind of running out of time to take an official," Cam Heyward said. "It was a couple weeks before the big game, and our weekends just aligned, and my mom was like, 'Let's see if we can do this. Just see if you like it.' It was unofficial, so it wasn't like they could roll out the red carpet."

Heyward had helped Peachtree Ridge High School win its Georgia Class AAAAA playoff opener on Friday night and, while then fighting a cold, he landed in Columbus with his mother Saturday morning, hopped in a rental car, drove to Ohio Stadium, parked with other fans in fields across Route 315, and walked toward the stadium. At least they assumed they were walking toward the stadium. "Cameron and I are walking with the flow of traffic, so we asked this couple, 'Are we going the right way to the game?' and they're like, 'Oh, yeah,' and they start telling us about how the woman had never been a football fan, but since moving to Columbus, she had become a fan," Charlotte Heyward said. "They said how they were going to the Schottenstein Center to watch the game, and we're like, 'You're not going to the game? You parked and you're going to watch it in an arena?' And they were like, 'Yeah, yeah, there's not enough seats [in Ohio Stadium], but it's an awesome experience, and we really believe in Coach Tressel and him as a person,' and they start telling me about his website."

What the Heywards were learning was that an overflow crowd for the game would be watching inside Ohio State's basketball arena because too many fans wanted to be a part of this. And they were learning that Ohio State coach Jim Tressel was offering life lessons online that went beyond football, and that football in Columbus went beyond the stadium and the players. The Heywards had family in Pennsylvania, but Charlotte didn't know Big Ten football well. "I look up at the signs and it says, 'The Best Fans in the Land.' And it just stuck to me, like, wow, you're appreciating the fans, not just the players," Charlotte said. "So we go to the game, and nobody's sitting down. And this is wearing me out. I'm tired. I just want to sit down. And Cameron to this day does not really like to watch football. He will rarely sit down and watch a game on TV. He just gets bored. He will watch it if he's studying something. So he was sick and kind of bored, and we went inside to eat, and he was like, 'I don't want to go back out there.'"

Her son didn't like being apart from the other players. So, nursing a cold, Heyward and his mom spent most of the second half watching from inside the OSU recruiting room at the stadium. After Ohio State's 42–39 victory, which sent the Buckeyes onto the national title game, the Heywards said some hellos without getting the official visit treatment. Then Heyward hung out with his player hosts, sophomore linebacker Laurinaitis, who had nine tackles against the Wolverines, and redshirt freshman defensive tackle Todd Denlinger. That pair was picked by linebackers coach Luke Fickell, who was leading the Heyward recruitment for the Buckeyes. "Luke always put me with the most boring people that wouldn't want to go out because that was me: boring," Laurinaitis said. "He said, "Cam's coming up, he's a big kid, but he doesn't want to do anything. You don't have to try to entertain him. Just hang out at your place.' I was like, 'Great.' Luke just made it seem like, 'Don't screw it up.'"

"We went out to Chipotle and then just played video games," Heyward said, "and then I was just like, 'I'm tired and I'm not feeling that well.' So I was the easiest guest he ever got."

The Heywards did see High Street the next day and got a feel for the campus. They met with basketball coach Thad Matta and watched a basketball practice because playing both sports in college was on Cameron's mind. And they did meet Tressel. "Charlotte wasn't really worried about whether he was going to be a good player or not," Tressel said. "She wanted to know what kind of program he was going to be in."

She heard that from Tressel. And it was exactly what she needed. "I was in awe," Charlotte said. "In my head I was thinking, *This was a man I could trust with my son.* By the time we left there, I had a sense of calm."

When they got to the Columbus airport, Cameron asked if he could buy an Ohio State T-shirt. His mother paused. That wasn't the type of request her son usually made. Something was happening with Cameron Heyward and Ohio State, even though for much of his life, the idea of a football scholarship for the son of former NFL running back Craig "Ironhead" Heyward would have been inconceivable. "We never thought Cameron would play sports," Charlotte said. "He was severely asthmatic as a child. Instead of getting a normal cold, he got scarlet fever. His asthma required hospitalizations for like a week. He tried baseball when he was little and he got tired running the bases. He'd hit home runs and say, 'I don't feel like running the bases.' He played soccer, but he was the goalie because he couldn't run. So he just was not that athletic kid. He loved to draw and he was a really happy-go-lucky kid. But sports did not look like it was it for him."

At age 10 he started playing basketball and danced at the foul line. But the next year, he improved and he was already big. So the basketball court was where Heyward found a home. He joined a better team, where he was still the biggest kid on the team but didn't start. That angered him, so he worked harder. Eventually, football came calling, and Charlotte and Craig relented. He was drafted onto a summer team in middle school by family friend Bobby Hebert, the former NFL quarterback and teammate of Craig's. As his coordination caught up to his body, Cameron then learned the game and started to love it, too. Craig would lean against the fence and shout encouragement during practice.

The family chose Whitefield Academy, a small, private school 45 minutes away, for his high school, and Charlotte said no to football as a freshman so he could take a year to adjust to the new environment. The coaches saw the new, big kid and invited him to join the team, and Charlotte said no again. They gave him a jersey. Charlotte said no a third time. Basketball in the winter was a possibility if the grades were there, but football in the fall was out. Sophomore year, Cameron was back, having realized how much he had missed football. And then in March 2005 during Cameron's sophomore basketball season, Craig had a stroke.

A decade into his NFL career, Craig Heyward had been diagnosed with cancer at the base of his skull in November 1998 and underwent 12 hours of surgery. He retired at the end of that season at age 32, when Cameron was nine. A gregarious personality and physical runner, Craig was now in a wheelchair after the stroke, just as his son's recruitment was taking off. The long drive to school was now too much as the family cared for Craig at home (Charlotte and Craig divorced in 2001 but maintained a strong friendship), so the decision was made for Cameron to transfer to the closer public school, Peachtree Ridge. Fourteen months later in May 2006, Craig died at the age of 39. "Craig did know Cameron was going to have the opportunity to play collegiate football. He would throw out his little comments I can't quote because sometimes they were infused with other words," Charlotte said, laughing. "And he was adamant about Cameron choosing the right school."

Cameron's parents met as sophomores at Pitt, and as a junior, Craig ran for 1,791 yards for the Panthers, earned first-team All-American honors, and then became a first-round NFL draft pick of the New Orleans Saints. Craig had a good relationship with Pitt coach Dave Wannstedt, and Charlotte, a Pittsburgh native, had family in the city. "I remember him telling me I should go to Pitt, his old stomping grounds," Cameron said.

But even if Cameron didn't want to attend his father's school, he did want his father's advice on a subject that Craig knew well. "He was going to be my crutch to help me through the process," Cameron said. "It was pretty tough. My dad was someone who had been through it and experienced it a lot and he was supposed to be there because I think every dad wants to experience that when their child is in the middle of the recruiting process. But he passed away, and my mom really stepped up."

Charlotte stepped into a world where her son's football talent was obvious, but on the basketball court, he was showing basketball and football skills alike. Cameron thought he wanted to play both sports in college, and there's nothing that catches the eye of defensive football coaches like big guys who can move on the basketball court. "I wanted to play basketball my whole life," Heyward said. "But then as you get older, you're like, I'm pretty good at football. Maybe I should just stick with this."

Heyward watched the Buckeyes on TV as a kid, and the family had Rust Belt ties. But there wasn't a strong Ohio State connection until Fickell was put onto Heyward by a phone call from Matta from an event in Orlando. "He said, 'I'm at this basketball tournament and I'm watching this kid. He's not a basketball player. But he's got to be a football player,'" Fickell recalled. "'He is literally bowling people over, going after balls, knocking guys all over the place.'"

When informed of the basketball player's name, Fickell recognized it. He knew that he was from Georgia, that he was Ironhead's kid, but not much else. "He hadn't played a lot of football," Fickell said. "The first time I went to his high school to see him was like a month after his dad passed away. I don't know if he still thought he was a basketball player, but Thad knew I had to check him out."

Ohio State defensive line coach Jim Heacock soon joined on a visit and saw the same thing: a future run stopper and quarterback menace currently grabbing rebounds and chasing down loose balls. "He never slowed down," Heacock said. "Your first impression is amazing. He's big and physical-looking. But when I watched him play basketball, the thing that really stood out to me was the aggressiveness he played with. Basketball tells you a lot. Do they run the court? Do they go after the ball? Will they dive on the floor? All those things. And he checked all those boxes."

Heacock had seen it before in another defensive lineman who had made a name for himself at Ohio State. Nine years earlier Heacock had recruited Ryan Pickett out of Zephyrhills High, a school 30 minutes outside Tampa, Florida. Pickett started three years at defensive tackle from 1998 to 2000 and then went pro early and was drafted by the St. Louis Rams in the first round in 2001. Ohio State's interest there also began with basketball. "I stopped by, and they happened to be practicing," Heacock said. "He might have been 310 pounds, but to watch him run the court, there was no doubt in my mind."

It was happening again. Heyward didn't top 300 pounds—he was more like 6'6" and 280 pounds—but the combination of a big man with agility, power, and a motor was enticing. Ohio State was hooked. He was a future defensive star in Fickell's mind. "I watched him practice before their state championship game or maybe their state semifinals," Fickell said. "After I watched that practice, I thought, *Oh my God, this is my favorite kid.*"

Ohio State just had to make sure Heyward felt the same way. With his mother asking tough questions and demanding smart answers from college recruiters, Heyward narrowed his final five choices to Florida, LSU, USC, Ohio State, and home state Georgia. This came during a period when the Bulldogs weren't regularly locking down the best players in Georgia. According to the 247Sports.com player ratings from 2007, Heyward was the 14th best recruit in the state in the Class of 2007. Only two of the 13 players ranked ahead of him committed to Georgia. "I was at [the Heywards'] house early on," Fickell said, "and I was at another recruiting fair in Georgia and I saw the whole Georgia staff. And I remember somebody saying, 'Hey, don't bash us, don't go in there bashing us. We're going to see him tonight.'"

Fickell told the Georgia coaches he didn't think Heyward would be leaving home. But when he met with Charlotte that night, she told him he had been under her wing for long enough. "I was like," Fickell said, "Oh, we can get this kid."

The Heywards were searching for the right answer. Again, this is how Heyward's football, family, and recruiting reality fit together during his high school days:

- In the fall of 2003 as a freshman at a small high school, he didn't play football.
- As a sophomore in the fall of 2004, he got back on the football field.
- In the spring of 2005, his father suffered a stroke.
- In the fall of 2005, he transferred to a bigger public school, but he had to wait for a waiver from the state high school association to grant him immediate eligibility and he wasn't sure until just before the season started that he'd be able to play. He broke out as a football player that fall, and the offers started coming.
- In May 2006 at the end of his junior year, his father died. He entered the summer before his senior year of high school mourning his father while seeking out his new football home.

So, of course, their recruiting process was delayed. No one was thinking much about that during his junior season as Craig's health worsened and Charlotte was caring for him. Craig could still go to games until he eventually lost his hearing. But Cameron stayed by his side, as did his two younger brothers, Corey and Connor, and their older half-brother, Craig Jr. "Cameron didn't really hang out with friends that junior year," Charlotte said. "He just wanted to be with his dad."

Late to the recruiting game, Cameron wanted to give himself as much time as possible to make a decision. The OSU unofficial visit popped up, but he didn't line up his official visits, the kind where schools could pay for his travel and put on a show, until January, just weeks before National Signing Day on the first Wednesday in February. He went to LSU on January 12, Florida on January 19, and Georgia on January 26. In the midst of that, the Bulldogs sent six coaches to watch him grab 10 rebounds and score 10 points during a Peachtree Ridge basketball game on January 23, 2007, which saw Heyward's team lose 76–59 to defending state champ Norcross. Who was also there? Fickell, LSU assistant Bradley Dale Peveto, and the Florida assistant who won the battle to sit next to Charlotte during the game—Greg Mattison, who a decade later would join the Ohio State staff. USC was too far away on the West Coast, though head coach Pete Carroll told the Heywards he only recruited first-round draft picks...which was the first time Charlotte realized her son's full potential.

So it was the three SEC schools and the Buckeyes that made up the final four. Under second-year coach Urban Meyer and about to beat the Buckeyes in the BCS National Championship, Florida made a push. "I had a pretty good visit with Coach Meyer," Heyward said.

Meyer would call Charlotte during the process and say how hard it was to reach Cameron. "He'd say, 'Hey, your son doesn't pick up the phone. Does he not like me?'" Charlotte said. "I said, 'He does like you, but he doesn't like the phone. It's becoming overwhelming for him.'"

Peveto, the upbeat LSU assistant, was relentless in expressing his interest with regular calls, and their visit with LSU head coach Les Miles in Baton Rouge, Louisiana, was fine. But Charlotte also remembered asking LSU defensive coordinator Bo Pelini how long he would be there, and Pelini was honest about his head coaching aspirations. He left to be Nebraska's head coach in 2008, which would have been Heyward's sophomore season there.

And in Charlotte's mind, the interest from Georgia, the school whose Athens campus was less than an hour from the Heyward home, wasn't strong enough early on. "Georgia was the last school to recruit him out of his top schools because I think they automatically take it for granted that you're a Georgia kid [and,] we don't have to do a lot to get you because everybody wants to go to UGA," she said.

When the Heywards visited Athens, Charlotte flashed her football knowledge. She had a specific idea of where her son should play in college. It wasn't only about the school, but also the position. The Heywards were interested in Cameron playing at least some defensive end, not just defensive tackle. The Bulldogs compared his potential to Richard Seymour, a former Georgia star defensive tackle who had been the No. 6 overall pick in the 2001 NFL Draft. "I asked to see their board," Charlotte said. "And that threw them off. They were like, who is this woman asking to see our recruiting board?…So they took me into this room, and I saw all these junior college players they were bringing in, and they were defensive ends. So I said, 'You're bringing in these JUCO players who are defensive ends. I know you're moving him strictly inside.'"

Charlotte said their visit also included plenty of time with the coach in charge of defensive tackles and little time with the coach in charge of defensive ends. "I didn't like that they were going around it with me," she said, "versus just saying, 'Yes, we see him as defensive tackle.'"

"My mom," Cameron said, "was like my agent."

With that the Bulldogs were on the outside looking in, and the final choice came down to Florida and Ohio State. "Urban really wanted him," Charlotte said. "But I think he tried to put a little too much pressure on Cameron and I think that pushed Cameron away."

So all that remained was a final official visit at last to the school that seemed to be leading the way. That trip to Columbus was lined up for the first weekend in February. But the player who had been hospitalized for asthma as a kid and who wasn't himself on that Ohio State visit in November had another issue. "He was coming on the last weekend to do a visit," Fickell said. "And he called me and said, 'Coach, I'm sick, I can't come.'"

But then Heyward, according to Fickell, informed him: "'I'm still coming to Ohio State. I'm committed.' So he committed without an official visit."

The unofficial visit for the Michigan game had been enough. Charlotte had known it as soon as her son wanted that shirt at the airport. Tressel believes the fact that Heyward had grandparents three hours away in Pittsburgh helped sell the school against three SEC options. "There was that comfort for everyone," Tressel said. "When you're recruiting a kid from that far away, you think, *Gosh, the parents and the grandparents and the cousins, they're never going to get to see him play.* Well, we had a little advantage that they were from Pittsburgh."

That did help. But the Buckeyes also sold the Heywards on the basics they sought. "Ohio State really had his heart," Charlotte said. "Coach Heacock, he said, 'I will teach him the inside and the outside of the line. I will make him as marketable as possible if he has aspirations to play in the NFL.'"

Fickell, who was 33 at the time and who lost the battle to sit next to Charlotte at that January basketball game, had done everything else to show the family how much the Buckeyes wanted Cameron to join them. "He wasn't pushy. He was just easy to relate to," Charlotte said. "He was young, and Coach Fick was just cool. It wasn't a lot of pressure. And they did their homework on Cameron, meeting with all his counselors and teachers, the administration, and they were like, 'Wow, he's a fantastic kid, great character.' My kids loved Luke, and we just developed a great friendship. He had become a fixture in our home."

Heyward still had to sign, which he'd do at his high school on Wednesday morning, February 7. Charlotte made her son call the coaches at Georgia, Florida, and LSU to tell them he'd be choosing the Buckeyes. "But Bradley Dale Peveto did not answer, I guess, because he was busy with other recruiting," Charlotte said. "So we're driving to the school, and as I'm pulling up, Bradley Dale calls and he's still trying to make his pitch, and I'm like, 'No, no, he's decided he's going to Ohio State.' Cameron was so relieved the whole recruiting process was over because he was not a real participant in the recruiting process. We waited to the last minute to go to schools. He wouldn't answer anybody's calls or texts. He was the worst recruit."

He immediately would become one of the best Ohio State players of his era. "This guy was a monster," Laurinaitis said. "Playing with him, there was no one you were more afraid of friendly fire from than Cam Heyward on a screen. Because if that big head hit you, you were going to be out."

Heyward almost immediately ascended to the starting lineup and he was named a freshman All-American, and Charlotte would become one of Ohio State's best recruiting assets. A continued force on the line, he made second-team All-Big Ten as a junior and played at a level that made declaring early for the NFL draft a possibility. After that 2009 regular season, Tressel was in Fort Wayne, Indiana, checking in on running back recruit Rod Smith in the first week of December when his cell phone rang. Wearing a topcoat on a cold, snowy day, Tressel stumbled to grab his cell phone and saw the caller ID said Charlotte was calling. "I thought, *Oh, shoot, I wonder if she's going to tell me that he's moving on?* You know how coaches are: we're paranoid," Tressel said. "She said, 'Well, first of all, I don't know what you've been reading, but Cam is not leaving Ohio State. He's staying and he's going to finish.' And I was like, whoa, that was the easiest recruiting job we ever did.' But then she went on to say, 'That's not really why I'm calling. I'm calling you about Bradley Roby.'"

That was future All-Big Ten cornerback, future NFL first-round pick, future Super Bowl 50 champion Bradley Roby, who at that point in time was a three-star recruit committed to Vanderbilt as a receiver. He was also a family friend of the Heywards and he played at Peachtree Ridge. Roby was three years younger than Heyward and didn't become a starter at Peachtree until his senior season. He was also primarily playing offense. Thanks to a high school coach who had played at Vanderbilt, the Roby family made several visits there, and his speed and potential got him an offer. Roby attended an Ohio State camp in June 2009 before his senior season, working out at receiver and corner. He thought it went just okay, and Ohio State didn't show a lot of interest. "He wanted to be a receiver, and we couldn't offer him as a receiver," Tressel said. "We told him we thought he could play defense, and he said he wanted to play receiver."

Not sure what other offers might come, Roby committed to Vanderbilt in July of 2009. But then he was convinced by his high school coaches to play cornerback as a senior, as they knew his 5'11" size and speed gave him a better shot at standing out on the other side of the ball.

"His recruiting blew up," said his mother, Betty Roby, a close friend of Charlotte's. "I feel like we went through the recruiting process twice."

The underrated receiver was now playing on both sides of the ball for Peachtree, as well as returning kicks and punts, and blossoming into a very intriguing cornerback prospect. By this time, Betty was regularly accompanying Charlotte to Ohio State games to watch Cameron play, and for the Iowa game on November 14, 2009, Bradley came along. As with Cameron previously, this was an unofficial visit without the full push from the Buckeyes. Roby had hurt his calf in his game the night before and was limping. It was cold. And when Charlotte suggested they call the coaches and go to the football headquarters at the Woody Hayes Athletic Center and look around, Bradley refused. "He said, 'I don't even know why I'm here,'" Charlotte said, "'They don't like me.'"

But Charlotte kept working. And Roby kept excelling at corner. At the postseason football banquet after the 2009 season, safeties coach Paul Haynes, who had also been involved in Cameron's recruitment, hoped to speak to Charlotte about Roby. Under Tressel, Ohio State had a policy of not going after committed players, and Tressel also didn't want to offer players until he met them in person. But Charlotte flew home after the banquet before Haynes could speak with her. He called when she landed in Atlanta, hoping to gauge Roby's interest, not wanting to extend an OSU offer if Roby, so previously disheartened by his Ohio State interactions, was out on the Buckeyes.

Charlotte, who had realized she left her car keys in Columbus, had already called a friend to pick her up from the airport. As she took the call from Haynes, Betty was already on her way. Then Betty and Charlotte had to push past Bradley's feelings of rejection and make him understand that Haynes really wanted to talk. Bradley agreed, but only if it was clear that Ohio State wasn't calling only because Charlotte made them. So Haynes was able to talk to Bradley. But somebody had to talk to Tressel.

Soon after, Charlotte dialed Tressel from outside her gym for that aforementioned call. She remembered standing outside, freezing because when she tried to go inside, the connection cut out. On the other end, Tressel listened in a Fort Wayne parking lot. Charlotte vouched for Roby. She explained what Roby was like, how smart he was. She talked about the Roby family, how Betty was a single mom who worked as an executive for Bank of America. By this time other schools, including Auburn, were very interested, and she explained that the Vanderbilt commitment wasn't going to stick regardless. "I said, 'Charlotte, we don't get into this, trying to steal other people's players,'" Tressel said. But he also remembered her sharing the news that a decommitment from Vanderbilt was on the way. "She said, 'He's opening up his recruiting, so you'd better get down here and see him because I want him at Ohio State and so does his mother.'"

According to Charlotte, Tressel then said, "I'm going to trust you on this one."

Ohio State then heard that Nick Saban and Alabama were on Roby as a corner as well, so the Buckeyes made their final visit and their final pitches. "Charlotte was in charge of the whole process," Tressel said.

Roby told Tressel and Haynes he was committing. But he had been the prize of Vanderbilt's recruiting class and he didn't want to make the switch public and hurt the Commodores. So into January, he stayed publicly committed to Vanderbilt and privately committed to Ohio State.

In the meantime, Vanderbilt was able to prepare to offer a last, late scholarship spot to Jordan Matthews, a receiver from Alabama who had been planning to walk on at Auburn. Matthews' mother found out about the scholarship spot because she and Betty had a mutual friend. Matthews made sense as a replacement because Vandy had viewed Roby as a receiver. By the time Matthews graduated four years later, he was the SEC leader in career catches and receiving yards. By the time Roby was done four years later, he was a two-time All-Big Ten pick. In the 2014 NFL Draft, Roby went No. 31 in the first round to the Denver Broncos, which was the same draft spot—No. 31—where Heyward had been picked three years earlier. Matthews went No. 42 and in the second round to the Philadelphia Eagles. "So we got two first-round draft choices because of Charlotte," Tressel said. "It wasn't what we did. We didn't do anything. It's not like we're these ace recruiters. That was all Charlotte."

By 2014 Cameron Heyward had established himself as one of the best defensive linemen in the NFL. Now more than a decade into his career, he has twice been named first-team All-Pro. Although he didn't choose to play college football in Pittsburgh, his dad's old stomping grounds came calling. It was the Pittsburgh Steelers who selected Heyward in the 2011 NFL Draft, and it's in Pittsburgh where, like his dad, he has become a football hero. "For it to come full circle," Heyward said, "I graduated from Ohio State, and we won the Sugar Bowl, and I have a torn elbow from the Sugar Bowl, so now I can't really work out at the combine, and there was so much uncertainty. But to watch the draft on TV and see the Steelers pick me—I never thought in a million years it would end up this way. It was one of those moments that will always live with me."

His first week at Ohio State, Heyward met volleyball player Allie Schwarzwalder. They dated throughout college and later married. They have three children, a son, Callen, and daughters Chloe and

Caia. The first time he visited Columbus, he was sick and bored. But it was there where he would lay the foundation for the rest of his life. "It's picking a school, knowing it's the right school, knowing what it's setting up for your future, then living that future," Heyward said, "and not having any regrets."

## CHAPTER 15

# Wyatt Davis,
# Class of 2017

Urban Meyer didn't normally drive the golf cart. When the Buckeyes head coach told a five-star offensive line recruit from California and his dad to climb in for a personal tour of Ohio State's campus, that was a sign of how serious the Buckeyes were about Wyatt Davis. How often did the boss take recruits on their initial tour of Ohio State? "Not often," said Ohio State recruiting director Mark Pantoni. "Not often."

Wyatt and his father, Duane Davis, had entered the Woody Hayes Athletic Center in June 2016 and were steps into a hallway lined with the history of OSU football—the stars, the coaches, the Rivalry. "They call it the longest hallway in college football," Wyatt Davis said, "and out comes Coach Meyer and I'm like, oh my gosh, this is crazy."

Duane remembers how Meyer shouted down the hall and asked, "Is that Wyatt Davis?" Sporting a large grin, Meyer then demanded that the teenager get in his office. "Typically with recruiting visits," Wyatt said, "you don't get to really interact with the head coach until toward the end of the visit...What was so funny about it was we're in the golf cart, and he's driving and we're going on the sidewalk, and there's people that are walking and they're doing double takes like, that's Coach Meyer! And it was hilarious."

Growing up in Los Angeles, Davis was in kindergarten when the University of Southern California won the second of back-to-back national titles under coach Pete Carroll in 2005. Davis was in fifth grade when Carroll coached his last season with the Trojans before heading to the NFL. As Davis grew into a football player, USC football faded into the background. Between 2010, when Davis entered sixth grade, and 2015, his junior year of high school, USC had four coaches in six years, finished in the top 10 just once, and didn't win a single Pac-12 title nor play in a Rose Bowl.

Plus, college sports in Los Angeles have a different feel. "L.A. is one of those cities where it's a bandwagon city," Davis said. "When certain teams are doing good, then the people will start showing up to the games. But what tripped me out about Ohio was just how die-hard the fans are. When I was running around with Coach Meyer on that golf cart, you would have thought the president was driving it. It was heavy duty. He took me to the library, he literally took me everywhere around campus."

That was no accident. That was Ohio State's version of rolling out the scarlet carpet and hoping it would stretch 2,250 miles from Columbus to Los Angeles. That day was a vital first step. But it was one day in a long-distance relationship. By the end of Ohio State's recruitment of Davis, Meyer was worried about the fact that USC coach Clay Helton was a character in the lives of the Davis family, the kind of almost-friend they'd see at the grocery store. Ohio

State was clearly the road team in this fight. Helton, who took over as head coach when Steve Sarkisian was fired in the middle of the 2015 season, had an inside local edge.

Duane had coached Helton's oldest son, Reid, in youth football, and Wyatt had played with Reid. Duane also helped coach Reid in high school; Helton's daughter, Aubrey, was in the same grade as Wyatt; and Helton's wife, Angela, was friendly with Wyatt's mother, Inge. And Helton, obviously, was very interested in the best lineman in the state. Wyatt had been offered by USC as a sophomore when Sarkisian was still the coach. Sarkisian had made the offer in person when the Davis family was on an unofficial visit, and Wyatt was so taken aback by the gesture that he cried. "At that point," Duane said, "I really believed Wyatt was gonna go to SC."

By the end of Wyatt's junior football season, Sarkisian was gone. But the replacement was in the produce aisle. "Clay lives in the same area that we do, and I've bumped into Clay and his wife many times," Duane said. "I've known Clay since he first got to USC. We have a relationship. We know each other very well definitely. We're not calling each other and saying, 'Let's get on the barbecue.' But when we see each other, we talk."

Later on, after Wyatt had committed to the Buckeyes, Meyer got a fuller picture of the Helton connection when he was talking with Duane and Inge. "Coach Meyer would always say, 'I just want to make sure you're still heading to the Midwest. We'd hate to lose you to SC because it's in the backyard.' And my wife said, 'Well, I can tell you Coach, we see Clay Helton all the time. He lives in our area.' And when my wife said that," Duane said, "Urban's face changed."

Even if Wyatt was committed, Helton was offering accidental reminders just by running errands. And even if USC wasn't peak USC, it was still home. "When I did receive that USC offer, being an L.A. kid, it was a big deal," Wyatt said. "I wasn't ready to commit to USC or anything, but I was super excited. It was awesome, especially for my mom. Since I was the baby of the family, she wanted me close."

Helton's proximity would haunt Meyer and serve as part of Ohio State's challenge in keeping the Davis commitment. The plan to keep that California connection would include sending offensive line coach Greg Studrawa to Los Angeles to almost live with the Davis family for a day before National Signing Day in February 2017.

But as Meyer drove the golf cart on that initial visit, he didn't know any of that. The Buckeyes just knew Davis could play, and he was here. "This is no knock against the other schools that were recruiting me," Wyatt said. "But he was the only head coach that was super hands-on."

"That right then was the difference maker," Pantoni said. "They knew that they were wanted, that they were a priority."

That showed how much the Buckeyes wanted to reach across the country and pull in a player with a Hall of Famer in his family. That's how eager the Buckeyes were to capitalize on the opportunity to expand their West Coast recruiting. In the 10 years before Davis and the Class of 2017, the Buckeyes signed 218 players, and only two of them were from the states of California, Oregon, Washington, Arizona, or Nevada.

One was receiver Michael Thomas, a lower-ranked California recruit who spent a transitional year at Fork Union Military Academy in Virginia before signing with the Buckeyes in the Class of 2012.

Thomas developed into a star at Ohio State and a superstar in the NFL with the New Orleans Saints. He was also the nephew of former USC star receiver Keyshawn Johnson. Thomas had an advanced understanding of college football, but his commitment to the Buckeyes was more of a one-off than a trendsetter. The Buckeyes weren't established on the West Coast yet.

And then there was Class of 2013 tight end Marcus Baugh, who was a top 100 recruit in the first full class of the Meyer era. But that didn't unleash Ohio State in Pac-12 territory either. The Buckeyes didn't sign a West Coast recruit in the next three classes before Davis came along. He was also the start of something. After signing two West Coast players in the 10 years before Davis, the Buckeyes would sign eight West Coast players in the four years after Davis. Someone had to vanquish Ohio State's hesitancy because the time and energy to recruit a player 2,000 miles away instead of 200 miles away grows exponentially. "You can end up wasting your time on guys," Studrawa said of the risk of long-haul recruiting, "because you've got to pass 7,000 schools to get there."

Time wasted on one faraway player can cost a program with closer, more realistic targets. Ohio State considers itself the home team anywhere it can drive to recruit, which means the Buckeyes are the favorites for almost every Midwest recruit on the map. Their connections in Florida have always been there. And then the Buckeyes are judicious in where they choose to chase players in other areas. It's not a strategy they often discuss publicly, but it's acknowledged by actions and head nods. Ohio State looks for weakness in home state teams, and the Buckeyes go where they have a chance to win. They've done it in Georgia at times, in Tennessee at times, and they did it when they went more forcefully into Michigan.

In Davis' 2017 recruiting class, they clearly did it in Texas, where after a slide at the end of the era of national championship coach Mack Brown, the Texas Longhorns struggled for three seasons under Charlie Strong, going 16–21 between 2014 and 2016. The Buckeyes jumped in, snaring three of the top five Texas high school players in the 2017 class in cornerback Jeff Okudah, linebacker Baron Browning, and running back J.K. Dobbins. They figured that expending the time there would be worth the investment—and they were right.

In the pursuit of a 2017 class that would include five five-star recruits and would rank No. 2 in the nation, they were doing the same thing in California with this special player. USC was down compared to its peak. The 2016 season was a step back up, as the Trojans beat Penn State in the Rose Bowl and finished No. 3 in the country. But it was too late by then—Davis had already committed to the Buckeyes. Over the previous six years, USC had lost 27 games. In the six years prior to that, they had lost 10 games. The Trojans weren't themselves, which created an opening. "Obviously, we don't go to California a ton," Studrawa said. "But if there's a special case and a special kid, that comes into play. So the first time I watched his film, I saw a guy that was so physical and got after it and just loved to play the game. He was raw technique-wise, but it was rare to find a guy that was so physical and that got after it the way he did."

So the Buckeyes got after it in recruiting Davis once they knew he was worth the time. But for that to happen, Davis first had to let the Buckeyes know that he existed. Beyond the state of Texas, the Buckeyes were hitting Las Vegas in the Class of 2017, where they would sign two players—quarterback Tate Martell and defensive tackle Haskell Garrett—and lose another commitment late in the process from receiver Tyjon Lindsey. All three played at Bishop Gorman High School, and Davis' Los Angeles high school, St. John Bosco, played Gorman in 2014, when they were all sophomores, and the schools played again in 2016, when all of them were seniors. As West Coast football high school powerhouses, the matchups made sense, and Davis developed a friendship with the players through the game and other football camps.

At this stage three things were happening in Davis' recruitment:

1. USC wasn't a dominant local power.
2. Davis was looking for a school where he could compete for a national title and realizing he'd likely have to leave home to accomplish that.
3. Ohio State was on his mind for a few family connections and because his older brother, David, had become a fan of the Buckeyes growing up, loving their defensive line and coach Jim Tressel. David did book reports on Tressel in school and he may have picked Ohio State in recruiting if the Buckeyes had offered. He went on to play defensive tackle at Cal. But some of that Buckeyes love rubbed off on his younger brother.

There were enough Ohio family threads to encourage that thinking. Wyatt's grandfather, Pro Football Hall of Famer Willie Davis, who died in 2020 at age 85, started his NFL career as a Cleveland Brown, which is why Duane Davis was born in Cleveland. After two seasons Willie was traded to Green Bay in 1960, where he developed into a Hall of Fame defensive end with the Packers and a core piece of the Vince Lombardi dynasty. Meanwhile, Duane's mother was from Cincinnati, and there were family members who still lived there.

That family link would encourage Ohio State to take Davis seriously when he showed interest from afar.

Davis was still open in his recruitment during his junior year when Bishop Gorman's Garrett committed to Ohio State in February 2016. So Davis asked Garrett and the other Gorman guys to put in a good word with the Buckeyes. "I was just like, 'Hey man, I would love to take a visit to Ohio State. If there's any way that you could tell the coaches about me, I'd love to go,'" Davis said.

Pantoni remembered the push. "They kept reaching out saying, 'There's this kid in California who keeps saying he loves Ohio State,'" Pantoni said. "And it's one of those, *Okay, is this real? Or is this just a highly-rated kid trying to get the offer?* And they were like, 'I'm telling you: they really want to visit.'"

That summer of 2016 between his junior and senior years, Wyatt and Duane planned a Midwest recruiting swing. Stops at Notre Dame, Northwestern, and Michigan were on the docket, and Duane asked Wyatt if they should add any other visits. "I said, 'Is there any school that if they offered you, it would change the game?'" Duane said. "And he said to me, 'Well, yeah Dad, it's still the same school it's always been.' I said, 'Wait a minute, you're not talking about Ohio State.' And he goes, 'Yeah, if they would offer me, I would go there in a second.'"

At that point Duane asked Bosco football coach Jason Negro to call Ohio State to see if there was any possible mutual interest there. But Duane did that while offering his son a warning. "I don't want you to get disappointed," he said. "But Ohio State doesn't come to California to get linemen."

For this one, they would. Negro called, film was sent, and when Studrawa got his eyes on Davis, he was in. The Buckeyes were quickly added to the Midwest itinerary, and Wyatt and Duane set off on a tour that would change their lives with Columbus, the final stop.

But always a fan of legendary Michigan coach Bo Schembechler, Duane said he was actually pulling for the Wolverines a bit in this recruiting race, especially after they had a good trip to Ann Arbor. "I'll just never forget: one of the Michigan coaches came up and goes, 'So you guys are going to Columbus tomorrow?' And he said, 'Why are you going to Columbus? It makes no sense. This is the place you want to be. Don't go to Columbus,'" Duane said.

Wyatt, though, wanted to go. And the next day, the Davises were in the golf cart. Soon after, they were in their rental car, driving from Columbus to Milwaukee for their flight home. "Wyatt was super, super quiet," Duane said. "I looked at him and said, 'What's up, man?' And he goes, 'I just really like it here.' And I said, 'Really?' And he said, 'Dad, can I commit?'"

Duane answered with advice about patience, pro and con lists, and not allowing yourself to be swayed by your latest visit. There was still plenty of time. And there was also the matter of the first school that had offered Wyatt during his sophomore year—Alabama. That offer had led to an unofficial visit to Tuscaloosa, Alabama, in January 2016, long before the Buckeyes were really on the radar. If Davis had a good idea that he was leaving California for college, the Midwest tour really could have been nothing more but a chance to confirm what seemed probable at that time—that he was headed to the SEC. "I had envisioned myself going out of state for college since middle school," Davis said. "If I wanted to reach my goals and take the next step and go to the next level, why wouldn't I go to a place that consistently produces linemen and is consistently competing for national championships?"

As Duane drove away from Columbus and west toward Milwaukee that June day, his son was a top 25 national recruit with football in the family and a swirl of offers in his head. He was an L.A. kid with USC connections and a USC offer. He was a five-star prospect whose first offer had come from Alabama and who had taken multiple unofficial visits to that school. And he was a physical Big Ten kind of player who had just taken a look at suitors like Michigan and Notre Dame.

Before the trip Duane would have guessed there was about a 90 percent chance his son would play for Alabama. Duane said that if Wyatt had never asked for his high school coach to contact Ohio State, "he's probably in Tuscaloosa."

So that's why Duane didn't take Wyatt all that seriously when he said he wanted to commit to Ohio State only hours after he had seen the campus for the first time. His fatherly advice was to hold off and to go through the entire recruiting process—or to at least get back to California first and think about it. But Wyatt was already thinking. "He didn't say a word for 45 minutes," Duane said. "He was really sad. He looked at me and kind of had tears in his eyes. And I said, 'You know what, Wyatt? If you want to commit right now, go ahead.' And he picked up the phone and he called Coach Meyer."

The decision wasn't announced until the next week. But it was made in that moment.

The Buckeyes just had to sweat out the next eight months until National Signing Day in February. It wasn't that Davis wavered; it was that distance increases uncertainty. The Buckeyes were stretched around the country with that '17 class, which would rank second in the nation. The 21 players they signed included just six playing high school football in Ohio as seniors. Of their 11 players ranked among the top 100 recruits, three were in Texas, three were in Florida, two were in Las Vegas, and one was in Maryland. Davis was in California and just one was in Ohio. Holding on to the class could be nearly as challenging as gathering it.

That's why Studrawa appreciated the fact that the one top-ranked Ohio player, offensive lineman Josh Myers from Miamisburg, told his future coach to spend his recruiting time elsewhere—like California. Because if you take an in-state player for granted, you can lose him just as fast as an out-of-state player. "It's happened to me," Studrawa said. "That's why my first thing was: that's not going to happen with Josh Myers."

Studrawa wouldn't neglect the in-state recruit to pursue the out-of-state recruit. He was in Miamisburg as much as possible. "After the third time, he's like, 'Coach, you don't have to come see me again,'" Studrawa said. "I said, 'You're important to our program, buddy, I'm not letting you go.' He goes, 'Coach, I'm not going anywhere. Go get whoever you need to get. I'm fine.' That was a huge relief for me because you can spend so much time taking care of your own backyard so that you don't risk losing that kid. Josh wasn't like that. He said, 'I'm a Buckeye, man.'"

The other thing he said was: "Go get Wyatt."

When the Buckeyes made back-to-back College Football Playoff appearances in 2019 and 2020, starting at center was Josh Myers of Miamisburg, Ohio. Starting next to him at right guard was Wyatt Davis of Los Angeles, California.

To lock that duo down, Studrawa had to be in Los Angeles in late January 2017. National Signing Day was Wednesday, February 1. Recruiting rules didn't allow on-campus contact by coaches from Sunday, January 29, through Signing Day. So on the next-to-last day of permissible contact, Friday, January 27, Studrawa didn't leave the side of Davis and his family. In Texas, running backs coach Tony Alford did the same for Dobbins. The Buckeyes had obtained these far-off pledges, and the goal was to box out any last-second competition by not leaving the scene. "I made Stud stay out there all day long," Meyer said, "just sit in his car if he wasn't in the house, just make sure we had the last word."

"I was in the school at 7:00 AM," Studrawa said, "hanging out, seeing the coaches because you're allowed to make a trip to the school. And when school ended, I went with Mom and Dad. We sat at the house, we had dinner, we had coffee, so I was with them until pretty much 10:00 that night. So I spent that entire last day that we could possibly spend at the school and then at the house."

Davis said in the final two months before Signing Day, the recruiting around him intensified. He said multiple schools per day were stopping by for in-home visits or approaching him in his car at school. Washington was among the schools showing genuine, consistent interest. Though Davis said that his coach told schools he was committed to the Buckeyes and not interested in talking, Bosco had so many other college prospects that college assistants would come by to discuss other players and then drag Davis into a conversation. At one point, Davis said one coach came to his classroom and pulled him out of a Spanish final and insisted on speaking with him.

Studrawa said schools came by that Friday as he sat with Negro, and the high school coach passed on the message that Davis was committed. But Studrawa said that Bosco had an open outdoor campus, so some schools messaged Davis directly and tried to meet with him that way. Davis would text Studrawa with what was happening and say he wasn't coming out to meet them. "That happened a couple times that day," Studrawa said. "And that's exactly what I was there for."

Meyer was concerned about Helton and USC, and Studrawa said he believed the Trojans held some local allure for Davis' parents. Pantoni said there was some smoke about a possible late push from Oregon. And Davis had asked the Buckeyes if he could just visit Washington with some friends, which set off some alarm bells in Columbus. "I had a lot of buddies on my team that were committed to Washington," Davis said. "At this point I had only taken one official visit—to Ohio State—and I was 100 percent in on Ohio State, didn't have any second thoughts about it. But my buddies were taking this trip to Washington, and in my head, I didn't see any harm to take this one last trip, especially since we never took trips at the same time. So I just thought it would have been cool. So I remember I called Coach Meyer and I said, 'Hey Coach, I have a quick question. If you're not okay with it, I won't do it.' And I heard him take this deep breath, and he was like, 'Please don't go on this trip.'"

Wyatt said he wouldn't go. But the day he would have gone was the day Studrawa was there. "That's when they sent Stud to basically make sure Wyatt didn't get on that plane to go visit Washington," Duane said with a laugh. "He came over to the house, and we entertained Coach Stud for the day."

Davis had been named California's Mr. Football by Cal-Hi Sports. He had been named the Southern California Player of the Year by the *Los Angeles Times*. And as Studrawa sat with Negro that Friday, Studrawa said he could see Davis in the school courtyard doing a television interview. "Here's the *L.A. Times* Player of the Year, Mr. Football in California getting ripped on the radio stations for going to Ohio State," Studrawa said. "And then they're interviewing him at the school and they're asking, 'Why are you leaving L.A.?' So a lot of guys can flip at the end and say that it's easier to stay home and not deal with it. So that was my concern: any last-minute late stuff. They try to guilt trip these kids. And the bottom line is: it's a young kid. All they've got to do is get one little piece in there. It's like a jury. All you've got to do is get one juror to say, 'No, no, no,' and then that hesitation is in there, and then the whole thing blows up."

On February 2, 2017, Davis became a Buckeye, part of a class with Okudah, Browning, Dobbins, Myers, defensive end Chase Young, and cornerback Shaun Wade that would carry the Buckeyes to an undefeated regular season in 2019 in Ryan Day's first year replacing Meyer.

In 2018 California receiver Chris Olave signed with Ohio State.

In 2020 Arizona prospects Jack Miller and Lathan Ransom, Washington receiver Gee Scott Jr., Los Angeles quarterback C.J. Stroud, and linebacker Kourt Williams—also from St. John Bosco—signed with Ohio State.

In 2021 Arizona defensive back Denzel Burke and Washington receiver Emeka Egbuka signed with Ohio State.

Davis took over as the starting guard for the last two games of 2018, held down that starting job in 2019 and 2020, and was named a unanimous first-team All-American for his play in his fourth and final year as a Buckeye in 2020. In the 2021 NFL Draft, he was taken in the third round by the Minnesota Vikings.

That day in June 2016, Meyer drove around a player who would become one of the best offensive linemen in recent Ohio State history. That golf cart also took the Buckeyes down a new recruiting road. The West Coast was now open for business.

CHAPTER 16

# Jim Otis,
# Class of 1966

Before he was a doctor, Jim Otis was just a little guy with a tough friend. No more than 5'6" and about 160 pounds, Otis had a college roommate who liked to box. So when Woody Hayes would step into a ring during his days at Denison University, Otis would introduce him and then man his corner. Hayes threw punches; Otis cleaned cuts. College in the mid-1930s prepared them for life—as a fighter and a fixer. Football would bring them together again in the late 1960s—as a mentor and a father.

That's what Jim Otis Jr. stepped into—by birth and then by choice. That meant he would face a boxing match of his own in his football career. There would be questions, he knew, about whether he earned his scholarship to Ohio State, or whether his path was cleared by his father's friendship with the head coach. But when you play football and Woody Hayes is one of your father's oldest friends, there's nothing to do but take it head on. Raise your gloves, step forward, absorb the blows, and keep moving.

First, with a bevy of other opportunities in front of him, Jim Otis Jr. had to reaffirm in his own mind that he wanted a football scholarship to Ohio State. And then he wanted to prove he deserved that scholarship in Ohio State's 1966 recruiting class at a time when Hayes, heading toward a 4–5 season in 1966, couldn't exactly be in the business of handing out scholarships as favors. During the history of Ohio State football, personal relationships have intertwined with the game. But there likely hasn't been a recruitment quite like the recruitment of Jim Otis. So he wanted to ensure there wasn't an Ohio State career quite like his either.

When Otis stepped off the field for his final time as a Buckeye in 1969, he did so as a first-team All-American, the team MVP, and the leading rusher in school history. He ran hard for that proof. (With modern offensive explosions and longer seasons, Otis' career rushing total of 2,542 yards ranked 18th in OSU history entering the 2021 season.) "The only thing I worried about going to Ohio State was I didn't want the kids on the team not to like me because they thought I was getting special treatment," Otis said. "But that didn't last very long because of how tough Woody was."

Hayes said he was tougher on Otis for that reason. Hayes wanted and needed Otis to handle the full measure of playing for Woody Hayes. It was at first a shock to the system for a player who had known Hayes only in the gentler light of a family friend. "When I went down there as a freshman, we would scrimmage the varsity, and I'd see how tough he was. And it bothered me a little bit in the beginning because I had never seen that side of Woody," Otis said. "But he didn't just pick on a few guys. He got everybody."

To have the chance to get to Ohio State, Otis first had to get into the backfield. As he started his junior year in 1964 at Celina High School—just more than 100 miles northwest of Ohio Stadium— Otis found himself quite a bit larger than his diminutive father (by now known to all as Doc Otis) and quite a bit larger than the average Celina High School football player. That wasn't the best path for carrying the ball at a small high school. "My varsity coach said, 'You're gonna have to play on the offensive line, Jim, because you're one of the biggest kids we have.' I think I weighed 185 or 190 pounds," Otis said. "And he said, 'This is where we need you.'"

An offensive lineman and linebacker, Otis blocked and tackled with an understanding of what it meant for his team and an overriding unease of what it meant for his football career. "I thought to myself, *I will never be able to go to Ohio State if I don't play fullback,*" Otis said.

Other than a note about his father participating in a golf auction, the first appearance in *The Lima News* of the Otis name came in a story from a Celina High win in 1963. Junior running back Alan Aikman ran for 158 yards and three touchdowns in a 46–6 victory against Bellefontaine, while Otis, a sophomore, scored once on a two-point conversion.

Two weeks into the next season, the nearby paper, *The [Greenville] Daily Advocate*, listed Celina's four leading rushers—Bill Fails and Aikman were on top, and Otis wasn't among them. Celina coach Norm Decker said of Aikman, a senior who'd rushed for 127 yards and four touchdowns in the last game, "You can depend on Aikman getting you two or three yards. He's so strong."

Otis was named in a list of defensive players. By mid-November with Celina in contention for the conference title in the Western Buckeye League, the backfield had shifted, as outlined in *The Daily Advocate*: "The Bulldogs are the only team to have beaten Wapakoneta, but the win was a costly one. Alan Aikman, one of Limaland's leading scorers early this year, sustained a knee injury that has kept him below par most of the season. Bill Fails, senior speedster, took up the slack in the Bulldog offense until he too was shelved with a knee injury and had two teeth knocked out in the Bellefontaine loss two weeks ago. Bulldog coach Norm Decker has done some nifty shuffling in his backfield all season to offset the effects of this rash of injuries, and one change makes him look like a magician. Jim Otis, who opened the season at tackle slot, was moved to fullback for the Wapak game and in six games has scored 72 points."

"What happened in the fourth game of the season—there's always a story like this—was our fullback got hurt, and our second-string fullback was sick with the flu," Otis said. "Dick Quilling was the quarterback, and he and I were best friends. What he and I had done, we had practiced all the plays. Every night after the regular football practice, the kids would come. And being in a farming community like that, all the kids drove, so they'd come down to the field and take their cars and turn the lights on, and we practiced like that."

When the fullback options dwindled, Quilling went to Coach Decker and advocated for a lineman who knew all the fullback plays. "You've got to give Otis a chance," Quilling told his coach.

Otis went in. Celina rallied from down 12 points, scoring on two fourth-quarter Otis touchdowns and adding a pair of two-point conversions to upset the Western Buckeye League favorites. "That was the beginning," Otis said of that first weekend in October.

Four years later on the first weekend of October in 1968, Otis would run for 102 yards and a touchdown in a 21–6 win against Oregon for an Ohio State team that would win a national championship. "It's funny. He wanted to learn so badly," Quilling said. "That's the amazing thing. Here's a kid who none of us even thought would start during his high school career. But he would work harder than everyone, and yes, we spent a lot of time together. And I encouraged him to keep doing it."

Otis kept it up, and Aikman, who had been such a force at the fullback position previously, never was quite the same after his injury. "I got put on defense to play both ways and I got my knee damaged," Aikman said. "That was my senior season, and I never really recovered fully."

Aikman went to Ohio State and walked on the football team and he said Hayes told him he'd be put on scholarship. Then something changed, and Aikman felt unfairly pushed aside and he decided to leave Ohio State. "I transferred to the University of Hawaii and was their starting fullback for a season," Aikman said.

He returned to Ohio State after that one season and he went on to earn his degree in civil engineering. But he was done with football. His former backup was just getting started.

At the end of his junior season at Celina, Otis had accounted for 72 points in just seven games and was named first-team all-conference, one of just two juniors joining nine seniors on the first-team offense, in the Western Buckeye League. He was once third team on his own squad, and now Otis was first team in the conference.

That served as a prelude to a dominant senior season. After two weeks Otis had 352 yards on 48 carries, and Decker was talking all-state. After four weeks Otis had 655 yards on 109 carries, and Decker told the *Dayton Daily News*: "Jim is really a bull runner. He goes looking for people. He has one ambition in life, and that is to play fullback for Woody Hayes at Ohio State. They're definitely interested in him, and the way he's played for us, I can see why."

In Week 5 Celina fell behind Wapakoneta 26–6 at the half, and, according to Otis, a friend of his father's who had come to the game said he was heading out to make the 22-mile drive back to Celina because of the lopsided score and bad weather. But he put the radio on for the drive. "I'm running the ball every down and scoring touchdowns, and we beat them 36–26," Otis said. "He came back."

Later that season *The Lima News* reported that Kenton High School tried an 11-man defensive line against Celina, but Otis ran through it anyway, rushing for 147 yards and three touchdowns in a 38–20 win. Taking inside handoffs in the T-formation, Otis was on top of defenses almost before they could move. "What I recognized was how explosive he was to the line," Quilling said. "It didn't make sense for somebody that big to be that quick. He was stocky, his thighs were enormous, but I'm sure that's where he got all that thrust."

Celina finished 9–0–1. In basically nine games (Otis barely played in one game because of a sprained ankle), he carried the ball 290 times for 1,680 yards and 24 touchdowns. He was named the third-team fullback on the Associated Press Class AA All-Ohio team. "With Aikman I was able to create a faking offense that worked really well," said Quilling, who himself was an all-league player also recruited by Ohio State. "Sometimes the other team wouldn't even know where the ball was. With Otis, if I can put it bluntly, he was one of the slower guys on the team, but one of the quickest guys that I've ever dealt with. I never dealt with a running back that got to the line of scrimmage faster than Jim Otis. As a quarterback you needed to get the ball clean and get it around or he'd be gone. He wasn't going to run for 40 yards, but he was going to get positive yardage every single time."

His full senior season at fullback confirmed what the partial junior season at fullback had indicated. Otis was good enough for Ohio State, which is all he ever wanted. When he was growing up with his three sisters, their father created a football field in their back-yard, and Otis Jr. played the game every day. Hayes would come out to Celina for a visit most summers, usually for his preseason physical, and Otis Jr. developed a child's clear vision of his future. When he was around the age of 10, he instructed his sisters to take photos of him playing football in the yard so they could send them to Hayes. Otis Jr. would attend Ohio State games with his father several times a year. If his father had business in Columbus, they might stop by for a visit. Hayes himself wasn't a regular presence in Otis Jr.'s life, but the idea of Hayes was. "If you talked to him when he was a young kid," Quilling said, "and said, 'What are you going to do with your life?' He'd say, 'I'm going to be an All-American fullback at Ohio State.' We just kind of looked around and said, 'Yeah right, that's not in the cards for you.'"

Otis kept shuffling the cards until it was. Still, as Otis finally established what kind of football player he was, he felt he owed himself at least a half-hearted attempt at the recruiting process. And to be clear: an actual offer from Hayes did not arrive until Otis had played his last high school football game.

That sprained ankle game? Otis was supposed to fly the next morning to Bloomington for a recruiting trip to Indiana University, but his dad nixed that. "He said, 'You've got to take care of that ankle,'" Otis Jr. said.

Plus, Doc Otis already considered his son a lock for the Buckeyes. There was also a visit to Miami (Ohio) with a few teammates for a game and a meeting with Miami coach Bo Schembechler. "We sat down," Otis said. "And he said, 'I know where you're going, Jim. I know you're going to Ohio State.' And I said, 'But Coach, if I don't go to Ohio State, I'll come here and play for you.'"

Hayes was the featured speaker at Celina's football banquet following the senior season for Otis and Quilling, and after that event, any inkling of Otis not playing for Ohio State was finally put to rest. "It was an awful nice thing for him to come to Celina and do our football banquet because the kids never forget that. It's their team, and someone special comes," Otis said. "I know my teammates would still remember that night, the night Woody Hayes came to Celina."

"To that town, Jim Otis was a big deal," Quilling said. "And Woody Hayes was an even bigger deal. So it was enormous."

"We're at the school," Otis said. "He came up to me, and he said, 'Hey, Jim, I've been invited to come to your home after the banquet and I want to get with you privately for a minute.' And I said, 'That'd be great, Coach.' He was always kind of a hero to me. We got out to my house and we were talking about Ohio State and the things I dreamed about doing and all that. And he said, 'Jim, we've recruited some other fullbacks. One of them is bigger than you. And we got another one that I think is a little faster than you are, and I want you to know that.' And I said, 'Well, Coach, are you offering me a scholarship?' And he said, 'Yes, yes I am.' And I said, 'Coach, we'll have to find out how good those other fullbacks are.'"

Doc Otis had, ironically, started his college career at Michigan, but a lack of focus and some academic issues caused his parents to pull him out and insist he attend a smaller college. That college was Denison, where he met Hayes. Now his old roommate was offering his son an Ohio State scholarship, and the beloved town doctor was insisting that he would pay for his son's education. "You won't be paying here," Hayes told his friend. "He deserves this scholarship, and that's what he's getting."

Otis stepped into the low ebb of Hayes' tenure in Columbus. While Otis was relegated by NCAA rules of the day to the freshman team in 1966, the Buckeyes managed only a 4–5 record, Hayes' second losing season in 16 years at Ohio State. In 1967 Otis was ready to play, and before the first game of his sophomore season, a 6,000-word story in *Sports Illustrated*'s September issue examined a growing campus apathy around the Ohio State football program, a reality viewed as both emblematic of the times and problematic for the Buckeyes. Woody's world wasn't what it once was. The story viewed Hayes more as a victim of the times than a cause of the disinterest. The article said, "Poor Woody, he is a raindrop being blamed for a flood."

But there also was a greater issue mentioned by author Robert Cantwell, a novelist by trade who freelanced for *Sports Illustrated* and wrapped this football examination of the Buckeyes around references to Columbus' own literary hero, James Thurber. The issue was recruiting. "Big Ten recruiting regulations, which are among the strictest in the country, have made it difficult to attract the best athletes," Cantwell wrote. "Six boys from Ohio played on the 1966 Nebraska team that won the Big Eight championship. Strict enforcement of the regulations is increasing the muscle gap between the Big Ten and other conferences."

Beyond that, Cantwell went so far as to question the entire athletic endeavor to which Otis had just pledged his loyalty. "Football's dominance on the campus is over," Cantwell wrote. "The dissolution of the Big Ten, or even the end of college football, can be discussed as calmly as any other current campus topic: the draft, Vietnam, or the questions of whether women visitors ought to be compelled to get out of men students' apartments by 2 o'clock in the morning."

In that uncertain environment with Otis now on varsity, the Buckeyes opened the 1967 season with three losses in five games, including a 41–6 home defeat to Purdue before a crowd of 84,069 that left Hayes thanking Purdue coach Jack Mollenkopf for pulling his starters early in the second half. Otis carried 18 times for 83 yards in the loss. All that Hayes could promise in the aftermath was that the Buckeyes wouldn't quit. They didn't, rallying to win their last four, including a 24–14 win against Michigan, in which Otis carried 24 times for 114 yards, and fellow back Rudy Hubbard propelled the Buckeyes with two early touchdowns. Some think the Michigan win saved Hayes' job.

It was now up to Hayes to save not only his livelihood, but also, according to the most dire warnings of preseason wordsmiths, the conference and the sport as well. He did it with recruiting. Hayes' 1967 recruiting class changed the face of Ohio State football. Quarterback Rex Kern, backs Leo Hayden and Larry Zelina, linebacker Doug Adams, and defensive linemen Jim Stillwagon and Mark Debevc were home state Ohio recruits. Receiver Jan White was from Pennsylvania, fullback John Brockington was from New York, defensive back Tim Anderson was from West Virginia, and receiver Bruce Jankowski and safety Jack Tatum were from New Jersey. They, too, would sit as freshmen and then emerge as sophomores. Of the 25 Buckeyes who played the most during a 10–0 season in 1968, just five were seniors. Eight were juniors, and 12 were sophomores.

The Super Sophs, as that recruiting class of 1967 would come to be known, exploded onto the scene and led, almost inarguably, the greatest season in Ohio State history. The national championship season of 1968 secured Hayes' legacy and set the standard for everything that would come after it. Every great recruiting class in Ohio State history since then is compared to the 1967 class, and Kern on offense and Tatum on defense established new standards for what Ohio State excellence looked like on each side of the ball.

At the center of all that sophomore talent was a familiar junior fullback. An Otis would stand by Hayes for much of his life. Long after those college days, Dr. Jim Otis, through the eyes of a physician, watched on television as Hayes punched Clemson player Charlie Bauman during the 1978 Gator Bowl, and Dr. Otis thought that Hayes didn't look like himself. Worried about Hayes' diabetes, Otis drove the 100 miles from Celina and picked Hayes up when the plane landed and took him to the hospital, as the coach's career at Ohio State was about to end with his firing the next day. Forty years later, Otis was still in his friend's corner.

Hayes died in 1987 at age 74. Dr. Otis died in 2013 at age 99. "He was this little guy, just full of piss and vinegar," Quilling said. "He was funny all the time. He was my doctor, and I'd go in, and we never even talked about medicine. All he talked about was football. And I'd leave the office and think, 'Why did I come in here? He didn't check me out.' But he was just one of these guys who lived life to the fullest."

More of a basketball player than a football player, Quilling accepted a scholarship from Hayes as well, wishing in the end he would have held out for potential basketball scholarships. Hayes had come to recruit Otis and he saw that the quarterback might fit at Ohio State as a defensive back. "The circumstances led Woody to me," Quilling said. "When you come from a poor family and your parents can't afford to pay for your school, when Woody Hayes offers you a scholarship, you take it."

Once on campus, Quilling realized he wasn't cut out for defense, so he found a role as the quarterback running the scout team against maybe the best young defense in the country. "I ran the second team against the first team every night in practice," Quilling said. "So every night in practice, I had the pleasure of getting hit by Jack Tatum and Jim Stillwagon. And actually, Tatum hurt me in the spring game my sophomore year. He dislocated my shoulder, and I never played after that. He was just a different kind of an athlete. He was so scary. In fact, Woody Hayes would say, 'You find out where that guy is and don't get your player hurt.' He was worried about that little swing pass, up in the air, and Tatum just leveling the guy. He was different. He was just really different."

So too, in his own way, was Otis. With all that sophomore talent on the 1968 team, nobody played more minutes than Otis. He rushed for 985 yards (then a school record) and scored 17 touchdowns (then a school record). He ran it 34 times for 143 yards and four touchdowns in a 50–14 win against Michigan and 30 times for 101 yards and a touchdown in the Rose Bowl win against USC. The Super Sophs surrounded him, but as was the case whenever he was on a football field, Otis often carried the load, even though he might not have had the most natural talent. "He really worked at it, and I think that's the key to anybody," Quilling said. "Jim really worked to develop the skills that he had. I admire him as a football player because he got every ounce out of his ability. And obviously the career he had at Ohio State is one of the best out of any running back there. Because I know Jim really well, I'm sure that in the back of his mind there was a little bit of doubt about, *Did I really deserve a scholarship, or was it a combination of me being a really good football player and Woody having a relationship with my dad?'* Well, Jim Otis earned every bit of that scholarship."

After a nine-year NFL career, Otis settled in St. Louis, his last football stop, and began a successful career in commercial real estate. He and his wife, Jan, raised two sons: Jeff, a quarterback at Columbia, and Jim, a preferred walk-on at Ohio State. For much of his success and joy in life, Otis credits his old coach for what Hayes taught on and off the field. "He was a great man," Otis said.

And a pretty good recruiter even in this case. Otis remembered a moment during his recruitment when a friend yelled out to Hayes as Otis was walking by. "Woody," he asked, "you think you got a chance to get the Otis boy?"

"If I can't get the Otis boy," Hayes said, "I will quit coaching."

CHAPTER 17

# TreVeyon Henderson, Class of 2021

Ryan Day understands being a recruiter in this era of college football. "It's not our job—or my job—to talk you into coming to Ohio State," said the head coach of one of the most successful programs in the nation. "Ten years ago it was kind of different. It was: how do you close? The head coach would come in and close the deal. And I don't think that's the case anymore."

On December 4, 2018, when Day sat at a news conference next to Urban Meyer for a transition from a three-time national championship coach to an assistant who had never been a head coach on any level, recruiting struck at the core of the timing of the move and at the looming questions in the moment. *Why now? Why Day?*

Meyer wanted to announce his resignation from Ohio State then—before the early signing period began for the Class of 2019 two weeks later because recruits had started asking about Meyer's future. "People will say, 'Why would you let recruiting get in the way?' That's a silly question," Meyer said during the discussion announcing the passing of the torch. "[If] you want to have a good team, you recruit and you recruit very hard. So that put a little push on it. And to be honest, I didn't want to mislead recruits."

That addressed the when. But what about the who? Day had proven himself as a quarterback developer and offensive play caller as Ohio State's offensive coordinator in 2017 and 2018, but could he maintain the level of talent that Meyer, one of the great modern recruiters, had infused the program with for the previous seven years? Could the Buckeyes under Day recruit like the Buckeyes had under Meyer?

Over the next two days in December 2018, Day hit four states personally on the recruiting trail. In January he flew back and forth from Ohio to Hawaii to visit offensive lineman Enokk Vimahi, a move that helped secure a commitment from the four-star prospect. Five-star Texas receiver Garrett Wilson, who had been discovered when Day was recruiting quarterback Matthew Baldwin at Wilson's Austin high school, reaffirmed a commitment to the Buckeyes. From the Columbus suburbs, five-star defensive end Zach Harrison picked the Buckeyes over Michigan after the transition. Only three players decommitted from Ohio State after Meyer's departure, and the Buckeyes finished with the No. 14 class in the country in 2019, according to 247Sports.com, not bad for a program in flux.

In 2020 the Buckeyes landed the No. 5 class. And amidst a global pandemic in 2021, the Buckeyes pulled in the nation's No. 2 class, a group that featured five-star players at quarterback, running back, receiver, offensive line, and defensive end. COVID-19 shut down college football recruiting in March 2020—one tiny piece of a worldwide crisis—as the NCAA called for a recruiting dead period on March 13, 2020, that would last for more than a year. That meant no in-person campus visits by recruits and no in-person visits by coaches to a player's high school or home. With many programs at a standstill, the Buckeyes over the next two weeks in March 2020 landed verbal commitments from four players who would eventually sign with Ohio State, and that run peaked with a pledge from a five-star running back who had never been to Columbus.

By that point 15 months after Day had taken over, the Buckeyes were so confident and collected in their recruiting and had covered such ground with the 2021 prospects early in the process that they made the shutdown work for them, especially when it came to running back TreVeyon Henderson. He was the player in the Class of 2021 that talent, circumstance, opportunity, and past misses dictated that the Buckeyes most needed to land.

For a position coach feeling some pressure, for a team craving a top-tier rushing threat, for a program seeking a lift in a world filled with uncertainty, for a recruiting operation earning confirmation that it was still connecting with kids, Henderson answered every question.

Running backs coach Tony Alford was hired by Meyer for the 2015 season and retained by Day, and Alford credits Day with Ohio State's continued recruiting prowess. "It starts with Ryan Day," he said. "It starts with the messages that are being delivered top down and the culture of this program. Coming to Ohio State and playing for Ohio State is hard. It's not for every player. It's not for everybody to coach here either. And that doesn't mean someone's good, bad, soft, whatever. It's just not for everybody. And we make no apologies for that. We're very transparent when we recruit that this is going to be hard. I'm not saying it's easy anywhere else, but I'm talking about here because you're going to be held accountable. It's a very transparent, in-your-face type of a program, where when you're doing well, you're lifted on a pedestal, and everyone sees you. And guess what? When you're not doing well, you're put out there for everyone to see you, too.

"You're out front and you're going to be held accountable in every aspect of your life. And some guys don't mind that. You're not going to be coddled. You're going to be forced to work. No one cares about how many stars you had out of recruiting or how many other schools offered you. No one cares. This is how we're doing our business. There's a culture that's been built here and established here way before me and will go on way after me. This is the culture, and we're not wavering. We're not going to change the culture for one or two players. You're going to change to become one of us or you're going to be gone. We're not gonna become you."

That recruiting approach had coalesced on Day's staff as the Buckeyes retained the successful recruiting structure from the Meyer era. Mark Pantoni remained as the trusted strategist and front-line evaluator at the top of the recruiting operation. The talent continued its trek to Columbus.

Alford brought in both Henderson and Evan Pryor as top 100 players at running back in the Class of 2021. Promoted to full-time assistant in 2018, receivers coach Brian Hartline signed nine receivers in the Classes of 2019, 2020, and 2021, and all of them were ranked among the top 100 overall players in their class. From opposite sides of the country, Ohio State signed the No. 1 receiver in 2020—Pennsylvania's Julian Fleming—and the No. 1 receiver in 2021—Washington's Emeka Egbuka. The room overflowed with talent. In offensive line coach Greg Studrawa's room, the Buckeyes signed a five-star lineman in five straight classes: California guard Wyatt Davis in 2017, Florida tackle Nicholas Petit-Frere in 2018, Georgia center Harry Miller in 2019, Ohio tackle Paris Johnson in 2020, and Texas guard Donovan Jackson in 2021. And Day's quarterback expertise meant five-star 2021 quarterback Kyle McCord joined the battle to replace Justin Fields in 2021, competing with C.J. Stroud, the No. 3 quarterback in the 2020 class and a borderline five-star, and four-star 2020 recruit Jack Miller.

On the defensive side, Day hired linebackers coach Al Washington away from Michigan and he helped raise that position's recruiting with a major linebacker haul planned for 2022. Meanwhile, defensive line coach Larry Johnson and defensive backs coach Kerry Coombs (who left the Buckeyes for two years but returned as the defensive coordinator in 2020) kept rolling as two of the top recruiters in the country. After Johnson developed elite defensive end recruits Joey Bosa, Nick Bosa, and Chase Young into the No. 3, No. 2, and No. 2 picks in the NFL draft, next up were 2018 borderline five-star Tyreke Smith, 2019 five-star Harrison, and 2021 five-star Jack Sawyer. And when Coombs returned to Ohio State, his first order of business was recruiting, where the talent of the defensive backs had dipped a bit. Highlighted by top 100 cornerback recruits Jakailin Johnson of Missouri and Jordan Hancock of Georgia, Ohio State signed six defensive backs from six different states in 2021.

Ohio State entices players for reasons that go beyond its football program. "What you do as a coach now is you create a vision of what you want the program to be culturally with the environment and the type of people that you want to bring in," Day said. "We have to check all those boxes off. And if so, okay, here's why we think it's a great fit for you and for us, and then we want you to choose to come here. The football development is a huge part of it, and we take a lot of pride in that. But it's also: what can Ohio State do for your life? Because even for the guys who play for a long time in the NFL, they still have to wake up and do something with the rest of their life. Ninety-nine percent of them are going to have to go make money. But even the 1 percent that doesn't have to make money, they still have to do something productive with the rest of their lives. So helping them find that passion while they're here is a huge part of it, I believe. And so again, we're not in the business of talking people into coming here because we want them to choose it for the right reasons."

Henderson wasn't coerced into attending Ohio State. "TreVeyon Henderson chose Ohio State for the right reasons," Day said. "We chose TreVeyon, but he then chose Ohio State. If he chose Ohio State, he's gonna have rough days here. Every kid does. Very rarely does the journey here at Ohio State go exactly how you think it's gonna go. And so when you hit those bumps in the road, you're going to work through those things because you chose it for the right reasons. You're not gonna go jump in the transfer portal because some coach talked you into it. I think that's really, really important right now, and that's what we're doing."

That's why when the Buckeyes first visited Henderson's high school in Virginia, they weren't there to talk anybody into anything. Washington was hired in early January 2019—less than a month after Day was named the new coach and less than a week after Meyer's final game as head coach in the Rose Bowl. At Michigan, Washington had been intensely recruiting Henderson. Up until Michigan's interest, Henderson's best offers were from Virginia, Virginia Tech, Duke, and Boston College, but the Wolverines were the first major school to extend an offer to Henderson late in his sophomore season. "After that," Henderson said, "I pretty much just blew up."

His recruiting blew up as his film blew up.

Henderson started in youth football as a running back, a natural with juke moves who followed in the footsteps of his older brother Ronnie Walker Jr., a running back at Hopewell High School in Virginia who was all-state and would commit to Indiana and play there for the 2018 and 2019 seasons before transferring to Virginia. But when Henderson started showing off his skills at Hopewell High, it was as a defensive back. "I thought that was the position I was going to be playing because I loved defense," Henderson said. "I loved being physical. I loved hitting people. So that's what I thought I was going to end up playing."

Then his team needed him. Late in his sophomore season, injuries wiped out the Hopewell running backs. Henderson, who had been showing off his shiftiness on kick returns, was installed as a Wildcat quarterback taking direct snaps. "I ended up scoring the game winner on like an 80-yard touchdown against a team we hadn't beaten in years," Henderson said. "That team was very good, and I ran the ball like two times, and they were hitting me behind the line. So we didn't go to that Wildcat formation until the end of the game, and everybody was telling me, 'You've got to score this, you've got to get this touchdown.' So everybody started flowing right, so I knew there was gonna be a cutback lane sooner or later. So I slowed down a little bit and I looked left, and the cutback lane was there and I hit it so fast. After that I was pretty much going. I couldn't hear anything. All I heard was me running."

And his life changing. That 79-yard touchdown with 4:06 to play on Thursday night, October 25, 2018, gave Hopewell a 7–0 win against Dinwiddie, a rival that hadn't lost a regular-season game since 2015 and hadn't lost to Hopewell since 2012. It gave Henderson new awareness of what his football career might be like. "That's kind of how I got started at running back in high school," he said.

When Michigan offered, the interest was on both sides of the ball. Washington as the linebackers coach and Jay Harbaugh, Jim's son, as the running backs coach were equally involved in the pursuit. "I had a great relationship with Jay Harbaugh," Henderson said.

The summer between his sophomore and junior years, Henderson and his mother, Lakeesha Hayes-Winfield, drove to multiple schools for unofficial visits. From Virginia to Virginia Tech to Michigan to Penn State to Tennessee to Georgia, Henderson's eyes grew wide with every stop. "Every time I visited new colleges, I was just like, dang, this is nice," Henderson said. "Every college I went to, the facilities just got better and better, so it was crazy."

But Ohio State was not one of those visits. Not yet. The Buckeyes and Alford got very interested early in Henderson's junior year as he started to put together electric junior film. "It only made me like him more," Alford said with a laugh.

Soon, there were regular conversations, as Alford got to know Henderson and his mother. Alford was looking for a connection while checking in on nearly every top running back in the Class of 2021. He also was looking for a guy who could carry a load. When Henderson signed with the Buckeyes in December 2020, he was listed at 5'11" and 195 pounds—in range of what running back J.K. Dobbins had been when he signed with the Buckeyes in 2017 and then took the starting running back role as a freshman. Dobbins left Ohio State at 217 pounds. "Our running backs are not 185-pound guys," Alford said. "But you look across the country and there are a lot of teams that play with a 185- or 190-pound tailback, and they have great success."

But Alford was looking for a back who could potentially handle 30 to 35 touches a game with speed, agility, and the ability to run between the tackles. He also was looking for instant impact after a few recruiting classes of not quite getting that at running back. As a top 50 national player from Texas, Dobbins was a huge get for Alford and the Buckeyes in the Class of 2017. He left Ohio State three years later as the second-leading rusher in OSU history behind only Archie Griffin. Dobbins also left with a bond with Alford that was as tight as family.

But the top OSU running back recruit in the Class of 2018, Brian Snead, was dismissed from Ohio State in 2019. That left 2018 back Master Teague, a recruit ranked in the 200s. The top running backs in the 2019 class, Steele Chambers and Marcus Crowley, were ranked in the 200s and 300s. And in the Class of 2020, the Buckeyes swung big on five-star Arizona running back Bijan Robinson, the No. 1 back in the class, but lost out on him to Texas. They also thought for a time they had Jaylan Knighton, a top 150 national player from Florida, but lost him to Miami. As a result, the running back in 2020 was Miyan Williams, a player ranked in the 600s nationally who was a late flip from Iowa State.

So like they had with Dobbins in 2017 or Ezekiel Elliott in 2013, the Buckeyes needed a top 50 national player at running back in 2021. "Coming off the year that we did when we lost Bijan Robinson, it was like I have to get this kid," Alford said. "I felt that a lot. If you go back, the heat we took as a program and I took as a position coach and the individual recruiter for not getting Bijan Robinson was a lot. You can argue if it was warranted or not. It is what it is. The bottom line is he's not here, and I'm responsible for it. So I'm not shirking responsibility. And you take the good with the bad, and he's not here, and we didn't get him. And there was a lot of angst among a lot of people that for whatever reason we didn't get him. Maybe there was some self-imposed pressure. Probably a lot. I have to get this kid. And I went after it, and it worked out."

Ohio State was far from the only school in pursuit, as Day, Alford, and Washington saw when they had a visit scheduled to swing by Hopewell High School to speak with Henderson's coach. When they arrived, Michigan coaches among the other staffs visiting Hopewell that day, and it pushed the Buckeyes back from their scheduled time. With other players to see in Virginia and a plane to catch for some visits farther South that same day, Day didn't think he had time to wait. "We were there, and the visit didn't work out exactly the way we planned," Day said. "We thought we'd spend some time with the coach and then have a chance to see TreVeyon, though you can't spend any time talking to him at that time. And the coach was kind of busy, and it was kind of a clunky visit. And then on the way out, we ran into the athletic director almost on the way out of the building. So we went back in and we spent some time with him, and he was a great mentor for TreVeyon and he was a great contact for us as well."

In Hopewell AD and track coach Kerry Gray, the Buckeyes had stumbled onto one of the most important people in Henderson's life. The aggravation of what might have been a lost visit quickly turned into a valuable new relationship. "Coach Gray was the one that really helped me narrow down my colleges," Henderson said. "He helped make my process so easy."

"If that AD doesn't walk by them in that moment," said assistant athletic director, player personnel Mark Pantoni, "Ryan's leaving the high school to go somewhere else."

Day wasn't going to stay and try to talk anyone into Ohio State. The Buckeyes had an appointment and if that didn't work, they were willing to leave. That way of approaching recruiting literally brought them directly into the path of their most important running back recruit in four years. That's not to say they would have been out on Henderson if Day had reached the parking lot and driven away. But there are little moments within the complicated and time-consuming recruiting process that can change everything. Bumping into the AD on the way out qualified as that. "I would say 100 percent it did," Day said. "There's a connection relationship phase in this thing, and sometimes it works and sometimes it doesn't. That doesn't mean it's going to make or break the recruitment, but it's a piece of the pie. And it's funny how things work out. It's hard because you can't spend two hours at a school and it's hard for these high school coaches because they have a lot of people coming at them. But then we had this beautiful visit, and the coach kind of came back in, and it all worked out. It felt like fate was involved a little bit there."

That AD meeting reinforced what Alford had established by that point, and Alford was developing a relationship with Henderson that included telling stories about Dobbins. "He kept asking about J.K. for weeks and weeks and weeks," Alford said. "I said, 'Me and J.K. have a father-son relationship. It really is. If you asked him, he'd tell you the same.'"

"I started to trust Coach Alford after that," Henderson said. "He took J.K. Dobbins under his wing, and they were so close and tight. And I just loved seeing that relationship between those two. And I actually talked to J.K. Dobbins, and he told me about his process, and I was able to start getting Coach Alford's trust and I started to believe his words."

Henderson then became very intrigued with the idea that Dobbins, a Texas native, had committed to Ohio State in March 2016 without ever visiting campus. As the pandemic hit, that idea became more entrenched in Henderson's mind because he was now in a situation where he could neither visit campus nor know how long the pandemic and the related recruiting restrictions would last. Henderson had planned to make some more visits over the summer before his senior season, but he didn't know what the future held. "I didn't know if the coronavirus was just gonna be like a couple months, and then they'd start business back up again," Henderson said. "I didn't want to be overwhelmed. So I wanted to commit. So I went ahead and sped up my process."

He did know how he felt about Ohio State based upon his interactions with the coaches and other players in the recruiting class from afar. "Once COVID shut things down," Day said, "it was all through Zoom and FaceTime and phone calls. We weren't able to spend time with them in person. So what we tried to do was build a relationship within the class. Typically, 10 to 15 years ago, the first time you met everybody was when you checked in for preseason camp. Now things have changed, and we really try to build the relationship within the class to help with that because there was a void there. They weren't able to get on campus and see it and feel it and touch it. So the easy thing to do is just throw up your hands, but what we tried to do is really build the class together. So we thought the relationship between the players really helped in that area. Guys like Trey that hadn't been here before could feel that family environment, so they'd feel comfortable coming here."

Still smarting from how the Robinson recruitment had played out, Alford warned Henderson that there wouldn't be any silent commitment, where a player tells the coaches he's coming but doesn't make a public declaration. And though it was an uncertain time, Alford didn't want Henderson to do it unless he was sure. "Once you do it, it's got to be over," Alford said. "If you're gonna do it, let's do it."

Alford had made it clear that the Buckeyes were taking two running backs in the Class of 2021, and Pryor, a top 100 player from North Carolina, committed on March 16. Henderson knew only one spot remained. "I didn't want to miss out on the opportunity," Henderson said.

So on March 27, 2020, Henderson committed to Ohio State.

As always, especially with top recruits, that didn't end the process for Henderson or the Buckeyes. Alford thought Oklahoma was the greatest threat to turn Henderson's head. Some thought Clemson was on the radar, but Alford believed their interest was on defense. And then there was Michigan, which had been on Henderson from the start. "They were probably a bigger player than most people think," Alford said. "And then it became Oklahoma because that's almost where he went."

Alford said he studies running back coaches at other schools to know how they recruit and what they push in recruiting so that he has a plan to counter whatever they say. Alford had a feel for what was happening. Yet as Signing Day approached in December, he grew more anxious about getting Henderson to be a Buckeye. "Two days before Signing Day, Oklahoma tried to pull some garbage and tried to say that we're still going to take Donovan Edwards," Alford said.

Edwards, the No. 4 running back in the Class of 2021, had been on Ohio State's radar and was still uncommitted at that point, but he was pointed toward Michigan, and the Buckeyes were locked on Henderson and Pryor. But Alford said Oklahoma was telling Henderson that the Buckeyes taking Edwards was a real possibility.

Alford had recruited Edwards earlier and he still had a strong relationship with him. So he asked Edwards to call Henderson and explain that there was nothing happening with the Buckeyes and Edwards. "I called Donovan and I said, 'I need you to make a phone call for me,'" Alford said. "I said, 'I need you to call Trey and tell him I have not recruited you since the day he committed back in March.' Have we talked? Yeah, me and him talk all the time. We continued to talk but not about recruiting. It was about just me being a part of his life and being an advocate for him in his life."

Edwards called Henderson. "Once I committed, a lot of false rumors started up," Henderson said. "It was just crazy. And that came up, saying that Coach Alford was recruiting a third running back. And I knew it wasn't true. But when you hear it from a lot of people, you start thinking, *Dang, maybe it is true.* And he got Donovan Edwards to hit me up and Donovan Edwards' head coach to hit me up."

Rumor quashed, Henderson and Pryor signed with Ohio State, and Edwards signed with Michigan on December 16, 2020, ending a recruiting cycle previously unseen in college football. The entire Class of 2021 had to make final college choices without the typical recruiting experience. The recruiting dead period extended into June 2021, affecting the Class of 2022 as well. The Buckeyes in 2022 were hoping to do what they hadn't quite done in 2021—land the No. 1 class in the country.

In October of 2020, Henderson came to Columbus for an unofficial event hosted by Sawyer, the Columbus-area defensive end recruit. Called the Buckeye Bash, it allowed more than 10 commits from the Class of 2021 to gather and hang out in a way they weren't allowed to at Ohio State because of the pandemic. It was Henderson's first trip to Columbus.

Henderson didn't play high school football as a senior because the fall season was canceled in Virginia and moved to spring. That was another thing he had in common with Dobbins, whose senior football season lasted one play when he suffered a season-ending ankle injury on his first carry of the first game in 2016.

By spring of what would have been his senior year of high school, Henderson was a Buckeye, early enrolled at Ohio State, and taking part in spring football practice. He rushed six times for 26 yards in the spring game in Ohio Stadium and caught five passes for another 29 yards. He had arrived at Ohio State in January. He and his older brother drove from Virginia in one car; his mother, grandmother, and younger brother drove in another. That's when he moved into his dorm. And that's when he entered the Woody Hayes Athletic Center for the first time.

He hadn't been there as a recruit. But whether in a pandemic or in more typical times, whether from Ohio or from out of state, whether a five-star or a three-star hidden gem, whether recruited by Woody Hayes or Earle Bruce or John Cooper or Jim Tressel or Urban Meyer or Ryan Day, Henderson arrived as so many had before and so many will again, taking the road to Ohio State with one goal: to be a Buckeye.

# Acknowledgments

I always flip straight to the acknowledgements and author bio in the back of books because my huge ego inevitably leads me to believe that I'm probably more qualified to write a book than whatever joker wrote it. Now that the positions are reversed, and I'm the joker, it's my sincere hope there are future authors reading this who are buoyed by their correct belief that if I could write a book, anyone can.

Honestly, I like my wife, Katie, my daughters, Kyra and Daria, and a select group of people in the world (my sister and her family, my mom, my in-laws, the former members of R.E.M., the guy who invented bacon, a handful of others). Those first three are who I think about when I wake up, who put up with me during the day, and whom I want to hang around with at night. I am a lucky man with a wonderful family and I never take that for granted. Sorry for the times when writing upstairs took time away from hanging out downstairs. You won't be able to get rid of me now. Love you guys. Also, my wife has always been my first editor, so she read this, but I would have put in the love thing anyway.

My sports editor at Cleveland.com, David Campbell, has been the guiding light of my career and he's why I came to cover Ohio

State sports for *The Plain Dealer* and cleveland.com. He's the most creative and caring sports editor I could imagine and he's made every day working for him a great adventure and pleasure. Thanks also to cleveland.com executive editor Chris Quinn, who has always supported our coverage. In an uncertain time for journalism, I have always been proud of where I work.

My four primary co-workers covering Ohio State, Nathan Baird and Stephen Means now and Bill Landis and Ari Wasserman in the old days, let me be part of a team, which is more fun than covering a beat on your own. I am the yelling part of the team. Thanks for your patience.

The sports information directors at Ohio State, Jerry Emig and Mike Basford, help me do my job every day and went above and beyond in assisting with this book.

It always amazes me that people ever give up their time to speak with journalists. Without their talent, their experiences, and their willingness to share them, these pages would be blank. So my heart-felt thanks and appreciation to every player, coach, and parent who shared their stories. Special thanks to Vernon Shazier, who I felt like was acting as my agent at some points in assisting with other interviews, and Charlotte Heyward, who I think could help even me get recruited by a college football team with her knowledge and passion.

The Ohio State coaches I've covered since 2005 have treated reporters well, and that's never a guarantee. So thanks to Jim Tressel, Luke Fickell, Urban Meyer, Ryan Day, and every assistant coach who helped with this book, as well as John Cooper, who I never covered daily but is always great to talk to.

Thanks to Tom VanHaaren for suggesting me as the Ohio State author for this series, following the Michigan and Alabama books. I hope this continues for every major college football program in the country. And thanks to Jeff Fedotin, the editor who shepherded a first-time author through the process and put up with every excuse I came up with for not getting my chapters done on time.

Finally, thank you to Ohio State fans, those who read cleveland. com, those who listen to our podcast, *Buckeye Talk*, those who subscribe to our OSU texts, and those who bought this book, or checked it out from a library, or found it discarded on the side of the road and rescued it. I'm not from Ohio and didn't grow up following the Buckeyes. I came to this state for a great job covering a fascinating team and found a devoted fanbase and insatiable readership and listenership who allow me to—get this—watch football and then talk about it and write about it for a living. What a deal. Without you, I'd just be a loud man scrambling for work. With you, I am a loud man with a podcast (seriously, listen to *Buckeye Talk*) who finally wrote a book.

# Sources

*Dayton Daily News*
*Quad-City Times*
*News-Reporter*
*Mansfield News Journal*
*South Bend Tribune*
*Pittsburgh Post-Gazette*
*Los Angeles Times*
*The Columbus Dispatch*
*The Daily Advocate*
*The Lima News*
*The Pittsburgh Press*
*The Washington Post*
247Sports.com
Cleveland.com
Ohiostatebuckeyes.com
*Sports Illustrated*
*Buckeye Bumper Crops*
ESPN Radio